Faking It: An International Bibliography of Art and Literary Forgeries, 1949 - 1986

compiled by James Koobatian

Special Libraries Association

Copyright © 1987 by Special Libraries Association
1700 Eighteenth Street, N.W.
Washington, D.C. 20009

Printed in the United States of America

FIRST EDITION

Cover photograph: Reid S. Baker © 1987

Library of Congress Cataloging-in-Publication Data

Koobatian, James, 1952—
  Faking it.

  Includes index.
  1. Arts—Forgeries—Bibliography.   I. Special Libraries
Association.   II. Title.
Z5956.F67K66   1987   [NX636]   702'.8'74   87-4419
ISBN O-87111-320-1

FOR

Sarah and Max

TABLE OF CONTENTS

Foreword   vii
List of Abbreviations   ix
Items of Special Interest   x
    Philosophical   1
    General   10
    Paintings   22
    Drawings   56
    Sculpture   61
    Ceramics   76
    Hallmarks   87
    Antiquities   89
    Inscriptions   97
    Coins   99
    Medallions   116
    Arms and Armor   117
    Brass   120
    Bronze   121
    Pewter   124
    Silver   125
    Goldsmithing   128
    Minerals, Gems, and Jewelry   129
    Glass   133
    Ivory and Bone   135
    Scrimshaw   136
    Icons   137
    Antiques   138
    Woodcraft   143
    Ethnographic Arts   143
    Prints   147
    Photography   151
    Maps   153
    Postage Stamps   155
    Diptych   157
    Tapestry   158
    Mosaics   158
    Miniatures   158
    Netsuke   159
    Cameos   159
    Bookplates and Bookbindings   160
    Music and Musical Instruments   161
    Scientific Instruments   163
    Postcards   164
    Papier Mâché   164
    Sale Stamps and Certificates of Authenticity   165
    Media   166
    Computer Art   166
    Technical   166
    Architecture   174

Patents   174
Literary   175
  (A) Literature   175
  (B) Manuscripts, Letters, and Documents   186
  (C) Thomas James Wise   193
  (D) Detection   199
Law   201
Chronological List of Some Exhibitions and
  Exhibition Catalogs of Fakes and Forgeries   215
Exhibition Reviews   223
Author Index   229

FOREWORD

In 1950, the Special Libraries Association published Robert George Reisner's *Fakes and Forgeries in the Fine Arts*, a comprehensive, classified bibliography covering the writings on forgery in the arts from 1848–1948. This bibliography both updates and expands Reisner's work. While this bibliography does not claim to be exhaustive, it does bring together citations to the great majority of works concerned with this troublesome yet fascinating subject.

Due to the international scope of the bibliography and the need to keep it to a manageable length, it was not possible to write annotations for most entries. Nevertheless, annotations have been published for many of the entries in various indexes, and the compiler has made every effort to refer the researcher to these abstracts whenever possible. References to these abstracts appear at the end of each citation. The names of the publications referred to have been abbreviated; a list of abbreviations appears on page ix.

The first section of the bibliography, *Items of Special Interest*, covers items related to art forgery deserving special mention for the researcher. The next section, *Philosophical*, concerns itself primarily with the moral, ethical, aesthetic, and psychological aspects of art forgery. The next section, *General*, is devoted to works which touch on two or more art forms. Following the *General* section are numerous sections devoted to various art forms from painting and sculpture, to miscellaneous art forms such as scrimshaw and papier mâché. The next section, *Technical*, covers scientific works related to art forgery which discuss two or more art forms. (Works concentrating on a single art form have been placed in their respective categories.) The *Patents* section lists two patents related to the subject of art forgery. The next section, *Literary*, covers various types of literary forgeries, including the detection of literary forgeries. The *Law* section covers the ever increasing legal literature on the subject of art forgery. Following the *Law* section is a listing of exhibitions of forgeries. If the compiler was successful in locating an exhibition catalogue to an exhibition, it has been listed below the exhibition entry. A list of exhibition reviews follows the list of exhibitions and the bibliography concludes with an author index. The bulk of the bibliography shares the same format with each section divided into as many as three sections: books, sections of books, and periodicals.

ACKNOWLEDGEMENTS

A small group of people contributed greatly to the compiling to this bibliography and it is with pleasure that I now mention their names. Bill Johnson of the Special Libraries Association offered his encouragement and editorial expertise to this project from the time when it was just an idea to its completion. Carolyn Rory, Librarian at the Whittier Public Library, California, through her determination and ingenuity, tracked down numerous hard-to-find articles for me to examine. I owe a huge debt to two special friends: Roger De Silva and Dr. Ross Scimeca, who offered their time and expertise in foreign languages so unselfishly. And, of course, there are Sharon Cunney and Mary Pierce, the two typists who so skillfully typed the manuscript.

LIST OF ABBREVIATIONS

AATA *Art and archaeology technical abstracts,* v.1–, 1955–. New York. Semi-annual. Title varies: 1955–1957, *Studies in conservation;* 1958–1965. I.I.C. Abstracts. Volumes for 1955–1956 were published by the International Institute for Conservation of Historic and Artistic Works, London; 1966–, published at the Institute of Fine Arts, New York University, for the International Institute.

ABM *Artbibliographies modern,* v.4, no.1–, Spring, 1973–. Oxford, European Bibliographic Center; Santa Barbara, California, Clio Press, 1973–. Semiannual. Supersedes LOMA: *Literature of modern art,* 1969–1971, and assumes its numbering.

RAA *Repertoire d'art et d'archeologie,* depouillement des periodiques et des catalogues de ventes, bibliographie de ouvrages d'art francais et etrangers, tome 1–67, 1910–1963; Nouvelle serie, tome 1–1965–. Paris, Morance, 1910–. v.1–. Quarterly beginning in 1973. Published under the auspices of the Bibliotheque d'Art et d'Archeologie of the University of Paris and, since 1945, of the Comite International d'Histoire de l'Art.

RILA *Repertoire internationial de la litterature de l'art. International repertory of the literature of art.* Sterling and Francinie Clark Art Institute, Williamstown, Massachusetts. Published by the J. Paul Getty Museum with the sponsorship of the College Art Association of America, ARLIS/NA (Art Libraries Society of North America), and the International Committee for the History of Art. Semiannual. 1975–. v.1–. Volume for 1975 was preceded by a number dated 1973, called "Demonstration issue."

G&U Gettens, Rutherford John and Usilton, Bertha M. *Abstracts of technical studies in art and archaeology, 1943–1952.* Washington, 1955, 408 p., index (Freer Gallery of Art. Occasional papers, v.2, no.2).

RGR Reisner, Robert George. *Fakes and forgeries in the fine arts: bibliography.* New York: Special Libraries Association, 1950, 58 p.

ITEMS OF SPECIAL INTEREST

Since its founding in 1968, the International Foundation for Art Research (IFAR) in New York City often acts as a court of last resort in resolving questions of attribution and authenticity. The foundation will arrange for laboratory tests on art objects and engage art experts for stylistic analysis of works of art on behalf of individuals, galleries, and museums. Fees charged are based on the types of tests performed. In addition to its activities in the areas of authentication and attribution, IFAR maintains an extensive stolen art archive (over 25,000 items) documenting stolen art from around the world. The foundation publishes *IFAReports* (formerly the Stolen Art Alert and Art Research News). Published ten times a year, *IFAReports* is necessary reading for individuals and organizations involved in purchasing valuable art. By publishing these reports, IFAR hopes to help curtail the proliferation of forgeries in the marketplace. Most of the journal, however, is devoted to reporting news on stolen art. Numerous photos in each issue illustrate the stolen art and forgeries reported. (See H. Harvard Arnason, "Introducing the International Foundation for Art Research," *Museum News* (USA) 50 no.8 (April 1972) 28–30; Lee Rosenbaum, "IFAR: art attribution for art history's sake," *Art in America* (USA), 63 no.2 (March–April 1975) 25,27.)

A two-page chart providing information on how to detect fakes of sixty 20th century Italian artists was published in the May–June 1977 issue of *Bolaffiarte* (Italy), vol.8 no.70, pp.48–49. The title of the article is "Vero o Falso? Se lo dice lui" (Real or fake? If he says so), P. Levi, editor. It lists frequency and quality of fakes, galleries that can offer expert advice, works that can be consulted to aid in authenticating artworks, and experts on the artists.

The section on forged coins in this bibliography, although extensive, is far from exhaustive. The best source to consult for purposes of supplementing this section is the outstanding *Numismatic Literature* index, published by the American Numismatic Society in New York. The coverage of the index is international in scope with lengthy abstracts. A detailed subject index facilitates access to the index.

The rare book room of the New York Public Library houses an extraordinary collection of forged literary works. It is not surprising that the N.Y.P.L. also has a considerable amount of literature on the subject of literary forgeries in its collection. Anyone doing extensive research in the subject will want to visit the library to examine its holdings. For those people who cannot travel to New York, the G.K. Hall Co. has published the *Dictionary Catalog of the Research Libraries of the New York Public Library 1911–1971*. The subject heading of "Literature—Forgeries, Frauds, etc." yields an impressive catalog of works on the subject.

Newspaper articles have been omitted from this bibliography. Newspapers are an excellent source for gathering news on art forgery, especially the legal aspects of the problem. Articles frequently appear in the *New York Times* and the *London Times*. An excellent service to supplement individual newspaper indexes and newspaper data bases is the *Review of the Arts: Fine Arts and Architecture*, published by Newsbank Inc., in New Canaan, Connecticut. This information service covers the arts in over 100 newspapers from over 100 cities across the United States. Articles on painting, sculpture, museums, individuals, fakes, and forgeries etc., are reproduced on microfiche. This service is monthly. A printed index is also published monthly and cumulated every four months.

Philosophical

Books

1

Dutton, Denis, (Editor). *The forger's art: forgery and the philosophy of art.* Berkeley: University of California Press, 1983, 276 p., illus.

A collection of 12 articles concentrating on the more technical philosophical-aesthetic aspects of art forgery. Contents: Han van Meegeren *fecit*, by Hope B. Werness; What is wrong with a forgery?, by Alfred Lessing; Forgery and the anthropology of art, by Leonard B. Meyer; Art and authenticity, by Nelson Goodman; Originals, copies, and aesthetic value, by Jack W. Meiland; The aesthetic status of forgeries, by Mark Sagoff; Art, forgery, and authenticity, by Joseph Margolis; Artistic crimes, by Dennis Dutton; Is, Madam? nay, it seems!, by Michael Wreen; Notes on forgery, by Monroe Beardsley; On duplication, by Rudolf Arnheim; The disappointed art lover, by Francis Sparshott; Bibliography; Index.

2

Echtheitsfetischismus? Zur Wahrhaftigkeit des Originalen. (A fetish for authenticity? On the truthfulness of originals). Symposion in der Carl Friedrich von Siemens Stiftung, München-Nymphenburg, 4–5 April 1979. Munich: Carl Friedrich von Siemens Stiftung, 1979, 70 p., illus. (Carl Friedrich von Siemens Stiftung, Themen 28).

Contents: Introductions by Eric Steingraber and Michael Petzet; Malerei, Plastik, Kunstgewerbe, by Stephan Waetzoldt; Architektur, Stadtbaukunst, by Alfred A. Schmid.

3

Mumford, Lewis. *Art and technics.* New York: Columbia University Press, 1952, 162 p.

Contents: Art and the symbol; The tool and the object; From handicraft to machine art; Standardization, reproduction, and choice; symbol and function in architecture; Art, technics, and cultural integration.

Sections of Books

4

Aagard-Morgensen, Lars. "Unfakables." *Danish Yearbook of Philosophy*, 15 (1978) 97–104.

5

Beardsley, Monroe C. "Redefining art," in *The aesthetic point of view.* Ithaca: Cornell University Press, 1983.

6

Benjamin, Walter. "The work of art in the age of mechanical reproduction," in his *Illuminations*, translated by Harry Zohn; edited and with an introduction by Hannah Arendt. New York: Schocken Books, 1969, pp. 217–251.

7

Bernstein, Cheryl. "The fake as more," in *Idea art: a critical anthology*, edited by Gregory Battcock. New York: E.P. Dutton & Co., Inc., 1973, pp. 41–45.
A discussion of the artworks of Hank Herron.

8

Bloch, Peter. Original—Kopie—Fälschung. (Original—copy—forgery). *Jahrbuch, Preussischer Kulturbesitz* 16 (1979) 41–72. 23 illus.

9

Gardner, Howard. "Illuminating comparisons: looking at fakes and forgeries," in his *Art, mind and brain*. New York: Basic Books, Inc., 1982, pp. 218–226.

10

Gardner, Howard. "Illuminating Comparisons in the Arts," in *Vision and artifact*, edited by Mary Henle. New York: Springer Publishing Company, 1976, pp. 105–114.
An essay inspired by the Fakes and Forgeries Exhibition at the Minneapolis Institute of Arts in 1973.

11

Goodman, Nelson. "Arts and authenticity" (Chapter III), in his *Languages of art: an approach to a theory of symbols*, 2nd Edition, Indianapolis: Hackett Publishing Co., Inc., 1976, pp. 99–123.

12

Janson, H.W. "Originality as a ground for judgment of excellence," in *Art and philosophy: a symposium*, edited by Sidney Hook. New York: New York University Press, 1966, pp. 24–31.

13

Kennick, William. "Expression, creativity, truth, and form." in *Art and philosophy*, edited by William Kennick, New York: St. Martin's Press, 1980.

14

Metz, Peter. Echt oder falsch? Eine Studie über Grundsätzliches (True or false? A study concerning the rules of inquiry). *Festschrift K. Oettinger*, 1967, pp. 465–477.

15

Rheims, Maurice. *The strange life of objects: 35 centuries of art collecting &
collectors*. Translated from the French by David Pryce-Jones, New York:
Atheneum, 1961, pp. 3, 48 147, 160–165, 211.

16

Rudner, Richard. "On seeing what we shall see," in *Logic and art*, edited by
Richard Rudner and Israel Scheffler. Indianapolis: Bobbs-Merrill, 1972,
pp. 163–194.

17

Unverfehrt, Gerd. 'Reproduktion' oder 'Graphisches Original?' Anmerkungen
zur Geschichte der Druckplatte. ('Reproduction' or 'Original Prints?'
Remarks on the history of the printing plate), in *Vom Jugendstil zum
Bauhaus: Deutsche Buchkunst 1895–1930*, edited by Joseph Lammers
and Gerd Unverfehrt, pp. 176–180, 2 illus.

Periodicals

18

Aagard-Morgensen, Lars. Caught without an answer. *Philosophical Studies*,
28 no. 1 (1 July 1975) 67–70.

19

Bachler, Karl. Zur Psychogenese des Kunstfälschers (On the psychogenesis
of the art forger). *Zeitschrift für Kunstgeschichte* (Germany), 3 (1949)
127–131.

20

Banfield, Edward C. Art versus collectibles: why museums should be filled
with fakes. *Harper's Magazine* (USA), 265 No. 1587, (August 1982) 28–34.

21

Battin, M. Pabst. Exact replication in the visual arts. *Journal of Aesthetics
and Art Criticism* (USA), 38 no. 2 (Winter 1979) 153–158.

22

Bazarov, K. Emperors with no clothes. *Art and Artists* (England), 12 no. 4
(July 1977) 34–36.

English abstract in ABM vol. 9 (1978) #1686.

23

Bloch, Peter. Gefälschte Kunst (Forged Art). *Zeitschrift für Asthetik und
allgemeine Kunstwissenschaft* (Germany), 23 no. 1, (1978) 52–75, 16 illus.

English abstracts in RILA vol. 6 (1980) #213, and ABM vol. 10 (1979)
#1603.

24

Bloch, Peter. Original, Kopie, Fälschung (Original, copy, forgery). *Pantheon* (Germany), 39 no. 4 (1981) 354–357, 7 illus.

25

Bosson, V. Kopior, repliker, pastischer, förfalskingar. (Copies, replicas, pastiches, forgeries). *Paletten* (Sweden), no. 1 (1974) 10–11, 6 illus.

26

Cahn, Steven M., and Griffel, L. Michael. The strange case of John Shmarb: an aesthetic puzzle. *Journal of Aesthetics and Art Criticism* (USA), 34 no. 1 (Fall 1975) 21–22.

27

Ceysson, Bernard. Le copie destructive. (The destructive copy). *Revue de l'Art* (France), no. 21 (1973) 119–124. Summary in English.

English abstract in ABM vol. 6 (1975) #0918.

28

Chamoux, Francois; Velmans, Tania; Grodecki, Louis; Gauthier, Marie-Madeleine; Schnapper, Antoine; Foucart, Bruno; and Chastel, Andre. Copies, repliques, et faux (Copies, replicas, fakes). *Revue d'Art* (France), no. 21 (1973) 5–31, 31 illus. Summary in English.

A five-part article (in French) by 7 authors analyzing the distinctions between copies, replicas and fakes, and how they have been viewed from antiquity through the 20th century. Contents of the article in English are: I. Antiquity, medieval in the Orient and the Occident: The arts of repetition; II. The Renaissance. The principle of imitation; III. The Classical age: The institutional copy; IV. The XIX century: The elusive models and the museum of copies; V. The XX century. Devaluation of the copy and proliferation of the fake.

29

Colin, Ralph F. Fakes and frauds in the art world. *Art in America* (USA), 51 (April 1963) 86–89; Reply with Rejoinder. J.T. Soby and A.H. Barr, Jr., 51 (October 1963) 143.

30

Courtney, Neil. The strange case of John Shmarb: an epilogue and further reflections. *Journal of Aesthetics and Art Criticism* (USA) 34 no. 1 (Fall 1975) 27–28.

31

Czerner, Olgierd. Wartosc authentyzmu w zabytkach. (The value of authenticity in historical monuments). *Ochrona Zabytkow,* (Poland) 27 no. 3 (1974) 180–183.

English abstract in AATA vol. 12 (1975) #12-141.

32

De Gaigneron, A. Le temps des copies. (The age of copies). *Connaissance des Arts* (France), no. 368 (October 1982) 87–95, 9 illus.

English abstract in ABM vol. 14 (1983) #1118.

33

De Meredieu, F. Sur quelques faux objets pastiches. (On some fake false objects). *Revue d'Esthetique* (France) nos. 3–4 (1979) 124–130.

English abstract in ABM vol. 16 (1985) #0245.

34

Del Renzio, T. Multiple authenticity. *Art and Artists* (England), 9 no. 4 (July 1974) 22–27, 10 illus.

On the aesthetic problems created by easily reproduced prints. English abstract in ABM vol. 6 (1975) #2770.

35

Döhmer, Klaus. Zur Soziologie der Kunstfälschung. (On the sociology of art forgery). *Zeitschrift für Ästhetik und Allgemeine Kunstwissenschaft* (Germany) 23 no. 1 (1978) 76–95.

English abstract in RILA vol. 6 (1980) #219.

36

Dutton, Denis. Artistic crimes: the problem of forgery in the arts, *British Journal of Aesthetics* (England) 19 no. 4 (Autumn 1979) 302–314.

37

Epperson, Gordon. The strange case of John Shmarb: some further thoughts. *Journal of Aesthetics and Art Criticism* (USA), 34 no. 1 (Fall 1975) 23–25.

38

Fell, H. Granville. The validity of fakes as works of art. *Connoisseur* (England), 117 (1946) 32–37.

39

Field, R.; Proute, H.; and Wayne, J. On originality. *Print Collectors' Newsletter* (USA), 3 no. 2 (May–June 1972) 26–29, 3 illus.

40

Fuller, Peter. Forgeries. *Art Monthly* (England), 1 (Oct. 1976) 7–9.

English abstracts in RILA vol. 3 (1977) #3851 and ABM vol. 8 (1977) #1432.

41

Goodman, Nelson. Reply to Sagoff. *Erkenntnis* (Netherlands), 12 (1978) 166–168.

42

Graak, K. Original—Reproduktion–Originalreproduktion? (Original—reproduction—original reproduction?) *Artis* (Germany) 31 no. 11, (November 1979) 16–18, 9 illus.

English abstract in ABM vol. 22 (1980) #1079.

43

Gracia, J.J.E. Falsificación y valor artístico. (Falsification and artistic value). *Revista de las ideas estéticas* (Spain), 29 no. 116 (1971) 33–39.

44

Hauben, R. Han van Meegeren: a study of forgery. *Bulletin of the Menninger Clinic* (USA) 31 no. 3 (1967) 167–176.

45

Hoaglund, John. Originality and aesthetic value. *British Journal of Aesthetics* (England) 16 no. 1 (Winter 1976) 46–55.

46

Ivins, William M., Jr. Ignorance, the end. *Bulletin of the Metropolitan Museum of Art* (USA), n.s. (1943–1944) 2–10, illus.

English abstract in G&U #188.

47

Kennick, Wiliam E. Art and inauthenticity. *Journal of Aesthetics and Art Criticism.* (USA), 44 (Fall 1985) 3–12. Discussion. 44 (Winter 1985) 191–192; 44 (Spring 1986) 291–292.

48

Koestler, Arthur. The anatomy of snobbery. *Anchor Review,* 1 (1955) 1–25.

49

Kulka, Tomas. The artistic and aesthetic status of forgeries. *Leonardo* (England) 15 no. 2 (Spring 1982) 115–117.

50

Kulka, Tomas. The artistic and aesthetic value of art. *British Journal of Aesthetics* (England) 21 no. 4 (Autumn 1981) 336–350.

51

Lang, Berel. A note on the location of paintings. *Journal of Aesthetics and Art Criticism* (USA) 31 no. 1 (Fall 1972) 115–116.

52

Lessing, Alfred. What is wrong with a forgery? *Journal of Aesthetics and Art Criticism* (USA) 23 no. 4 (Summer 1965) 461–471.

53

Levinson, Jerrold. Aesthetic uniqueness. *Journal of Aesthetics and Art Criticism.* (USA) 38 no. 4 (Summer 1980) 435–450.

54

Linnenkamp, Rolf. Über Originalität und ihre Grenzen (On originality and its boundaries). *Pantheon* (Germany), 39 no. 3 (July–September 1981) 202–203, 2 illus.

English abstract in RILA vol. 11 (1985) #137.

55

Marabottini, A. Falsificazioni e disconoscimenti nell'arte contemporanea. (Forgeries and repudiations in contemporary art). *Problemi di Ulisse* (Italy) 12 no. 76 (1973) 156–169.

English abstract in ABM vol. 6 (1975) #4820.

56

Margolis, Joseph. Aesthetic appreciation and the imperceptible. *British Journal of Aesthetics* (England) 16 no. 4 (Autumn 1976), 305–312.

57

McFee, Graham. Adam made Me. *British Journal of Aesthetics.* (England) 18 no. 4 (Autumn 1978) 373–377.

English abstract in ABM vol. 12 (1981) #0728.

58

McFee, Graham. The Fraudulent in art. *British Journal of Aesthetics* (England), 20 (1980) 215–228.

59

Melot, Michel. Le frontières de l'originalité et les problèmes de l'estampe contemporaine. (The frontiers of originality and the problems of contemporary prints). *Revue de l'Art* (France), no. 21 (1973) 119–124. Summary in English.

60

Meyer, Leonard B. Forgery and the anthropology of art. *Yale Review* (USA) 52 (December 1962) 220–233.

61

Mitchells, K. The aesthetic status of art reproductions. *British Journal of Aesthetics* (England) 5 no. 1 (January 1965) 70–73.

62

Radford, Colin. Fakes. *Mind* (England) 87 (1978) 66–76.

63

Ralls, Anthony. The uniqueness and reproducibility of works of art: a critique of Goodman's theory. *Philosophical Quarterly,* 22 (1972) 1–18.

64

Resolato, G. Notes psychanalytiques sur le vol et la dégradation des oeuvres d'art. *Museum Unesco* (France) 26 no. 1 (1974), 21–25, 1 illus.

65

Sagoff, Mark. On the aesthetic and economic value of art. *British Journal of Aesthetics* (England) 21 no. 4 (Autumn 1981), 318–329.

66

Sagoff, Mark. The aesthetic status of forgeries. *Journal of Aesthetics and Art Criticism* (USA) 35 no. 2 (Winter 1976) 169–180.

67

Sagoff, Mark. Historical Authenticity. *Erkenntnis* (Netherlands), 12 (1978) 83–93.

68

Sagoff, Mark. On restoring and reproducing art. *Journal of Philosophy*, (USA), 75 no. 9 (September 1978) 453–470.

69

Saidenberg, N. Copies, pastiches, repliques. (Copies, pastiches, replicas). *Galerie/Jardin des Arts* (France) no. 132, (December 1973) 34–37, 12 illus.

70

Sipos, George. On the reproduction of works of art. *Journal of Aesthetics and Art Criticism* (USA) 32 no. 1 (Fall 1973) 107–108.

71

Stalker, Douglas F. Goodman on authenticity. *British Journal of Aesthetics* (England) 18 no. 3 (Summer 1978) 195–198.

72

Steele, Hunter. Fakes and forgeries. *British Journal of Aesthetics* (England) 17 no. 3 (Summer 1977) 254–258.

73

Thompson, C. Why do you need to see the original painting anyway? *Visual Resources* (USA) 2 pt. 1–3 (Fall 1981–Spring 1982) 21–36, 12 illus.

74

Van Holst, Niels, Kunstafälschungen in alter und neuer Zeit. Ein beitrag zum Verständnis des Falles Lubecker Marienkirche. *Weltkunst* (Germany) 23 no. 3 (1953) 4.

75

Waetzoldt, Stephan. Echtheits-Fetichismus. (Authenticity-fetishism). *Berliner Museen* (Germany) no. 16 (1979) 10–13.

76
Webster, William E. Music is not a notational system. *Journal of Aesthetics and Art Criticism* (USA) 29 no. 4 (Summer 1971) 489–497.

77
Wreen, Michael. Counterfeit coins and forged paintings: caveat emptor. *Analysis*, 40 (1980) 146–151.

General

Books

78

Arnau, Frank (Pseud.). *Three thousand years of deception in art and antiques.* TR. From the German by J. Maxwell Brownjohn. London: Jonathan Cape, 1961, 349 p., illus., bibliog., index.

The bibliography of Arnau's book (pp. 331–339) is especially valuable for older, European works. Contents: Part I: The lure of forgery. Part II: The forger's methods; (1) Paintings, (2) Sculptures, (3) Printed works, (4) Objects d'art, (5) Ceramics, (6) Textiles, (7) Furniture. Part III: The limits of the forger's art. Part IV: Art forgers; (1) Dossena, the human anacronism, (2) Thirty van Goghs in search of a painter, (3) Twentieth-century Vermeers, (4) Malskat, (5) Through a glass darkly; Corot, Menzel, Leibl, Courbet, Duveen, (6) Some cases in brief. Bibliography. Index.

79

Arnau, Frank. *Kunst der Fälscher, Fälscher der Kunst. 3000 Jahre Betrug mit Antiquitäten.* (2 völlig neu bearb. Ausg.) Düsseldorf, Wien: Econ-Verlag, 1969, 396 p., illus. (Das moderne Sachbuch, 85).

80

Arnau, Frank. *Arta falsificatorilor, falsificatorii artei.* (Translated from the German.) Bucharest: Meridiane, 1970, 364 p., illus.

81

Arnau, Frank. *L'art des faussaires et les faussaires de l'art.* Paris: R. Laffont, 1960, 342 p., illus.

82

Arnau, Frank. *Umeňi padělatelů-padělatelské uměňí. Tři tisíce let podvodů se starožitnostmi.* (Translated from the German). Prague: Orbis, 1973, 237 p., illus.

83

Arnau, Frank. *Arte della falsificazione, falsificazione dell'arte.* (Trans.) Milan: G. Feltrinelli, 1960, 398 p., illus.

84

Ballo, Guido. *Vero e falso nell'arte moderna.* Torino: La Bussola, 1962, illus.

85
Cole, Sonia Mary. *Counterfeit.* New York: Abelard-Schuman, 1957, 209 p., illus., index.

Contents: (1) Forgeries, (2) Forgers: financial and political motives, (3) Psychological cases, (4) Thirty thousand manuscripts, (5) Flint Jack, (6) The "Creator" of first editions, (7) The restorer of medieval murals, (8) The Moulin Quignon Jaw, (9) The Calaveras Skull, (10) The Piltdown Puzzle, (11) The detectors: prehistoric, (12) The detectors: artistic, literary and 'criminal'; Epilogue; References; Index.

86
Constable, William George. *Forgers and forgeries.* New York: Harry N. Abrams, Inc. 1945, 23 p.

English abstract in AATA vol. 5 (1964–65) #4477.

87
Demeure, Fernand. *Les Impostures de l'art.* (The imposters of art). Paris: F. Chambriand, 1951, 222 p.

88
Glückselig, Josef. *Atentáty na umĕni.* Prague: ČTK-Pragopress, 1971, 197 p., illus.

Essays on forgeries and vandalism.

89
Goll, Joachim. *Kunstafälscher* (Art forgery). Leipzig: E.A. Seemann, 1962, 253 p., illus., index.

90
Goodrich, David L. *Art fakes in America.* New York: Viking Press, 1973, 246 p., illus., bibliog., index.

Contents: Introduction. (1) The faking of American art, past and present, (2) The curious case of Henri Abraham Abel Haddad, (3) The marketplace, (4) Fakes in American museums, (5) Detection, (6) Lawsuits, (7) Prints and sculpture, (8) Rogues' gallery, (9) What can be done? Selected bibliography (pp. 225–235); Index.

91
Isnard, Guy. *Faux et Imitations dans l'art.* Librairie Arthène Fayard, 18, rue du Saint-Gothard, Paris XIV, 1959, 324 p., illus.

French abstract in AATA vol. 2 (1958–59) #1857.

92
Jaeger, Jerome Thomas. *How to detect art swindles in classical and renaissance paintings, illuminated manuscripts, drawings, prints and sculptures.* Albuquerque, New Mexico: Gloucester Art Press, 1982, 137 p., illus.

93

Jeppson. Lawrence. *The fabulous frauds: fascinating tales of great art forgeries.* New York: Weybright and Talley, 1970, 338 p.

"Lawrence Jeppson's narrative has all the suspense of a detective novel, whether he is describing the nineteenth-century theft of the Mona Lisa or the twentieth-century escapades of jet-set charlatans. He tells of fakes that were created for outright sale, fakes that were created to order, fakes that were created so that the originals could be stolen, and fakes created to be destroyed in order to collect insurance . . . ." (From the book jacket.)

94

Kurz, Otto. *Fakes.* (2nd revised and enlarged edition). New York: Dover Publications, 1967, 348 p., illus., index.

A standard handbook for collectors and students since it was first published in 1948. Contents: I. Painting; II. Classical paintings and mosaics; III. Illuminated manuscripts; IV. Drawings; V. Prints; VI. Stone sculpture; VII. Terra-cotta, VIII. Sculpture in Wood, IX. Ivory Carvings, X Bronze sculpture; XI. Chinese bronzes; XII. Goldsmiths' work; XIII. Pottery and porcelain; XIV. Glass; XV. Furniture; XVI. Tapestries; XVII. Book-bindings. XVIII. Fakes without models; XIX. Conclusion; Appendix; Index.

95

Kurtz, Otto. *Falsi e falsari* (Trans.) Venice: N. Pozza, 1961, XXIX + 362 p., illus.

96

Kurtz, Otto. *Faux et faussaires.* Translated from the English (2nd ed.) by J. Chavy. Paris: Flammarion, 1983, 371 p., illus.

97

Libman, Mikhail Iakovlevich, and Ostrovskij, G. *Poddel'nye šedvry.* Moscow: Sovetskii Khudožhnik, 1966, 110 p., illus., bibliog., pp. 3–4.

98

Mendax, Fritz. (Pseud.) *Aus der Welt der Fälscher.* (From the World of the Forger). Stuttgart: Kohlhammer, 1953, 306 p., 22 plates.

99

Mendax, Fritz. *Art fakes and forgeries.* Translated from the German by H.S. Whitman. New York: Philosophical Library, 1956, 222 p., illus., index.

100

Mendax, Fritz. *Le monde des faussaires.* (Translated from the German.) Paris: La Table ronde, 1956, 288 p., illus.

101

Mendax, Fritz. *Uit de wereld der vervalser.* Voorhoute: Foreholte, 1956, 255 p., illus.

102

Meyer, Karl E. *The plundered past: the traffic in art treasures.* 2nd ed. London: Penguin Books, 1977, 303 p., 10 illus., bibliog.

English abstract in ABM vol. 9 (1978) #4623.

103

Mills, John FitzMaurice and Mansfield, John M. *The genuine article: the making and unmasking of fakes and forgeries.* New York: Universe Books, 1982, 240 p., 96 illus., index. (Reprint. Originally published: London: British Broadcasting Corp., 1979).

Contents: Forward, (1) The art of duplicity, (2) Antiquities, (3) Ceramics, (4) Coins, (5) Documents, (6) Furniture, (7) Jewelry, (8) Paintings, drawings and prints I, (9) Paintings, drawings and prints II, (10) Scientific instruments, (11) Sculpture, carving and modeling, (12) Stamps, (13) Miscellany, acknowledgments, Index.

104

Neuburger, Albert. *Echt oder Fälschung?: die Beurteilung, Prüfung und Behandlung von Altertümern und Kunstgegenständen: eine Handbuch für Museumsleiter, Sammler, Liebhaber Händler, Chemiker usw.* Gutersloh: Prisma-Verlag, 1978, 204, 46 p., 116 illus. Bibliog. (pp. 182–188), Index. A photoreproduction of the 1924 edition.

105

Savage, George. *Forgeries, fakes and reproductions: a handbook for the collector.* London: Barrie & Rockliff, 1963, XIII, 312 p., illus., index.

Contents: Introduction, I. Antiquity, II. Furniture, III. Metalworks, IV. Carvings, in various materials, V. Ceramics. VI. Glass, VIII. Painting and drawing, VIII. The collector, the restorer, and the forger. 12 Appendixes, Bibliography, and Index.

106

Schüller, Sepp. *Fälscher, Händler und Experten. Das zwielictige Abenteuer der Kunstfälschungen.* Munich: Heyne, 1965, 253 p., 54 illus., index.

107

Schüller, Sepp. *Forgers, dealers, experts: strange chapters in the history of art.* Translated from the German by James Cleugh. New York: G.P. Putnam and Sons, 1960, 200 p., 54 illus.

Sections of Books

108

Alsop, Joseph. *The rare art traditions: the history of art collecting and its linked phenomena wherever these have appeared.* New York: Harper and Row, pp. 156–159, passim.

109

Bonner, Gerald and Noble, Joseph Veach. "Arts, fraudulence in the," in *The New Encyclopedia Britannica*, 15th edition. Chicago: Encyclopedia Britannica, Inc., 1983, vol. 2 pp. 89–93, bibliog.

Contains an introduction signed by the editor; an article on literary forgery, by Gerald Bonner; and an article on forgery in the visual arts, by Joseph Veach Noble. Includes a brief bibliography.

110

Brandi, Cesare, et al. "Falsification and forgery," in *Encyclopedia of world art*. New York, Toronto and London, 1961, vol. 5, cols., 333–350, plates 225–238. (Also published in Rome under the title *Enciclopedia universale dell'arte*, under the auspices of Instituto per la Collaborazione Culturale).

Contents: The nature of falsification, by Cesare Brandi; History of falsification; falsification of antique works, by Licia Vlad Borrelli; Falsification of medieval and modern art, by Giovanni Urbanni; Falsification of Oriental works, by Mario Praden; Falsification of tribal and pre-Columbian art, by Frederick A. Peterson; Procedures for detection of forgery, by Licia Vlad Borrelli; Bibliography, by Licia Vlad Borrelli and Giovanni Urbani.

111

Brandi, Cesare. *Teoria del restauro*. (Theory of restoration). Giulio Einaudi Editore S.p.A., Torino:Italy, 1977, 154 p. The appendix contains an article on the distinction between a copy, imitation, and falsification of an art object.

English abstract in AATA vol. 16 (1979) #1112.

112

David, Emmanuel, and Le Roterf, Hervé. *Le métier de marchaud de* tableaux: entretiens avec Hervé Le Boterf (The art dealer's profession: conversations with Hervé Le Boterf). Paris: Editions France-Empire, 1978, 283 p.

English abstract in ABM vol. 13 (1982) #1345.

113

Ehresmann, Donald L. "Forgery", in the *McGraw-Hill dictionary of art*. New York: McGraw-Hill, 1969, vol. 2, pp. 420–421, bibliog.

114

Faxon, Alicia Craig. "Fakes, frauds and forgeries," in her *Collecting art on a shoestring*. Barre, Massachusetts: Barre Publishers, 1969, pp. 51–55, 114.

115

Herchenroder, Christian. *Die Kunstmärkte:Sammelgebiete, Museumspolitik, Auktionsstrategien, Messemärkte, d. grossen Sammler, Fälschungen, Wert d. Expertise* (The art market: collecting, museum politics, auction strategies, mass market, the serious collector, fakes, value of expertise). Düsseldorf: Econ, 1978, 336 p., illus., bibliog., index.

116
Kelly, Francis. "Forgery," in his *Art restoration: a guide to the care and preservation of works of art.* New York: McGraw-Hill, 1972, pp. 193–213.

117
Lutterotti, Otto. "Zum Problem der Kunstfälschungen" (On the problem of art forgery), in *Festschrift L.C. Franz* (Austria), 1965, pp. 271–276, 4 illus.

118
Mustilli, Domenico. "Falsificazione," in *Enciclopedia dell'arte antica, classica e orientale.* Rome: Enciclopedia Italiana, vol III, pp. 576–589, illus., bibliography.

119
Osborne, Harold. "Forgery", in *The Oxford companion to art.* Oxford: Oxford University Press, pp. 430–431.

120
Rosenbaum, Lee. "The grand goofs," in her *The complete guide to collecting art.* New York: Alfred A. Knopf, 1982, pp. 148–153.

121
Savage, George. "Forgery, art", in the *Encyclopedia Americana, international edition.* Danbury, Connecticut: Grolier Incorporated, 1985, vol. 2 pp. 595–597.

122
Wraight, Robert. "Forgeries, fakes, and fiddles," in his *The art game.* New York: Simon and Schuster, 1966, pp. 79–105.

123
Zeri, Federico (Editor), et al. *Storia dell'arte italiana Parte 3, Situazioni momenti indagini; vol. 3, Conservazione, falso, restauro.* (History of Italian art. Part 3. Situations, moments, investigations; vol. 3, Conservation, forgeries, restoration). Torino: Einaudi, 1981, 534 p., 341 illus., index. (Storia dell'arte italiana, 10).

For contents of the entire volume, see RILA vol. 9 (1983) #239.

Periodicals

124
Auxion de Ruffé, R.d.'. Fraude et imitations dans l'art chinois (Frauds and imitations in Chinese art). *Marco Polo* (Hong Kong), 1 (1939–1940) 77–87, illus.

125
Bloch, Peter. Gefälschte Kunst (Forged art). *Zeitschrift für Asthetik und allgemeine Kunstwissenschaft* (Germany), 23 no. 1 (1978) 52–75, 16 illus.

126

Bower, Anthony. the double-dealers. *Art in America* (USA) 56 no. 4 (July 1968) 58–67, illus.

127

Chastel, André. Le musée du faux (The museum of forgery). *Médecine de France* (France), no. 52 (1954) 41–42.

General article on forgeries of all ages.

128

Clark, Kenneth. Forgeries. *History Today* (England) 29 no. 11, (November 1979) 724–733, illus.

"Lord Clark examines the history of forgeries in art and discusses the motives of the forgers and the reasons for which what now seem to us obvious forgeries were accepted in their time as authentic. He concludes with a discussion of the ethical problems raised by forgeries." (From the abstract to the article.)

129

Davis, Frank. More frauds, good and not so good. *Illustrated London News* (England) 241 (6 October 1962) 526, illus.

130

Davis, Frank. Not what they seem. *Illustrated London News* (England) 11 August 1962, p. 216, illus.

131

Esterow, Milton. Buyers, sellers, and forgers: the strange new art market. *Harpers* (USA) 234 no. 1405 (June 1967) 83–86.

132

Fell, H. Granville. Looting and faking. *Connoisseur* (England), 114 (1944) 54.

133

Findlay, George. On Fakes and over-restored works of art. *The Bulletin of the South African Museums Association* (South Africa) 10 no. 5 (1973) 186–188.

134

Fleming, Stuart J. Rouge's gallery of fakes. *Unesco Courier* (English edition, Paris), 34 (March 1981) 24–26, 34, illus.

An excerpt from Fleming's book *Authenticity in art; the scientific detection of forgery.* See #1295.

135

Fritz, R. Kokosnootbokalen, vervaardigd in de Nederlanden van de 15de tot de 18de eeuw. Geschiedenis en kunstgeschiedenis. *Antiek* (Netherlands) 13 no. 10 (1978–1979) 673–731, illus. Summary in English.

French abstract in RAA 1979 #9387.

136

Gilmour, P. The art of reproduction. *Arts Review* (England) 31 no. 4, (2 March 1979) 80–82, 3 illus.

English abstract in ABM vol. 10 (1979) #5052.

137

Gimlin, Joan S. Art and antique frauds. *Editorial Research Reports* (USA) 27 March 1968, 223–240.

138

Gould, Cecil. The ethics of faking: imitation and deception in art and antiques. *The Listener* (England) 65 (6 April 1961) 622–623.

139

Harris, Richard. A reporter at large: the forgery of art. *The New Yorker.* (USA) 37 no. 31 (16 September 1961) 112–145.

An interview with Sheldon Keck.

140

Harrisson, Caviness M. De convenientia et cohaerentia antiqui et novi operis: Medieval conservation, restoration, pastiche and forgery. *Intuition und Kunstwiss.* (Mél. H. Swarzenski), (Germany), 1973, p. 205–221, 13 illus.

141

Headington, Ann. The great Cellini and his roster of famous fakes. *Connoisseur* (USA), 216 no. 896 (September 1986) 98–103, 9 illus.

Portrait of controversial Giuseppe ("Pico") Cellini, connoisseur, critic, master detector of fakes.

142

Held, Julius S. Alteration and mutilation of works of art. *The South Atlantic Quarterly* 62 no. 1 (Winter 1963) 1–28, illus.

143

Hoving, Thomas. The game of duplicity. *Metropolitan Museum of Art Bulletin* (USA) 26 (1967–1968) 241–246.

144

Jones, Brenda. A fistfull of forgers. *Sunday Times Magazine,* (England) 8 March 1970, 46–47. Photos by Jon Milton.

General article on famous forgers and forgeries in the arts.

145

Kalma, J.J. Bedrog, bedriegers en bedrogenen. *Vrije Fries* (Netherlands), 55 (1975) 5–13.

146

Kent, Norman. [Editorial]. For the ring of crystal. *American Artist* (USA) 28 (March 1964) 3, 58.

A brief editorial on the forgery of artworks and the intent of the artist forger.

147

Kotschenreuther, H. Betrogen nach allen Regein der Kunst. III. Fälschen, eine Wissenschaft (Deception in all the established arts III. Forgery, a science). *Artis* (Germany), 27 no. 4 (1975) 16–20, 8 illus.

148

Krajick, Kevin. Stumbles, fumbles, and fakes. *Connoisseur* (England) 215 (Jan. 1985) 20–21.

A lighthearted look back at some of the more amusing sales at Sotheby's auction house on the occasion of their 100th birthday in 1985.

149

Kubler, Arnold. Falsch oder Ächt. *Du: Die Kunstzeitschrift,* (Switzerland), (April 1953) 6–34, 43 illus.

A broad ranging discussion of forgeries in numerous art forms, including a painting of Rudolf Koller, copied by August Voirol; a forgery of van Meegeren; Roman Italian ivory of the 11th century; the forgeries of Bastianni, etc.

French abstract in RAA 1953 #1795.

150

Lapouge, Gilles. Gefälschte Bilder, gefälschte Steine, gefälschte Handschriften (Forged paintings, forged jewelry, forged signatures). *Antares* (Germany), no. 8 (1956) 60–62.

151

Leerinck, Hans. In de werkplaats der kunstvervalsers. *Phoenix,* (Netherlands), 2 (1947) 42–48.

General article on forgeries in art and archaeology,

152

Leisching, Eduard. Über Kunstfälchungen (Concerning art forgery). *Alte und Moderne Kunst* (Austria), no. 67 (1963) 36; no., 68 (1963); 37; no. 69 (1963) 30.

153

Lockner, H.P. Vor der Münze bis zur Sonnenuhr. Wie man galvanoplastische Abformungen erkennen kann (From coins to sunclocks. How one can recognize galvanized castings). *Kunst und Antiquitäten* (Germany) no. 3 (1977) 51–54, 5 illus.

French abstract in RAA 1980 #11232.

154

Loew, Fernand. Fer, ferriers, forgerons, fabricants de faux au 15ᵉ s. Relations entre Neuchâtel, Fribourg et la Souabe. *Musee neuchâtelois*, 3ᵉ sér., 9 (1972) 33–52, 5 illus.

155

Makes, Frantisek. Konsthartsernas roll vid konstförfalskning. (The role of artisans in art forgery), *Paletten* (Sweden) no. 1, (1974) 13–15, 10 illus. English abstract in ABM vol. 8 (1977) #5069.

156

Morse, Earl. Fakes, frauds and free rides: confessions of a collector of chinese art. *Connoisseur* (England), 214 (December 1984), 90–93, illus.

157

Mueller, H. Fälschungen auf dem Pekinger Kunstmarkt. (Forgery from the Peking art market). *Ostasiatische Zeitsshrift* NF 3 (1926) 70–76, illus.

158

Musper, Theodor. Fälschungen und Verfälschungen in der bildenden Kunst (Falsification and forgery in the pictorial arts). *Kunstchronik* (Germany), 7 (1954) 271.

159

Petschek, W. Quanto vale il mio Picasso? (How much is my Picasso worth?) *Bolaffiarte* (Italy), 5 no. 38 (March 1974) 36–39, 7 illus.

An experiment by the author to find out how careful New York buyers are in authenticating art before they offer to purchase it. She took an authentic Picasso drawing to several buyers of which only one asked for legal authentication of the drawing.
English abstract in ABM vol. 6 (1975) #6209.

160

Reberschak, S.F. (Interviewer). L'ex direttore dei musei di Francia ha scritto un dossier esplosivo. Falsi: i collezionisti non possono difendersi (The ex-director of the museums of France has written an explosive dossier: fakes—collectors cannot defend themselves). *Bolaffiarte* (Italy), 10 no. 85 (January–February 1979) 44, 1 illus.

An interview with Jean Chatelain, former Director of the Museums of France, about a book, he is writing about fakes.
English abstract in ABM vol. 10 (1979) #5417.

161

Robbins, Chris. The great art forgers. *Observer Magazine* (England), 9 May 1976, pp. 24–27, ports., illus.

162

Rogers, Derek. The anatomy of forgery. *The Arts Review* (England), 15 no. 25 (28 December 1963–11 January 1964) 10.

General interest article on the nature of art forgeries. Mention of van Meegeren, forgeries in modern paintings and George Savage's book, *Forgeries fakes and reproductions: a handbook for the collector* (#105).

163

Savage, George. Are forgeries so frequent? *The Studio* (England),164 no. 834 (October 1962) 150–152, illus.

164

Savage, George. Forgeries and forgers. *Studio International* (England), 174 no. 891 (July/August 1967) 62–63.

165

Schrade, Hubert. Das Problem des Kunstfälschertums (The problem of forgery in art.) *Universitas* (Germany), 18 (1963) 1299–1310.

166

Simpson, Colin, and Sewell, Brian. Delusions of grandeur? *Sunday Times Magazine* (England), 25 March 1984, pp. 20–24, illus.

Portrait of Ante Topic-Minara and an assessment of his art collection (mostly fakes) which is valued at over 4 billion dollars. The collection is housed in Marshall Tito's villa overlooking Zagreb, in north Yugoslavia.

See also Thomas Hoving's book *The king of the confessors* for Hoving's account of how he purchased a (authentic) medieval ivory cross—one of the Metropolitan Museum of Art's most prized possesion—from Topic-Minara. (#1073).

167

Slánský, B. Copies, forgeries and expertises. *Zprávy Památkové Péce* (Czechoslovakia), 16 no. 3 (1956) 144–152.

English abstract in AATA vol. 2 (1958–1959) #1271.

168

Ślesiński, Marek, K. Metody fałszowania przedmiotów z metali (Techniques of forging metal objects). *Ochrona Zabytków* (Poland), 35 no. 3–4 (1982) 187–192. Summary in English.

English abstract in AATA vol. 22 (1985) #22-1106.
French abstract in RAA 1985 #3060.

169

Solomon, Stephen. Nelson Rockefeller turns his passion for art into a business. *Fortune* (USA), 98 no. 8 (23 October 1978) 72–75, illus.

On Rockefeller's controversial decision to sell accurate reproductions of his art works.

170
Unsigned Article. A fake is a fake is a fake. *Country Life* (England), 160 no. 4131 (2 September 1976) 580.

Very brief article with general thoughts on fakes and reference to forger Tom Keating.

171
Unsigned Article. Hints on spotting fakes. *Business Week* (USA), 27 October 1973, p. 110.

Brief article warning against fake art on the market.

172
Unsigned Article. Let the buyer beware. *Newsweek* (USA), 69 (19 June 1967) 112–114, illus.

General article on the different types of art forgeries on the market.

173
Unsigned Article. Ein Säkulum Kunstfälschungen (A century of art forgeries). *Das Kunstwerk* (Germany), 8 no. 6 (1954) 37–43, 7 illus.

French abstract in RAA 1954 #1309.

174
Vinter, Vlastimil. Kulturní památky a otázka jejich autentičnosti. *Architektura ČSSR* (Czechoslovakia), 28 (1969) 282–284, 5 illus. Summary in Russian, English, French and German.

175
Wilhelm R. Sammler, Händler und Fälscher in China. *Cinesische Blätter für Wissenschaft und Kunst* (Germany), 1 no. 2 (1926), 66–77.

176
Witt, P. Falszerstwa w afekcie. *Sztuka* (Poland), 5 no. 2 (1978), 48–53, 8 illus. Summary in Russian and English.

French abstract in RAA 1980 #105.

177
Wykes-Joyce, M. Forgers in perspective. *Arts Review* (England), 28 no. 19 (17 Sept. 1976) 485, 487.

English abstract in ABM vol. 8 (1977) #1433.

178
Zevi, Franco (Interview). Il mercato è invaso dai falsi, ma ci sono anche dei 'falsi' con credenziali di stato: I falsi da museo. (The market is invaded by fakes, but there are also fakes bearing state credentials: museum fakes). *Bolaffiarte*, (Italy), 8 no. 74 (Nov.–Dec. 1977) 9–11, 5 illus.

English abstract in ABM vo. 9 (1978) #1678.

Paintings

Books

179

Aries, R.S. *Le faux dans la peinture et l'expertise scientifique* (Fakes in painting and scientific expertise), Monte Carlo, Prochim, 1965, 103 p.

180

Avermaete, R. *Naweeën van het geval Vermeer-van Meegeren*. Brussels: Paleis der Academiën, 1974, 21 p.

181

Brandhof, Marijke van den. *Een vroege Vermeer uit 1937: achtergronden van leven en werken van de schilder/vervalser Han van Meegeren*. (An early Vermeer of 1937: life and work of the painter/forger Han van Meegeren). Utrecht: Het Spectrum, 1979, 168 p., 142 illus., bibliog., index.

182

Burroughs, Alan. *Art criticism from a laboratory*. Westport, Connecticut: Greenwood Press, 1971, xxiii, 227 p., illus. Reprint of 1938 edition.

183

Coremans, Paul B. *Van Meegeren's faked Vermeers and De Hooghs:* a scientific examination. Translated from the French by A. Hardy and C.M. Hutt. Amsterdam: J.M. Meulenhoff, 1949, viii, 40 p., 76 plates.

184

Corradini, Juan. *Radiografía y Macroscopía del Grafismo de Pedro Figari* (Radiography and photomacrography of Pedro Figari's drawing technique). Buenos Aires, Argentina: Museo Nacional de Bellas Artes, 64 p., 81 illus., bibliog.

English abstract in AATA vol. 17 (1980) #17-523.

185

Cotter, Maurice J.; Meyers, Pieter; van Zelst, Lambertus; and Sayre, Edward V. *Authentication of paintings by Ralph A. Blakelock through neutron activation of autoradiography*. Report BNI 17215 1972, 29 p. (1972). Brookhaven National Laboratory, Upton, New York.

English abstract in AATA vol. 10 (1973) #10-732.

186

Cotter, Maurice J.; Meyers, Pieter; van Zelst, Lambertus; Olin, C.H.; and Sayre, Edward V. *Study of the materials and techniques used by some 19th century oil painters by means of neutron activation autoradiography*. Report, Brookhaven National Laboratory 18629, 53 p., 1973.

Research on paintings by Ralph A. Blakelock.
English abstract in AATA vol. 12 (1975) #12-353.

187

Coutot, Maurice. Académie des beaux-arts. *Vrais ou faux dans la peinture moderne: communication faite à la séance du mercredi 31 mai 1978* (True or false in modern painting: communication made at the meeting of Wednesday, 31 May 1978). Paris: Institut de France, 1978, 22 p.

188

Dantzig, Maurits Michel van. *Pictology: an analytical method for attribution and evaluation of pictures.* Edited by the van Dantzig Foundation, with a preface by T.S. Buchner. Leinden: E.J. Brill, 1973, XVI, 112 p., 59 illus., (2 color).

English abstract in ABM vol. 8 (1977) #4190.

189

Dantzig, Maurits Michel van. *Vincent? A new method of identifying the artist and his work and of unmasking the forger and his products.* Amsterdam, 1953.

190

Decoen, Jean. *Vermeer-van Meegeren, scandale ou vérité?* (Vermeer-van Meegeren, scandal or truth?) Knokke-Le Zoute: Jean Decoen, 1968, 85 p.

191

Decoen, Jean. *Vermeer-van Meegeren, back to the truth.* Translated by E.J. Labarre. London: A. Donker, 1951.

192

Decoen, Jean. *Retour à la vérité, Vermeer-van Meegeren: deux authentiques Vermeer* (Back to the truth, Vermeer-van Meegeren: Two authentic Vermeers). Rotterdam: A. Donker, 1951, 60 p., illus., facisms.

193

Doudart de la Grée, Marie Louise. *Het fenomeen Getramatiseerde documentaire over het leven van de kunstschilder Han van Meegeren.* The Hague: Omniboek, 1974, 72 p., 8 plates.

194

Doudart de la Grée, Marie Louise. *Ich war Vermeer. Die Fälschungen des Han van Meegeren.* (I was Vermeer. The forgeries of Han van Meegeren). Translated from the Dutch by H. Stifter. Gütersloh, Bertelsmann, 1968, 235 p., illus.

195

Ferré, Jean. *Lettre ouverte à un amateur d'art pour lui vendre la mèche.* Paris: A. Michel, 1975, 214 p., index.

196

Grabar, Igor. *Novootkrytyj Rembrandt.* (A newly uncovered Rembrandt). Moscow: Academy of Sciences, 1956, 88 p., illus. Summary in German.

English abstract in AATA vol. 2 (1958–1959) #1143.

197

Hours, Madeleine. *Le Secret des Chefs-d'Oeuvre—L'oeuvre d'art est matière avant d'être message.* (Secrets of the Old Masters: the work of art is medium before being a message). Paris: Denoel/Gonthier, Bibliothèque Médiations, 1982, 168 p., 14 plates.

English abstract in AATA vol. 19 (1982) #19-476.

198

Isnard, Guy. *Les pirates de la peinture.* (The pirates of painting). Paris: Flammarion, 1955, 185 p., illus.

French abstract in AATA vol. 2 (1958–1959) #2167.

199

Isnard, Guy. *Vrai ou faux?* (True or false?) Paris: Robert Laffont, 1974, 381 p., plates.

200

Joni, Icilio Federico. *Le memorie di un pittore di quadri antichi: con alcune descrizioni sulla pittura a tempera e sul modo di fare invecchiare i dipinti e le dorature* (Memories of a painter of antique paintings: with some descriptions concerning tempera painting and the way to age paintings and gilt decorations). Preface by Umberto Baldini. Firenze: Sansoni, 1984, x, 282 p., 15 illus. Originally published c1931.

The autobiography of I.F. Joni, painter, and forger of 14th and 15th century Italian style paintings.

201

Keating, Tom; Norman, Geraldine; and Norman, Frank. *The fake's progress: being the cautionary history of the master painter and simulator Tom Keating as recounted with the utmost candor & without fear of favor to Frank Norman; together with a dissertation upon the traffic in works of art by Geraldine Norman* [entitled Art trading and art faking], London: Hutchinson & Co. (Publishers) Ltd., 1971, 272 p., leaf of plate, 12 pages of plates: illus., facisms, ports., appendix.

English abstracts in AATA vol. 20 (1983) #20-662; RILA vol. 4 (1978) #3013; ABM vol. 8 (1977) #5641. See also #216.

202

Kilbracken, John Raymond Godley, Baron. *Fälscher oder Meister? Der Fall van Meegeren.* (Forger or master? The case of van Meegeren). Translated by F. Polakovics. Vienna, Hamburg: Zsolnay, 1968, 291 p., 38 illus.

203

Kilbracken, John Raymond Godley, Baron. *The master art forger: the story of Han van Meegeren.* Agincourt [Ont.]: Book Society of Canada, 1966, 135 p., illus., ports.

204

Kilbracken, John Raymond Godley, Baron. *The master forger: the story of Han van Meegeren.* London: Home and Van Thal, 1951, 223 p., illus.

205

Kilbracken, John Raymond Godley, Baron. *The master forger: the story of Han van Meegeren.* New York: Wilfred Funk, 1951:, 223 p., illus.

206

Kilbracken, John Raymond Godley, Baron. *Van Meegeren: master forger.* New York: Charles Scribner's Sons, 1967, 197 p., index, Appendix I. Chronology; Appendix II. Principle data on the forgeries.

207

Kilbracken, John Raymond Godley, Baron. *Van Meegeren: a case history.* London: Nelson, 1967, 197 p., 24 plates.

208

Kilbracken, John Raymond, Godley, Baron. *Van Meegeren ou la vic d'un faussaire.* [Translated from the English]. Paris: Mercure de France, 1969, 253 p., plates.

209

Kurz, Otto. *Art forgeries and how to examine paintings scientifically. Albuquerque, New Mexico: Gloucester Art Press, (Foundation for Classical Reprints), 1982, 115 p., illus. Reprint of 1901 edition.*

210

Kurz, Otto. *Art forgeries and how to examine paintings scientifically.* Deluxe edition. Albuquerque, New Mexico: Gloucester Art Press, 1979. Reprint of 1948 edition.

211

Mailfert, André. *Au pays des antiquaires, confidences d'un "maquilleur" professionnel.* Paris: Flammarion, 1954, 171 p., illus.

212

Mailfert, André. *Au pays des antiquaires, confidences d'un maquilleur professionnel.* [Nouvelle édition]. Paris: Flammarion, 1968, 189 p., plates.

213

Maltese, C. *Vero e falso in un'opera di pittura.* Genova: Commune di Genova. Ass. Att. Culturali, 1977, Vedere nel museo. 1, 36 p., 48 illus.

214

Moiseiwitsch, Maurice. *The van Meegeren mystery: a biographical study.* London: Arthur Barker, 1964, 204 P., index, 8 plates.

Contents: Part one. Apprenticeship with the Masters 1889–1915; Part two. Disenchantment 1916–1934; Part three. The Magnificent Fraud 1934–1944; Part four. The Goering Affair 1944–1947; Index.

215

Myers, P. Gay. *The technical investigation and conservation treatment of an alleged Ming Dynasty wall painting.* M.A. Thesis, Oberlin College, Oberlin, Ohio, 1978, 103 p., 14 illus.

English abstract in AATA vol. 16 (1979) #16-1503.

216

Norman, Geraldine (Editor) *The Tom Keating catalogue: illustrations to the fake's progress.* Introduction by Geraldine Norman. London: Hutchinson & Co. (Publishers) Ltd., 1977, 104 p., 116 illus., facisms, ports.

English abstract in ABM vol. 8 (1977) #5642;
AATA vol. 20 (1983) # 20-683. See also #201.

217

Peyrefitte, R. *Scene di caccia. La vita straordinaria di Fernand Legros.* [Translated from the French]. Milan: Garzanti, 1978, Memorie documenti, 409 p.

218

Porkay, Martin. *Rembrandt, andere Leute und ich* (Rembrandt, other people and me). Wetzlar: Pegasus, Verlag, 1959, 268 p., illus.

219

Porkay, Martin. *Die Abenteuer zweier unechter Rembrandts* (The adventures of two fake Rembrandts) Munich: Lama Verlag, 1963, 72 p., plates, ports.

220

Schüller, Sepp. *Falsch oder Echt? Der Fall Van Meegeren* (True or false? The case of van Meegeren). Bonn: Brüder Auer, 1953, 74 p., 17 plates (1 color).

221

Stein, Anne-Marie. *Three Picassos before breakfast: memoirs of an art forger's wife.* As told to George Carpozi, Jr. New York: Hawthorne Books, 1973, 192 p., illus.

222

Vermeer de Delft: Une affaire scandaleuse de vrais et de faux tableau (Vermeer of Delft. A scandalous affair of true and false paintings). Brussels: Cahier des Arts, 1958, 106 p., illus.

223

Werner, A.E. *Scientific examination of paintings*. London, 1952, 15 p. (Royal Institute of Chemistry. Lectures, Monographs, and Reports, no. 4).

English abstract in G&U #1120.

224

Wright, Christopher. *The art of the forger*. New York: Dodd, Mead & Company, 1985, 160 p., illus., index. Includes a "Chronology of the appearance of the paintings described as possible forgeries."

"A specialist in seventeeth century art, Christopher Wright presents formidable evidence that some of the world's most renowned paintings are in fact the work of forgers. . . . Documentation and reproduction of undoubted works by Georges de La Tour at the outset of the book, assist readers in becoming familiar with the painter's style in order to reach their own conclusions about suspect paintings from the evidence presented. . . . Mr. Wright provides a gripping narrative with all the appeal of a good detective story." [From the book jacket.]

Sections of Books

225

Atkins, Guy. *Asger Jorn: the crucial years, 1954–1964. A study of Asger Jorn's artistic development from 1954 to 1964 and a catalogue of his oil paintings from that period*. London: Lund Humphries; New York: Wittenborn, 1977, 1000 illus., bibliog., biogs., exhibition list, catalog of works.

Includes a chapter on Jorn forgeries.
English abstracts in RILA vol. 4 (1978) #3000; ABM vol. 8 (1977) #1914.

226

Brandt, Walfried; Danninger, Edgar; and Straub, Rolf E. "Untersuchung zu einer Bernhard Strigel zugeschriebenen Darstellung der "Heiligen Antonius Eremita" in der Staatsgalerie Stuttgart", (Examination of a painting (Holy Antony Eremita) attributed to Bernhard Strigel (State Gallery, Stuttgart)), in *Jahrbuch der Staatlichen Kunstsammlungen Baden-Wurttemberg*, 5 (1968) 33-121.

English abstract in AATA vol. 7 (1968–1969) #7-1611.

227

Chandra, Moti. *The technique of Mughal painting*. Lucknow: U.P. Historical Society, Provincial Museum, 1949, xi, 108 p., 10 plates, index.

Includes a section on faked pictures.
Contents of book in G&U # 1028a.

228

Cotter, Maurice J.; Meyers, Pieter; Van Zelst, Lambertus; Olin, C.H.; and Sayre, Edward V. "A study of the materials and techniques used by some XIX century American oil painters by means of neutron activation autoradiography," in *Applicazione dei metodi nucleari nel campo delle opere d'arte. Congresso internazionale, Rome-Venezia, 24–29 Maggio 1973,* (Applications of nuclear methods in the fields of works of art. International congress, Rome-Venice, 24–29 May 1973). Rome: Accadamia Nazionale Dei Lincei, 1976, pp. 163–203. Summary in Italian.

Research on paintings by Ralph A. Blakelock.
English abstract in AATA vol., 14 (1977) #14-1008.

229

Davidson, Harold G. *Edward Borein: cowboy artist.* New York: Doubleday, 1974, 189 p., 169 illus.

Includes a discussion of Borein fakes.
English abstract in ABM vol. 10 (1979) #0945.

230

Fernier, Robert. *La vie et l'oeuvre de Gustave Courbet: catalogue raisonné. Tome 2: Peintures 1866–1877, dessins, sculptures.* (The life and work of Gustave Courbet: catalogue raisonné. Vol. 2: Paintings 1866–1877, drawings, sculptures). Lausanne; Paris: Bibliotheque des Arts, 1978, 750 + illus. (8 color), maps, index.

A two-volume set; vol. 2 contains a section on the sale of Courbet forgeries.
English abstracts in RILA vol. 7 (1981) #7043; ABM vol. 13 (1982) #1282.

231

Fu, M. and Fu, S. *Studies in connoisseurship: Chinese paintings from the Arthur M. Sackler collection in New York and Princeton.* With a preface by W.C. Fong, and an introduction by A.M. Sackler. Princeton, New Jersey: Princeton University Press, 1973, 375 p., 413 illus., bibliog.

English abstract in ABM vol. 9 (1978) #2852.

232

Goodrich, Lloyd. "A note on forgeries," in his *Albert P. Ryder.* New York: George Braziller, Inc., 1959, pp. 117-120.

233

Harper, J. Russell. *Krieghoff.* Toronto, Ontario; Buffalo, New York; London: University of Toronto Press, 1979, 204 p., 164 illus., bibliog.

Includes a chapter on Krieghoff imitations and forgeries.
English abstract in ABM vol. 12 (1981) #6240.

234

Hayes, John. "The problem of Gainsborough Dupont", (appendix 1) and "Copyists, Imitators and Influence" (appendix 2), in his *The landscape paintings of Thomas Gainsborough: a critical text and catalogue raisonné, volume one* (critical text). Ithaca, New York: Cornell University Press, 1982, pp. 187–236; 237–298. Also includes an 8 page, annotated bibliography on Gainsborough and his work as a landscape painter.

235

Keisch, Bernard. "Art and the atom: two dating methods based on measurements of radioactivity," in *Application of science in examination of works of art*. Research Laboratory, Boston Museum, 1973, pp. 193–198, illus., tables.

English abstract in AATA vol. 11 (1974) #11-642.

236

Koningsberger, Hans (and The Editors of Time-Life Books). "A legacy of mystery," in *The world of Vermeer 1632–1675*. New York: Time Incorporated, 1967, pp. 169–185, illus.

237

Laurie, Arthur Pillans. *The technique of the great painters*. London: Carroll and Nicholson Ltd., 1949, 192 p., plates, illus.

Contains a section on forgeries.

238

Lugt, Frits. "Echt oder unecht?" (True or false?), in *Festschrift E. Trautscholdt*, 1965, pp. 11–14.

239

Roskill, Mark. "Forgery and its detection: the hand of Hans van Meegeren," in his *What is art history?* New York: Harper and Row, 1976, pp. 154–167, illus.

240

Sedova, E.N. "Principles of examination of the works of art attributed to I.K. Aivazovski," in *Paris: International Council of Museums. ICOM Committee for conservation. 5th Triennal Meeting, II* (1–8 Oct. 1978), Zagreb. Paris: International Council of Museums, 1978, non paged.

241

Stechow, W. "On an early painting by Stefan Lochner," in *Kölner Bericht zur Kunstgeschichte* (Germany), 1 (1977) on Stefan Lochner (Koln Congress 1974) 122–126, 4 illus.

French abstract in RAA 1979 #11908.

242

Zeri, Frederico. *Diari di Laboro* (Diaries of my work). Bergamo: Emblema, 1971, 91 p., 115 photographs (107 b + w, 8 color).

Contains an article about a faker of Italian works.
English abstract in AATA vol. 9 (1972) #9-280.

Periodicals

243

Accorsi, C. Ecco l'elenco dei falsi de Chirico riprodotti en catalogo (The fake de Chiricos which are in his catalogue. *Bolaffiarte* (Italy), 10 no. 91 (Summer 1979) 28–33, 60 illus.

English abstract in ABM vol. 11 (1980) #1010.

244

Accorsi, C. and Gianferrari, E. Cinquecento o 5 mila i Sironi 'Macchiati'? (5 hundred or 5 thousand 'Micchiati' Sironis?) *Bolaffiarte* (Italy), 4 no. 34 (November 1973) 66–67, 8 illus.

English abstract in ABM vol. 6 (1975) #3104.

245

Althöfer, H. Echt oder falsch? Kennerschaft und Wissenschaft (Genuine or fake? Connoisseurs and science). *Weltkunst* (Germany), 47 no. 1 (1977) 18–20, 3 illus.

246

Bell, Lynne. Kaufe nie ein Bild, von dem die Copie im Louvre hängt (Never buy a picture if there is a copy hanging in the Louvre). *Artis* (Germany), no. 10 (1967) 10–12, 5 illus.

247

Bender, C. Over vervalsing van schilderijen. *Wetenschap. Tijd.*, 13, (1953) col. 336–344, 4 illus.

248

Bertrand, G. Le tableau d'après le tableau (Paintings which are 'after' other paintings). *Revue d'Esthétique* (France), 27 no. 1 (January–March 1974) 57–76, 6 illus.

English abstract in ABM vol. 6 (1975) #2496.

249

Blunt, Anthony. Poussin studies: early falsifications of Poussin. *Burlington Magazine* (England), 104 (November 1962) 486–498, illus. Reply by R.E. Spear 106 (May 1964) 234, illus.

250

Bogdan, Radu. Andreescu intre autentic şi fals. Metode de cercetare şi expertizà, în trecut şi prezent (Andreescu between real and false. Methods of research and expertise, formerly and today). *Studii si cercetari de istoria artei* (Romania) 22 (1975) 95–118, 9 illus. Summary in French. English abstract in RILA vol. 3 (1977) #2293. French abstract in RAA 1976 #3681.

251

Bosch, Lodewyk. Het wetenschappelijk onderzoek van schilderijen. *Phoenix* (Netherlands), 2 (1947/1948) 15–20, 3 illus.

252

Brachert, Thomas. Gemäldefälschungen. Praktische Hinweise zu ihrer Erkennung. 1. Teil (Practical hints in recognizing forged paintings. Part 1). *Weltkunst* (Germany), 44 no. 9 (1974) 769–771, 7 illus.

253

Brachert, Thomas. Gemäldefälschungen. Praktische Hinweise zu ihrer Erkennung. 2. Teil. (Practical hints in recognizing forged paintings. Part 2). *Weltkunst* (Germany), 44 no. 10 (1974) 861–863, 19 illus.

254

Brachert, Thomas. Gemäldefälschungen, Möglichkeiten ihrer Bekämpfung. Eine Studie (Forged paintings, possibilities of halting the activity). *Schweizerisches Institut für Kunstwissenschaft* (Switzerland), 1966, pp. 39–86, 44 illus.

255

Brealey, John M. and Meyers, Pieter. [Letter].*The Fortune Teller* by Georges de La Tour. Burlington Magazine (England), 123 no. 940 (July 1981) 422, 425, 2 illus.

256

Breek, R., and Froentjes, W. Application of pyrolysis gas chromatography on some of van Meegeren's faked Vermeers and Peter de Hooghs. *Studies in Conservation* (England), 20 no. 4 (1975) 183–189, 6 illus.

257

Bromley, D. Allan. Neutrons in science and technology. *Physics Today* (USA) 36 no. 12 (December 1983), 30–39.

The use of autoradiography to detect alterations in paintings. English abstract in AATA vol. 21 (1984) #21-26.

258

Brooks, Valerie F. The thrill of a lifetime. *ARTnews* (USA), 84 no. 5 (May 1985) 19–20, illus.

New York art dealer Alain Tarica claims *The Annunciation,* attributed to Dirk Bouts, is a forgery. The J. Paul Getty Museum, which is said to have paid $7 million for the tempera on cloth painting, thinks otherwise.

259

Bunney, Sarah. Tree ring dating for paintings is thrown into doubt. *New Scientist* (England), no. 1440 (24 January 1985) 37.

English abstract in AATA vol. 22 (1985) #22-1974.

260

Cagiano de Azevedo, Michelangelo. La *Polimnia* di Cortona e Marcello Venute (Marcello Venuti and the Cortona *Polymnia*). *Storia dell'arte* (Italy), 38–40 (January–December 1980) 389–392, 2 illus.

English abstract in RILA vol. 9 (1983) #5685;
French abstract in RAA 1981 #8868.

261

Cagiano de Azevedo, Michelangelo. Falsi settecenteschi di pitture antiche. *Bollettino dell'Instituto Centrale del Restauro* (Italy), no. 1 (1950) 41–43, 3 illus.

French abstract in RAA 1950–1951 #2451.

262

Cahill, James. Collecting Chinese painting. *The Arts* (USA), 37 no. 7 (April 1963) 66–72, illus.

263

Chastel, A. A propos d'un faux primitif. Les liens de la figure et du décor (Regarding a false primitive. The connections between the figures in the painting). *Kunsthist. Forsch. O. Pächt* (Austria), 1972, pp. 199–204, 5 illus.

French abstract in RAA 1974 #10017.

264

Checkland, S.J. The Tom Keating saga. *Arts Review* (England), 31 no. 5 (16 March 1979) 110, 112, 133.

English abstract in ABM vol. 10 (1979) #6063.

265

Clines, Francis X. The science of fraud detection: newer techniques of fluorescence, mass spectrometry, thermoluminescence outwitted by master art forger. *Science Digest* (USA) 85 no. 2 (Feb. 1979) 23–26.

Portrait of forger David Stein.

266

Colin, Ralph F. Fakes and frauds in the art world. *Art in America* (USA), 51 no. 2 (1963) 86–89, 3 illus.

Includes reproductions of forgeries of Manet, Feninger, and Monet.

267

Constable, W.G.A. A discovery and a warning. *Bulletin of The Museum of Fine Arts* (Boston), 41 no. 245 (1943) 51–54.

The cleaning of a painting, believed to be of Mme. de Bourboulon by Hubert Drouais, revealed that the painting had been mostly repainted by a restorer.

English abstract in G&U #1097.

268

Coremans, Paul. L'affaire des faux Vermeer, documents de complément. *Maandblad voor Beeldcnde Kunsten. Vereeniging van Vrienden der Aziatische Kunst* (Netherlands), 26 (1950) 199–203, 5 illus.

English abstract in G&U #170;
French abstract in RAA 1950–1951 #2454.

269

Cotter, Maurice J.; and Sayre, Edward V. Neutron activation analysis of oil paintings by Ralph A. Blakelock. *Bulletin of the American Group—The Institute for Conservation of Historic and Artistic Works* (USA), 11 no. 2 (1971) 91–106, 6 illus.

English abstract in AATA vol. 9 (1972) #9-223.

270

Cotter, Maurice J. Neutron activation analysis of oil paintings. *American Scientist* (USA), 69 no. 1 (January–February 1981) 17–27, illus.

English abstract in AATA vol. 18 (1981) #18-436.

271

Cotter, Maurice J., and Taylor, Kathleen. Neutron activation analysis of paintings. *Physics Today* (USA), 16 no. 5 (1978) 263–271.

English abstract in AATA vol. 15 (1978) #15-1446.

272

Coutot, M. Vrais ou faux dans la peinture (True and false in modern painting). *Academie des Beaux-Arts* (France), no. 16 (1978) 3–22.

273

De Marly, Diana. Indecent exposure: the costume inconsistencies of *The Cheat. Connoisseur* (England), 206 no. 827 (January 1981) 1–3, 2 illus.

English abstract in RILA vol. 10 (1984) #1710.

274

De Towarnick, Frédéric, and Malet-Buisson, Agathe. Automating art frauds: assembly-line techniques revolutionize art forgery. *Atlas World Press Review* (USA), 25 (March 1978) 26–28, illus.

Excerpt from *Le Point,* conservative Paris weekly (in English).

275

De Wild, A. Martin. De *Emmausgangers* van "Vermeer" een ideale vervalsing? *Olie* (Netherlands), no. 11 (1948) 3.

276

De Wild, A. Martin, and Froentjes, W. De Natuurwetenschappelijke bewijsvoering in het proces van Meegeren. *Chemisch-Weekblad. Nederlandse Chemische Vereniging* (Netherlands), 45 (1949), 269–277, 7 illus.

277

Deblaere, A. Het geval van Meegeren of het laboratorium in de kunstwereld. *Streven* (Amsterdam-Brussels), 3 (1950) 31–40, 3 illus.

278

Decker, A. A tale of money, intrigue and old masters. *ARTnews* (USA), 83 no. 2 (1984) 55–65, 10 illus.

279

Dokić, Dušan. Ispitvanje autentičnosti portreta kneza Blagajskoj (Question of the authenticity of the portrait of the Prince of Blagaj). *Zbornik Zaštite Spomenika Kulture* (Belgrade, Yugoslavia), 8 (1957) 57–69, 10 macrophotographs.

English abstract in AATA vol. 2 (1958–1959) #2166.
French abstract in RAA 1957 #1828.

280

Efremov, A. Van Goyen in colectia Muzeului de Arta (Van Goyen in the collection of the Museum of Art). *Studii Muzeale* 3 (1966) 106–118.

English abstract in AATA vo. 6 (1966–1967) # (6)-El-33.

281

Erkelens, J. De gebroeders Abraham en Jacob van Strij: een biografie van twee Dordtse schilders. *Oud Holland* (Netherlands), 90 no. 3 (1976) 186–190, illus. Summary in English.

Biography of the brothers Abraham and Jacob van Strij. The subject of forgery centers on copies after Cuyp that Jacop painted which, it is said, may have been sold as originals. Also mentioned is the claim that Jacob added figures to original Cuyp paintings.

282

Esterow, Milton. Who painted the George Washington portrait in the White House: *ARTnews* (USA), 74 no. 2 (February 1975) 24–28.

English abstract in AATA vol. 12 (1975) #12-359.

283

Ewald, F. Studien zur Alterbestimmung von Oelgemälden durch Schmelz-versuche an Farbschichtproben (Research and experiments to determine the age of oil paintings by means of glaze-tests on painting-layers), *Fette, Seifen, Anstrichmittel* (Germany) 65 no. 4 (1963) 358–368.

English abstract in AATA vol. 8 (1970–1971) #8-822.

284

Ewing, Robert. The case of the spurious Madonna. *Palacio* (USA) 75 no. 1 (1968) 5–8.

Painting in the Museum of New Mexico discovered to be a forgery, painted in 1848.

285

Fell, H. Granville. [Editorial]. The so-called 'French Primitive;' an exposure and a recantation. *Connoisseur* (England), 117 (1946) 126–127.

286

Feller, Robert L., and Keisch, Bernard. Identifying works of art: a diagnostic problem. *Abbottempo* (Canada), Book 4 (1970) 12–27, illus.

English abstract in AATA vol. 10 (1973) #10-737.

287

Feller, Robert, and Keisch, Bernard. Kunstwerk und Kunstfälschung: Identifizierung mit neuen Methoden (Works of art and art forgeries: identification with the help of new methods). *Universitas* (Germany), 28 no. 9 (1973) 1009–1012.

English abstract in ABM vol. 5 (1974) #4765.

288

Fernier, Robert. Pata et Courbet, ou Courbet empatassé. *Gazette des Beaux-Arts* (France), 80 (July 1972) 83–90, illus., por.

289

Ferretti, Fred. Echoes of Clifford Irving's 'Fake'. Fernand Legros: I "Never knowingly sold fake paintings." *ARTnews* (USA), 72 no. 4 (April 1973) 31–32.

290

Fleming, Stuart J. Detecting art forgeries. *Physics Today* (USA), 33 no. 4 (April 1980) 34–39.

291

Fong, Wen. Chinese album and its copy. *Princeton Museum Record* (USA), 27 no. 2 (1968) 74–78, illus.

On an album attributed to Tao-Chi, dated 1685.

292

Fong, Wen. The problem of forgeries in Chinese painting. *Artibus Asiae* (Switzerland), 25 no. 2–3 (1962) 95–140, 26 illus.

French abstract in RAA 1962 #10891.

293

Foucart, Jacques. Rubens: copies, repliques, pastiches (Rubens: copies, replicas, pastiches). *Revue de l'Art* (France), no. 21 (1973) 48–55. Summary in English.

294

Frankfurter, Alfred M. [Editorial]. The art of imitating art. *ARTnews* (USA), 52 no. 1 (March 1953) 15.

295

Frinta, Mojmír Svatopluk. Drawing the net closer: the case of Ilicio Federico Joni, painter of antique pictures. *Pantheon* (Germany), 40 no. 3 (July/September 1982) 217–224, 20 illus. Summary in English and German.

English abstract in AATA vol. 20 (1983) #20-650;
French abstract in RAA 1983 #1150.

296

Frinta, Mojmír Svatopluk. The quest for a restorer's shop of beguiling invention: restorations and forgeries in Italian panel painting. *The Art Bulletin* (USA), 60 no. 1 (March 1978) 7–23, 70 illus., diags.

English abstracts in RILA vol. 5 (1979) #635 and AATA vol. 15 (1978) #15-1453.
French abstract in RAA 1978 #8696.

297

Froentjes, W., and De Wild, A. Martin. [Correspondence]. A forged Frans Hals. *Burlington Magazine* (England), 92 no. 571 (October 1950) 297.

Partition-chromatography analysis revealed the painting *Boy Smoking A Pipe* to be a forgery. See the August 1924 issue of Burlington Magazine for Dr. C. Hofstede de Groote's article on the re-discovery of the picture.

298

Gerascenko, I, and Ivanov, V. Podlinnik ili poddelka? (An original or a forgery?). *Hudožnik* (USSR), 16 no. 8 (1974) 57–59, 2 illus.

Analysis of a painting by L. Turzanskij, entitled *Landscape with Horse*.

299

Getlein, Frank. Fakes, forgeries, foolishness. *New Republic* (USA) 156 (27 May 1967) 32–34.

General article on fakes and forgeries in painting.

300

Gill, William J. Strange story of Walter Chrysler, Jr. art scandal: colossal collection of fakes. *Life* (USA), 53 no. 18 (2 November 1962) 80–84, 86–87, illus.

301

Grundl, R. Gegendarstellung zu der Serie Kokoschka-Fälschungen. *Weltkunst* (Germany), 53 no. 10 (1983) 1374, 6 illus.

Grundl discusses the Heinz Spielmann articles on Kokoschka forgeries. French abstract in RAA 1983 # 13385.

302

Grundmann, Günther; and Sedlmaier, Richard. Die Malereien in Chor der Lübecker Marienkirche (The pictures in the choir-loft of the Marienkirche in Lübeck). *Kunstchronik* (Germany), 5 (1952) 324–331.

French abstract in RAA 1952 #8177.

303

Grundmann, Günther; Rossman, Ernst; and Hirschfeld, Peter. Lübeck. *Deutsche Kunst unde Denkmalpflege* (Germany), 1955, pp. 81–108, 33 illus.

English abstract in AATA vol. 2 (1958–1959) #1267.

304

Harris, Leon. After the sting: how the Kimbell Museum acquired a fake and what it is doing with it. *Connoisseur* (England), 214 (June 1984) 43–46, illus.

305

Harrison, John. Problems in pictures: a study of famous forgeries. *Artist* (England), 41 (June 1951) 84–86, 96, illus.

306

Herbert, Robert L. Le faux Millet (The false Millets). *Revue de l'Art* (France), no. 21 (1973) 56–65. Summary in English.

307

Hochfield, Sylvia. Can the *Fortune Teller* be trusted? *ARTnews* (USA), 81 no. 6 (Summer 1982) 73–78, 3 illus.

English abstract in RILA vol. 9 (1983) # 6280.

308

Hochfield, Sylvia. Portrait of a President. *ARTnews* (USA), 74 (February 1975) 28–30, illus.

On the portrait of George Washington.
English abstract in AATA vol. 12 (1975) #12-372.

309

Hochfield, Sylvia. The Watercolorgate affair. *ARTnews* (USA), 75 no. 8 (October 1976) 49–50, 1 illus.

On forger Tom Keating.

310

Hochfield, Sylvia. The White House Washington portrait. *ARTnews* (USA), 81 no. 1 (January 1982) 61–66, 6 illus.

English abstract in AATA vol. 19 (1982) #19-475.

311

Hoover, Eleanor. Who needs Dufy and Matisse? Jean-Jacques Montfort made it by faking them for actresses and kings. *People Weekly* (USA), 10 no. 23 (4 December 1978) 83–84, illus.

312

Hormats, Bess. Hitler and other Führers: one man loves the Führer's own works, but everyone loves a fake. *Art & Antiques* (USA), December 1984, pp. 13, 15–16, 1 illus.

Paintings by Adolf Hitler, painted before the First World War, have become collectors' items. Billy F. Price, a Third Reich memorabilia collector, paid German researchers to compile a book of Hitler's paintings, and has published it in English under the title *Hitler the Unknown Artist*. Authenticating paintings by Hitler is difficult and it is believed that some, possibly many, of the paintings in the book are not by Hitler.

313

Hutchinson, John. Sir Hugh Lane and the gift of the Prince of Wales to the Municipal Gallery of Modern Art, Dublin. *Studies* (Ireland), 68 (Winter 1979) 277–287, illus.

On the controversy, at the turn of the century, concerning the authenticity of a painting by Corot. The painting was eventually proven to be a french copy of a painting by Geza Meszoly, painted in 1877, in the National Museum, Budapest.

314

Irving, Clifford. Fake: the artist behind the greatest art swindle of the twentieth century tells how he bilked millionaires, museums, and art experts. *Look* (USA), 32 no. 25 (10 December 1968) 46–51, 54–58, 61, illus.

Excerpts from Clifford Irving's book *Fake!*

315

Isnard, Guy. La Joconde et les Joconde (The Mona Lisa and the Mona Lisas). *Jardin des Artes* (France), no. 30 (1957) 357–364, 24 illus.

316

Jedrzejewska, Hanna. Yellow lead pigments and their possible use in detecting fakes. (Correspondence). *Studies in Conservation* (England), 4 (1959) 78.

English abstract in AATA vol. 2 (1958–1959) #2168.

317

Keck, Sheldon. Radiation and optical techniques in the visual examination of paintings. *Applied Optics* (USA), 8 (January 1969) 41–48.

English absrtact in AATA vol. 8 (1970–1971) #8-825.

318

Keerdoja, Eileen. A former art forger keeps on painting. *Newsweek* (USA), 101 no. 4 (24 January 1983) 9, 1 illus.

Brief portrait of forger David Stein.

319

Keisch, Bernard. Dating works of art through their natural radioactivity: improvements and applications. *Science* (USA), 160 no. 3826 (26 April 1968) 413–415.

Authenticating paintings through dating white lead.

320

Keisch, Bernard; and Callahan, R.C. Sulfur isotope ratios in ultramarine blue: application to art forgery detection. *Applied Spectroscopy* (USA), 30 no. 5 (1976) 515.

English abstract in AATA vol. 14 (1977) #14-1025.

321

Knut, Nicolaus. Marco und infrarot Untersuchung der Signatur von Rembrandts "Männlichen Bildnis" in Braunschweig (Marco and infrared examination of the signature on Rembrandt's *Male Portrait* in Braunschweig). *Maltechnik-Restauro* (Germany), 2 no. 1 (1973) 40–43.

English abstract in AATA vol. 10 (1973) #10-744.

322

Krohner, Anita. Untersuchung eines Tafelbildes (Examination of a panel picture). *Bildende Kunst* (Germany), 3 (1980) 119–121, 5 illus.

English abstract in RILA vol. 8 (1982) #6807.

323

Lappe, L. Beruehmte Faelscher: van Meegeren, de Hory, Malskat und Keating (Famous forgers: van Meegeren, de Hory, Malskat and Keeting). *Die Waage* (Germany), 23 no. 3 (1984) 111–118, 13 photos.

English abstract in AATA vol. 22 (1985) #22-611.

324

Lari, G. Falsi e contraffazioni. Due acqueforti di Jacopo Palma il Giovane. *Conoscitore di Stampe* (Italy), no. 49 (1980) 46–49, 5 illus.

French abstract in RAA 1981 #8968.

325

Lazović, Miroslav. Quelques corrections au catalogue *Les icônes dans les collections suisses, Musée Rath, Genève, 1968. Musees de Geneve* (Switzerland), no. 115 (1971) 6–8, 5 illus.

French abstract in RAA 1971 #3185.

326

Levantal, P. L'affaire Vermeer rebondit. *Connaissance Arts* (France), no. 237 (November 1971) 90–101, 174.

327

Lomize, O. Iskusnaja fal'sifikacija. *Hudožnik* (USSR), 18 no. 6 (1976) 60–62, 4 illus.

French abstract in RAA 1977 #9017.

328

Loughrey, Brian, and Taylor, Neil. Jonson and Shakespeare at chess? *Shakespeare Quarterly* (USA), 34 (Winter 1983) 440–448.

On the controversy surrounding the painting *Ben Johnson and William Shakespeare playing at chess.* Attempts to determine who the painter was and if it is really Shakespeare in the picture have been unsuccessful.

329

Makes, Frantisek. Syntetiske harpixer og deres rolle i forfalskede malerier (Synthetic resins and their role in forged paintings). *Meddelelser om Konservering* (Denmark), 2 no. 6 (1975) 177–188.

English abstract in AATA vol. 13 (1976) #13-379.

330

Marceau, Henri. Photographic aids and their uses in problems of authenticity in the field of paintings. *Proceedings of the American Philosophical Society* (USA), 97 (1953) 686–712, 38 illus.

English abstract in AATA vol. 1 (1955–1957) #137;
French abstract in RAA 1953 #1798.

331

Marconi, Bohdan L. La découverte d'un faux tableau de Philips Wouwerman. Analyse du style et recherche technologique (The discovery of a false Philip Wouverman. Stylistic analysis and technological investigation). *Bull. Inst. Roy. Patrimoine Artistique. Miscellanea in Memorium Paul Coremans (1908–1965)* (Belgium), 15 (1975) 224–230, 7 illus.

English abstract in AATA vol. 13 (1976) #13-1036;
French abstract in RAA 1977 #2328.

332

Marijnissen, Roger H. De van Meegeren—affaire of de gevolgen van een niet bedwongen ontroering (The van Meegeren controversy or the consequences of an uncontrolled emotion). *Snoecks*, 74, Snoeck-Ducaju, Ghent, pp. 196–209 (1974).

English abstract in AATA vol. 11 (1974) #11-213.

333

Marijnissen, Roger H. On scholarship: some reflections on the study of early Netherlandish painting. *Mededelingen van de Koninklijke Academie voor Wetenschappen, Letteren en Schone Kunsten van België*, 11 no. 4 (1978) 3–14, 2 photos. Summary in Dutch.

English abstract in AATA vol. 21 (1984) #21–783.

334

McIntyre, Arthur. Fake Pollocks fool Australian art establishment. *Art Monthly* (England), 18 (July–August 1978) 4–6, illus.

English abstracts in RILA vol. 5 (1979) #7817 and ABM vol. 10 (1979) #3139.

335

McWhirter, William A. How art swindlers duped a virtuous millionaire. *Life* (USA), 63 no. 1 (7 July 1967) 52–54, 56–58, 61, illus.

Fake paintings purchased by Algur H. Meadows.

336

Mesuret, Robert. Le faux Goya de musées de Provence (Forgeries of Goya in the museums of Provence). *La Revue du Louvre et des Musées de France* (France), 13 no. 4–5 (1963) 183–194, illus.

337

Miyoshi, Tadaki.; Ikeya, Motoji.; Kinoshita, S.; and Kushida, T. Laser induced fluorescence of oil colors and its application to the identification of pigments in oil paintings. *Japanese Journal of Applied Physics* (Japan) 21 no. 7 (1982) 1032–1036. In Japanese.

English abstract in AATA vol. 21 (1984) #21-1908.

338

Muether, H.E.; Balazs, N.L.: Voelkle, W.; and Cotter, Maurice J. Neutron autoradiography and the Spanish forger. *Museum of Applied Science Center for Archaeology* (USA), 1 no. 4 (June 1980) 112–113.

English abstract in AATA vol. 17 (1980) #17-1361.

339

Neugass, Fritz. Enthüllungen von Kunstfälschungen in Amerika. (Revealing the art forgeries in America). *Weltkunst* (Germany), 37 (1967) 537, 728.

340

Nugass, Fritz. Profil eines Bildfälschers. Elmyr de Hory (Profile of an art forger. Elmyr de Hory). *Kunstwerk* (Germany), 22 no. 5–6 (1968–1969) 13–15.

341

Neve, Christopher. Light out of darkness: Claude Lorrain's *Liber Veritatis* revealed. *Country Life* (England), 161 no. 4152 (27 January 1977) 184–185, 4 illus.

English abstract in RILA vol. 4 (1978) #1339.

342

Norman, Frank. Lying low with Tom Keating. *New Statesman* (England), 10 September 1976, pp. 338–339.

343

Norman, Geraldine. Il falsario che ha sconvolto il mercato dell'arte (The forger who has upset the art market). *Bolaffiarte* (Italy), 7 no. 64 (November 1976) 28–29, 1 illus.

On forger Tom Keating.
English abstract in ABM vol. 8 (1977) #5640.

344

O'Connor, Rod. The case of the isotopic artist. *Journal of Chemical Education* (USA), 57 no. 4 (1980) 271.

English abstract in AATA vol. 17 (1980) #17-1368.

345

Pantazzi, Sybille. The Donna Laura Minghetti Leonardo: An international mystification. *English Miscellany* (Italy), 16 (1965) 321–348, 4 illus.

French abstract in RAA 1966 #1851.

346

Parlasca, K. Pseudo-alexandrinische Schuhe: gefälschte Malereien auf Hadra-Vasen. *Archäologischer Anzeiger* (Germany), no. 1 (1976) 78–84, illus.

347

Pelzel, T. Winckelman, Mengs, and Casanova: a reappraisal of a famous eighteenth century forgery. *Art Bulletin* (USA), 54 no. 3 (September 1972) 300–315, 6 illus.

348

Pickering, Paul. Genuine fakes. *Art and Antiques* (USA), Summer 1986, p. 23, 1 illus.

The Art Faker's Collective, formed about 1984 in Italy, consists of 300 artists who specialize in painting and selling legally documented fakes. They have held successful exhibitions in Rome and Milan. Each painting is accompanied by a certificate stating that it is a genuine copy.

349

Pieper, Paul. Zwei deutsche Altarflügel des 13, Jahrhunderts im Britishen Museum (Two German altar wings of the 13th century in the British Museum). *Niederdeutsche Beitrage zur Kunstgeschichte* (Germany), 3 (1964) 215–218, 9 illus.

French abstract in RAA 1964 #5253.

350

R. Un falsario d'eccezione: van Meegeren. *Critica d'Arte* (Italy), 8 (1949–1950) 411–416, 2 illus.

351

Ragghianti, Carlo Ludovico. L'affaire van Meegeren. *Sele Arte* (Italy), no. 17 (1955) 56–67, 26 illus., 1 color plate.

French abstract in RAA 1955 #1293.

352

Raines, Robert. Watteau and "Watteaus" in England before 1760. *Gazette des Beaux-Arts* (France), 89 no. 1297 (February 1977) 51–64, 7 illus. Summary in French.

English abstract in RILA vol. 4 (1978) #5745.
French abstract in RAA 1977 # 5611.

353

Raynor, William. The case against Simone. *Connoisseur* (England), 214 (October 1984) 60, 62, 64, 68–71, illus.; Discussion. 215 (April 1985) 161–162.

The controversy surrounding the authenticity of Simone Martini's portrait *Guido Riccio da Fogliano at the Siege of Montemassi*, one of the most treasured frescoes of the Sienese, 10 feet high by 30 feet long, in the Sala del Mappamondo, on Siena's Palazzo Pubblico.

354

Requiem für einen Fälscher (Requiem for a forger). *Artis* (Germany), 29 no. 3 (1977) 10–14, 10 illus.

On the forger Elmyr de Hory.

355

Rewald, John. Modern fakes of modern pictures. *ARTnews* (USA), 52 no. 1 (1953–1954) 16–21, 46–49, 33 illus.

English abstract in AATA vol. 2 (1958–1959) #1269.

356

Robbins, C. I terroristi del mercato (The terrorists of the market). *Bolaffiarte* (Italy), 7 no. 64 (Nov. 1976) 30–35, 13 illus.

On David Stein, Elmyr de Hory, and Fernand Legros.
English abstract in ABM vol. 8 (1977) #5066.

357

Roettgen, S. Storia di un falso: il *Ganimede* di Mengs. *Arte illustrata* (Italy), no. 54 (1973) 256–270, 13 illus.

French abstract in RAA 1974 #2181.

358

Rosenberg, Pierre. The *Fortune Teller* by Georges de La Tour [Letter]. *Burlington Magazine* (England), 123 no. 941 (August 1981) 487–488.

English abstract in RILA vol. 9 (1983) #6281.

359

Rossmann, Ernst. Scientific examination of wall paintings in the choir of the Marienkirche in Lübeck in reference to the Lübeck picture forgery methods. *Deutsche Kunst und Denkmalpflege* (Germany), 2 (1955) 99–105.

English abstract in AATA vol. 2 (1958–1959) #1270.

360

Roth, Toni. Fälschungen in der Malerei. Moglichkeiten und Grenzen der Erkennung und Beweisführung (Forgery in paintings. Possibility and boundary for recognition and proof). *Die Kunst und das Schone Heim* (Germany), 83 (1971) 81–85, 9 illus.

361

Rousseau, Theodore. The stylistic detection of forgeries. *Metropolitan Museum of Art Bulletin* (USA), 26 no. 6 (1967–1968) 247–252.

A discussion of Han van Meegeren's Vermeer forgery *Christ and the Pilgrims at Emmaus.*

362

Russell, John. La farce de van Meegeren (The farce of van Meegeren). *L'Oeil* (France), no. 14 (1956) 5–11, 7 illus.

363

Savage, George. Forgeries of modern works. *Studio International* (England), 175 no. 896 (January 1968) 54–55.

364

Savage, George. Uncovering the forger's methods. *Studio International* (England), 174 no. 893 (October 1967) 178–179.

365

Scheper, Hinnerk. Restaurieren und Berufsethos (Restoration and professional ethics). *Deutsche Kunst und Denkmalpflege* (Germany), 1955, pp. 109–111.

Concerning the fresco forgeries at Lübeck.

366

Schurr, Gérald. More picture fakes. *Connoisseur* (England), 165 no. 665 (July 1967) 189.

A Fauve canvas signed Derain and two watercolors by Raoul Dufy, to be auctioned at Pontosie near Paris, were discovered to be forgeries.

367

Secrest, Meryle. Memo to a forger. *Saturday Review* (USA), 9 no. 10 (September–October 1983) 24–27, illus.

General interest article on forgeries in paintings.

368

Sewell, Brian. The *Fortune Teller* by Georges de LaTour [letter]. *Burlington Magazine* (England), 123 no. 942 (September 1981) 549–550.

English abstract in RILA vol. 9 (1983) #6282.

369

Sewell, Brian. Keating's last laugh. *Art and Antiques* (USA), December 1984, pp. 16, 18, 1 illus.

Christie's sells 204 forgeries—a sellout—by Tom Keating that it pulled from his estate after his death in February 1984.

370

Seyffarth, Richard. Eine Fälschung und ihr Vorbild (A forgery and its model). *Keramik-Freunde der Schweiz* (Switzerland), no. 45 (1959) 28, 2 illus.

371

Seymore, Charles Jr. The Jarves "Sassettas" and the *St. Anthony altarpiece*. *Walters Art Gallery Journal* (USA), 15–16. Special Technical Issue (1952–1953) 34–45, 97, illus.

English abstract in AATA vol. 1 (1955–1957) #141.
On two paintings: *The Temptation of Saint Anthony by a Demon in the form of a Woman*, and, *The Flagellation of Saint Anthony by Demons*.

372

Shepard, Richard F. Why and how they stole the *Mona Lisa*. *ARTnews* (USA) 80 no. 3 (February 1981) 125–127.

English abstract in AATA vol. 18 (1981) #18-1442.

373

Shirey, David L. Faking it. *Newsweek* (USA), 72 no. 9 (26 August 1968) 82, illus.

Portrait of forger David Stein.

374

Slánský, B. O kopiích falsifikátech a expertisách. *Zpravy Památkove Péče* (Bulletin of the Service of the Historic Monuments) (Czechoslovakia), 16 (1956) 144–152, 4 illus.

375

Sonnenburg, Hubertus Falkner von. Gemäldefälschungen dem Zeitgeschmack entsprechend (Forgery in paintings conform to the fashion of the times) *Weltkunst* (Germany), 47 no. 20a (special issue) (21 October 1977) 2152–2155, 7 illus.

English abstract in AATA vol. 17 (1980) #17-1384.

French abstract in RAA 1978 #3642.

376

Sonnenburg, Hubertus Falkner von. Maltechnische Gesichtspunkte zur Rembrandtforschung (Technical viewpoint of Rembrandt's portraits). *Maltechnik* (Germany), 82 no. 1 (1976) 9–24, 11 illus. Summary in English.

French abstract in RAA 1976 #6496.

377

Sonnenburg, Hubertus Falkner von. Stilgemaelde und kuenstliche Alterung (Archaeizing paintings and artificial aging). *Weltkunst* (Germany), no. 20a (October 1975) 1846–1847.

English abstract in AATA vol. 17 (1980) #17-1381.

378

Sonnenburg, Hubertus Falkner von. Unechte Gemälde (Fake paintings). *Weltkunst* (Germany) 49 no. 13 (1 July 1979) 1678–1681, 21 illus.

English abstract in AATA vol. 17 (1980) #17-1383.

379

Spencer, Charles. Master faker. *Art and Artists* (England), 6 no. 2 (May 1971) 78, illus.

Brief article on forger Elmyr de Hory.

380

Spielmann, Heinz. Kokoschka-Fälschungen. Zur Gegendarstellung von Richard E. Grundl (Kokoschka forgeries. A response to Richard E. Grundl). *Weltkunst* (Germany), 53 no. 11 (1983) 1508–1513, 6 illus.

French abstract in RAA 1984 #6219.

381

Spielmann, Heinz. Kokoschka-Fälschungen I: Verzeichnis der gefälschten, gefälscht signierten oder falsch zugeschriebenen Gemälde aus dem Archiv des Künstlers (Kokoschka forgeries I: list of forged paintings, paintings with forged signatures, or falsely attributed paintings from the artist's archive). *Weltkunst* (Germany), 52 no. 2 (January 1982) 124–129, 68 illus.

French abstract in RAA 1982 #5971.

382

Spielmann, Heinz. Kokoschka-Fälschungen II: Verzeichnis der gefälschten, gefälscht signierten oder falsch zugeschriebenen Gemälde aus dem Archiv des Künstlers (Kokoschka forgeries II: list of forged, falsely signed or wrongly attributed paintings from the artist's archive. *Weltkunst* (Germany), 52 no. 3 (February 1982) 204–210, 102 illus.

French abstract in RAA 1982 #5972.

383

Spielmann, Heinz. Kokoschka-Fälschungen III: Verzeichnis der gefälschten, gefalscht signierten oder falsch zugeschriebenen Gemalde aus dem Archiv des Künstlers (Kokoschka forgeries III: list of forged paintings with forged signatures or falsely attributed paintings from the artist's archive). *Weltkunst* (Germany), 52 no. 4 (1982) 292–299, 95 illus.

French abstract in RAA 1982 #9244.

384

Spielmann, Heinz. Kokoschka-Fälschungen IV: Zu Fälschungen der Aquarelle und Gouachen (Kokoschka forgeries IV: to the forgeries of watercolors and gouaches). *Weltkunst* (Germany), 53 no. 3 (1983) 214–224, illus.

French abstract in RAA 1983 #9846.

385

Squire, John P. Coremans: van Meegeren faked Vermeers and de Hooghs. *Illustrated London News* (England), 1950, I, pp. 62–63, 8 illus.

386

Stankiewicz, Daniela. Wrocławski obraz Lukasza Cranacha Starszego *Madonna pod jodłami*. *Biuletyn Historii Sztuki* (Poland), 27 (1965) 348–357, 9 illus.

387

Sterling, Charles. Le émules des primitifs (The emulators of the primitives). *Revue de l'Art* (France), no. 21 (1973) 80–93, 39 illus. Summary in English.

388

Šujskij, K. K istorii odnogo otkrytisa. *Khudožnik* (USSR), no. 10 (1969) 57–58, 1 illus.

389

Swanson, V.G. Lawrence Alma-Tadema: his forgers and his imitators. *Nineteenth Century* (USA) 3 no. 4 (Winter 1977) 66–70, 19 illus.

Swanson's article includes a list of 29 imitators and forgers of L. Alma Tadema.

English abstract in ABM vol. 10 (1979) #0056.

390

Teodosiu, A. Aspecte privind studierea unei picturi pe baza raporturilor dintre structura fizică a stratului de culoare și suport. *Revista Muzeelor si Monumentelor. Seria Muzee* (Romania), 13 no. 6 (1976) 60–65, 16 illus. Summary in French.

French abstract in RAA 1977 #10626.

391

Turner, Evan H. A current general problem . . . and a specific issue. *Canadian Art* (Canada), 20 no. 2 (March/April 1963) 108–111, illus.

The increase of fakes on the Canadian art market, and the authenticity of a particular Tom Thomson sketch.

392

Unsigned article. Bass embroiled. *Newsweek* (USA), 71 no. 8 (19 February 1968) 87, illus.

The controversy over the authenticity of several paintings in the Bass Museum of Art, Miami Beach, Florida.

393

Unsigned article. Bargain-basement masters? *Time* (USA), 60 no. 17 (27 October 1952) 90.

Brief article on forger Lothar Malskat.

394

Unsigned article. Carbon-14 and art forgeries. *Chemistry* (USA), 46 no. 6 (June 1973) 18–19.

395

Unsigned article. Chemical standards may authenticate art works. *Science News Letter* (USA), 88 (6 November 1965) 296.

On the work of Dr. William A. Hoffman of Denison University (Greenville, Ohio) in developing chemical standards to authenticate paintings.

396

Unsigned article. Chrysler's controversial century. *New Statesman* (England), 64 (14 December 1962) 865–866.

An exhibition of paintings owned by Walter Chrysler, Jr. was entitled "The Controversial Century: 1850–1950." The title of the exhibition was prophetic as many of the paintings were suspected to be forgeries.

397

Unsigned article. Detecting forgeries in paintings. *Chemistry* (USA), 41 (May 1968) 5, illus.

398

Unsigned article. Fake Madonna. *Time* (USA), 65 (30 May 1955) 75, illus.

The National Gallery of London's *Virgin and Child with an Angel* by Francesco Francia (15th century), is declared a fake.

399

Unsigned article. Fake or Jake? *Newsweek* (USA) 69 no. 2 (22 May 1967) 110–111.

On the many fakes in Algur H. Meadows' collection.

400

Unsigned article. Forger's art: a van Meegeren "Vermeer," and its famous source. *Illustrated London News* (England), 238 (7 January 1961) 23, 4 illus.

401

Unsigned article. Forgery at the National Gallery: the *Virgin and Child with an Angel* attributed to Francesco Francia. *Museum Journal* (England), 55 (June 1955) 73.

402

Unsigned article. Forging ahead. *ARTnews* (USA) 73 (November 1974) 106–107.

An exhibition of Han van Meegeren's legitimate paintings. Eighteen canvases were excluded from the exhibition, at the request of van Meegeren's daughter, an art expert, who claimed they may be forgeries.

403

Unsigned article. Forgery in the National Gallery. *Newsweek* (USA), 45 no. 22 (30 May 1955) 78.

The National Gallery of Art, in London, discovers its *Virgin and Child with an Angel* by Francesco Francia (15th Century), is a forgery.

404

Unsigned article. Forging a career. *Newsweek* (USA), 76 no. 15 (12 October 1970) 105.

Brief article on forger David Stein.

405

Unsigned article. Fresco faker: German forges gothic church art. *Life* (USA), 34 (12 January 1953) 49–50, illus.

Brief article on forger Lothar Malskat.

406

Unsigned article. Gilt-framed securities. *Sunday Times Magazine* (England), 8 March 1970, pp. 36–37, illus.

Brief portrait of forger Elmyr de Hory.

407

Unsigned article. The greatest art sensation of the decade: the authenticity of Vermeer's *Christ at Emmaus* challenged. *Illustrated London News* (England), 207 (1945) 500–501.

408

Unsigned article. Meadow's luck: millionaire's collection largely fakes. *Time* (USA) 89 no. 20 (19 May 1967) 94, 97, illus.

The Algur H. Meadows collection.

409

Unsigned article. More on modern fakes. *ARTnews* (USA), 52 no. 6 (October 1953) 10.

Letters of Marc Chagall and Christian Gilbert Stiebel (Paris dealer) concerning forged Chagall paintings, and forgery in general.

410

Unsigned article. Mystery of the Madonna. *Connoisseur* (England), 136 no. 548 (October 1955) 118.

The *Virgin and Child with an Angel* in the National Gallery, London, is found to be a 19th Century forgery.
English abstract in AATA vol. 2 (1958–1959) #2169.

411

Unsigned article. Palming off the Palmers. *Time* (USA), 108 (13 September 1976) 64.

Tom Keating and his forged Samuel Palmers.

412

Unsigned article. Picasso's fakes and other stories. *ARTnews* (USA), 73 no. 6 (Summer 1974) 16–17.

After his death, Picasso's personal collection of 44 paintings was donated to the Louvre on the condition that the collection not be broken up and the paintings be exhibited together. Some of the pictures are believed to be fakes, and others have been criticized as "inferior." This article discusses the various problems the Louvre experienced in trying to meet the requirements placed on exhibiting the collection, which was donated by Picasso's son, Paulo, and his widow, Jacqueline.

413

Unsigned article. Rembrandt, Vermeer, Hals, you name it, Bass says he's got it. *Life* (USA), 67 no. 17 (24 October 1969) 44–45, illus.

Forgeries in the Bass Art Museum, Miami Beach, Florida.

414

Unsigned article. Reproductions de faux tableaux de Matisse et de Picasso (Reproductions of false paintings of Matisse and Picasso). *Cahiers d'Art* (France), 27 no. 1 (July 1952) 92–94, illus.

415

Unsigned article. Sargent in combat. *Newsweek* (USA), 70 no. 14 (2 October 1967) 88.

As many as 40 John Singer Sargent forgeries discovered in London.

416

Unsigned article. Secondhand Saint. *ARTnews* (USA), 76 (December 1977) 24 +, illus.

A Grünewald forgery.

417

Unsigned article. A sin of omission: the Kimble Museum discovered a forgery and bravely told the public—a year and a half later. *Texas Monthly* (USA), 12 (August 1984) 100, illus.

The Kimble Museum's prized Romanesque Apse is declared a forgery.

418

Unsigned article. Speeding up fluorescence tests. *Chem. Week.* 115 no. 23 (1974) 43.

English abstract in AATA vol. 12 (1975) #12-642.

419

Unsigned article. Still life with pasta. *Newsweek* (USA), 65 no. 26 (28 June 1965) 42, illus.

Brief article on an Italian forgery ring specializing in modern masters.

420

Unsigned article. Tom Keating [Obituary]. *Time* (USA), 123 no. 9 (27 February 1984) 104.

421

Unsigned article. True or False? *Time* (USA), 61 no. 5 (2 Feb. 1953) 50, illus.

Brief article on art expert André Schoeller of Paris.

422

Unsigned article. The two Francias—the National Gallery forgery exposed by X-rays. *Illustrated London News* (England), 226 (1955) 910–911.

English abstract in AATA vol. 2 (1958–1959) #2170.

423

Unsigned article. Van Meegeren—final chapter. *Art Digest,* 24 no. 20 (15 September 1950) 11.

The property of Han van Meegeren was auctioned off in Amsterdam after his death. Painter C.J. Snoeijerbosch claimed he painted two of the pictures being sold as van Meegerens. The legitimate works of van Meegeren brought in an average of $200 each.

424

Unsigned article. Van Meegeren: how many were fooled? *Art Digest,* 25 no. 20 (15 September 1951) 15, illus.

425

Unsigned article. Van Meegeren on his own. *ARTnews* (USA), 75 (Summer 1976) 24.

A legitimate van Meegeren painting—a farmyard scene—sells for $450.

426

Unsigned article. What next, the *Mona Lisa? Life* (USA), 68 no. 4 (6 Feb. 1970) 34–35, illus.

Portrait of forger Elmyr de Hory.

427

Unsigned article. Which painting is worth $1,000? *Life* (USA), 30 (9 April 1951) 69–70, 72, illus.

Forger Jean Pinson-Berthet and his forged Vlamincks and Utrillos.

428

Urdareanu, E. Ceretari si rezultate in legatura cu autenticitatea tabloului *Natura Statica* semnat Ion Andreescu de la Muzeal Zambaccian (Research and results concerning the authenticity of the *Still Life* attributed to Ion Andreesco from the Zambaccian Museum). *Studii Muzeale* (Romania), 3 (1966) 193–215.

English abstract in AATA vol. 6 (1966–1967) #(6)-El-34.

429

Van Os, H.W. Op het spoor dan een vervalser (On the trail of a forger) *Spiegel hist.,* 6 (1971) 80–87, 11 illus.

On the forger I.F. Joni who specialized in Italian primitives.

430

Van Thiel, P.J.J. Het Rijksmuseum in het Trippenhuis, 1814–1885 (IV): kopiisten en fotografen (The Rijkmuseum in the Trippenhuis, 1814–1885 (IV): copyists and photographers). *Bulletin van het Rijksmuseum* (Netherlands), 30 no. 2 (1982) 63–86, 104–106, 18 illus. Summary in English.

English abstract in ABM vol. 14 (1983) #1116.

431

Verzele, M. Bijdrage tot het opsporen van fenolaldehyde harsen in schilderijen. *Chemisch Weekblad* (Netherlands), 52 (1956) 335–339, 8 illus.

French abstract in AATA vol. 1 (1955–1957) #975.

432

Vielhaber, CHR. Grosse Namen im Zwielicht: Hochgeschaetzt und tief gefallen (Famous names in twilight: high esteemed and deeply fallen). *Die Waage* (Germany), 23 no. 3 (1984) 104–110, 11 photos.

English abstract in AATA vol. 22 (1985) #22-426.

433

Walker, Richard W. Is it a Bouts? Yes, says the Getty. *ARTnews* (USA) 85 no. 6 (Summer 1986) 42, 1 illus.

Controversy over the authenticity of the *Annunciation*, a rare tempera on canvas, attributed to Dirk Bouts, 15th century Flemish painter. The Getty Museum is said to have paid $7 million for the painting.

434

Waterman, Edward C. Master forger: the strange case of the art genius who could outpaint the old master whose work he forged. *Design Magazine* (USA), 62 (May 1961) 213.

The story of Han van Meegeren.

435

Wehlte, K. Was ging in Lübeck vor? (What had happened in Lübeck?). *Maltechnik* (Germany), 61 (1955) 11–21, 8 illus.

436

Weil-Cachin, Françoise. Le faux tableaux impressionnistes. *L'Information d'Histoire d'Art* (France), 2 (1957) 81–86, 9 illus.

437

Weinberg, R. Alter Meister oder meisterhafte Fälschung? *Du; Die Kunstzeitschrift* (Switzerland), no. 9 (1985)86 + .

On Dieric Bouts.

438

Wicker, Brian. Ars gratia artis?: where legitimate pastime ends and forgery begins. *Commonweal* (USA), 104 no. 20 (30 September 1977) 622–624.

Comments on forger Tom Keating, with additional thoughts on forgery in general.

439

Wilda, Tadeusz. L'expertise des signatures artistiques. *Bulletin du Musée national de Varsovie* (Poland), 21 no. 1 (1980) 7–24, 22 illus.

English abstract in RILA vol. 8 (1982) #266.

440

Wolfe, Lester. A quake in the world of art: tremors high on the Richter scale of righteousness. *Technology Review* (USA), 83 no. 6 (May–June, 1981) A2–A4, 1 photo.

English abstract in AATA vol. 18 (1981) #18-1460.

441

Wright, Christopher. Cheat? *Connoisseur* (England), 105 no. 826 (December 1980) 230–231, 5 illus.

English abstract in RILA vol. 9 (1983) #6283.
On paintings attributed to Georges de La Tour.

442

Wright, Christopher; and de Marly, Diana. Fake? *Connoisseur* (England), 205 no. 823 (September 1980) 22–25, 2 illus.

English abstract in RILA vol. 9 (1983) #6284.
French abstract in RAA 1981 #1977.
On the authenticity of *The Fortune Teller*, attributed to Georges de La Tour.

443

Wright, Christopher, and Sewell, Brian. Two cautionary tales. *Art and Artists* (England), 187 (April 1982) 6–9, illus.

444

Zurcher, E. Imitation and forgery in ancient Chinese paintings and calligraphy. *Oriental Art* (England), NS 1 (1955) 141–146, illus.

Media

445

Editorial. Forgery on television. *Burlington Magazine* (England), 102 no. 692 (November 1960) 465.

Comments on the BBC television program on Han van Meegeren's forged Vermeers.

446

Fake? Produced by WNET with RM Productions for BBC TV. Color, sound, 60 minutes. Narrated by Robert MacNiel. The Brand New Illustrated Journal of the Arts, 1981.

A documentary on the controversy surrounding the authenticity of *The Fortune Teller*, attributed to Georges de La Tour.

English abstract in AATA vol. 19 (1982) #19-1983.

447

Sewell, Brian. Where Fake? went wrong. *Art and Artists* (England), no. 189 (June 1982) 8–9.

The BBC documentary television program on the authenticity of *The Fortune Teller,* attributed to Georges de La Tour.

Manuscript Collections

448

Dabo, Leon. Material relating to James McNeill Whistler, including photographs of Whistler forgeries painted by a Whistler student (Harper Pennington) and verified as forgeries by Dabo, a letter inquiring about a forgery, and clippings relating to Whistler. Also included are 14 oils copying classic figures and scenes painted by Dabo drawn in 1918, and miscellany. Total: ca. 50 items. Gift of Mrs. Leon Dabo, May 11, 1972.

From the card catalog of the Manuscript Collections of the Archives of American Art, Smithsonian Institution, Washington, D.C.

Drawings

Books

449

Ost, Hans. *Das Leonardo-Porträt inder Königlichen Bibliothek Turin und andere Fälschungen des Giuseppe Bossi* (The portrait of Leonardo in the Biblioteca Nazionale, Turin, and other forgeries by Giuseppe Bossi). Berlin: Mann, 1980, 128 p., 56 illus., bibliog. (Gebr..uder-Mann-Studio-Reihe).

English abstract in RILA vol. 8 (1982) #6164. For a review of Ost's book see Sylvia Ferino-Pagden's article in *Kunstchronik* (Germany), 35 no. 1 (1982) 34–40, 5 illus.

(In German). Ferino-Pagden attributes the drawing to Leonardo. See also #468 for a reply by Ost to Ferino-Pagden.

450

Varnedoe, J. Kirk T. *Chronology and authenticity in the drawings of Auguste Rodin.* Ph.D. Dissertation, Stanford University (1972), 350 pp. (Dissertation Abstracts International: Order No. 72–30, 714).

English abstract in ABM vol. 8 (1977) #2898.

451

Walker, Rainforth Armitage. *How to detect Beardsley forgeries.* Bedford, England: R.A. Walker, 1950, 31 pp. 7 plates.

Contents: Beardsley forgeries; published drawings; unpublished drawings: appendix.
Publication was limited to 250 copies.

Sections of Books

452

Brown, Jonathan. "Copies, imitations, fakes, and and works by followers"; "Signatures and inscriptions"; and "Checklist of rejected attributions," in his *Murillo and his drawings.* Princeton: New Jersey, The Art Museum, Princeton University, 1976, pp. 38–53; 185–186, illus.

453

Hayes, John. "Assistants, pupils and imitators," in his *The Drawings of Thomas Gainsborough.* New Haven and London: Yale University Press, 1971, vol. 1 (Text), pp. 64–91.

454

Perrig, Alexander. "Authenticity problems with Michelangelo. The drawings on the Louvre Sheet No. 685," in the book *Authentication in the visual arts,* edited by H.L.C. Jaffe, J. Strom van Leeuwen and L.H. van der Twell, pp. 17–56, 19 illus., 50 refs.

English abstract in AATA vol. 19 (1982) #19-307.

Periodicals

455

Allodi, Mary. Forgery: who signed Bartlett's name. *Rotunda* (Royal Ontario Museum), (Canada), 1 no. 3 (1968) 10–21, 17 illus.

French abstract in RAA 1969 #9844.

456

Davidson, R. Bartlett forgeries: Coke Smyth originals: Royal Ontario Museum in Toronto. *Antiques* (New York), 97 no. 2 (February 1970) 202, 204, 208, illus.

457

Dreyer, Peter. "Tizianfälschungen des sechzehnten Jahrhunderts; Korrekturen zur Definition der *Delineatio* bei Tizian und Anmerkungen zur Datierung seiner Holzschnitte" (Sixteenth century Titian forgeries: a corrected definition of Titian's *delineatio;* comments on the dating of his woodcuts). *Pantheon* 37 no. 4 (October–December 1979) 365–375, 20 illus.

Summaries in English and French.
English abstract in RILA vol. 7 (1981) #1509.

Concerning a series of forged "woodcut sketches" taken from the reverse image details of Titians woodcut entitled *The Sacrifice of Abraham.* Among the forged drawings mentioned are *Forest Landscape* and *Abraham Making His Way to the Place of Sacrifice.*

458

Fell, H. Granville. [The Connoisseur Divan]. Beardsley forgeries. *Connoisseur,* (England), 125 no. 516 (June 1950), pp. 123–124.

Brief article concerned primarily with R.A. Walker's 31-page pamphlet on Beardsley forgeries. See #448.

459

Fuller, Peter. Property Values. *New Society* (England), 30 June 1977, pp. 663–664.

Portrait of forger Tom Keating.

460

Grigson, Geoffrey. The Samuel Palmer situation. *Times Literary Supplement* (England), 15 July 1977, p. 852.

Tom Keating's forged Samuel Palmers.

461

Kurz, Otto. Forgeries of marginal drawings in the style of Leonardo da Vinci. *Raccolta vinciana,* (Italy), 18 (1960) 27–44, 6 illus.

462

Mahon, Denis. An eighteenth-century faker of Guercino's drawings. *Apollo* (England), 109 no. 206 (April 1979), 315, 4 illus.

English abstract in RILA vol. 6 (1980) #6128.
French abstract in RAA 1980 #9154.

463

Meyboom, P.G.P. Some Nilotic scenes in eighteenth-century drawings of Roman wall paintings. *Mededelingen van het Nederlands Historisch Instituut te Rome*, 41 (1979), 59–65, 16 illus.

English abstract in RILA vol. 7 (1981) #1423.

Forgeries believed to be by Gaetano Piccini based on a reproduction of the *Barberini Mosaic* in Palestrina by Agapito Bernardini.

464

Meulenkamp, W.G.J.M. Aubrey Beardsley, John Lane en Leonard Smithers: een tekenaau en zijn uitgevers (Aubrey Beardsley, John Lane and Leonard Smithers: a draughtsman and his publishers). *Antiek* (Netherlands), 17 no. 3 (October 1982) 139–151, 14 illus. Summary in English.

This article centers primarily on Beardsley and his two principal publishers, Smithers and Lane. Also included is a discussion of Beardsley forgeries exhibited in New York in 1919.

English abstract in ABM vol. 14 (1983) #0724.
French abstract in RAA 1983 #6714.

465

Neugass, Fritz. Rodin: echt oder falsch (Rodin: true or false) *Weltkunst* (Germany), 42 (1972) 94–95, 3 illus.

466

Nicolson, Benedict. [Editorial] The Keating affair. *Burlington Magazine* (England), 119 no. 886 (January 1977) 3.

Reply by Geraldine Norman. 119 (March 1977) 196–197.

467

Olson, Roberta Jeanne Marie. 'Caveat Emptor': Egisto Rossi's activity as a forger of drawings. *Master Drawings* (USA), 20 no. 2 (Summer 1982) 149–156, illus, 28 refs.

The author concludes that Egisto Rossi (19th century sculptor) is responsible for forgeries of drawings by such masters as Raphael, Desiderio da Settignano and 19th century drawings as well, especially Lorenzo Bartolini and Antonio Canova.

English abstracts in ABM vol. 15 (1984) #7403; RILA vol. 10 (1984) #3180; and AATA vol. 20 (1983) #20-401.

468

Ost, Hans and Ferino Padgen, Sylvia Diskussion. Neues zum Turiner Leonardo-Porträt? (Discussion. New information on the Turin Leonardo portrait?) *Kuntschronik* (Germany), 35 no. 5 (1982) 163–172, 5 illus.

Discussion concerning Hans Ost's book *Das Leonardo-Porträt inder Koniglichen Bibliothek Turin und andere Falschungen des Giuseppe Bossi (#449). See also #446.*

469

Paras-Perez, Rodolfo. Notes on Rodin's drawings. *Art Quarterly* (USA), 30 (1967) 126–137, 10 illus.

470

Perrig, Alexander. On the corpus of 'Michelangelo' drawings. *Drawing* (USA), 1 no. 6 (March–April 1980) 127–132, 15 illus.

English abstract in RILA vol. 7 (1981) #5450.

471

Rhyne, Charles B. Constable drawings and watercolors in the collections of Mr. and Mrs. Paul Mellon and the Yale Center for British Art: Part II. Reattributed works. *Master Drawings* (USA), 19 no. 4 (Winter 1981) 391–425, 19 illus., 64 refs., 8 plates.

English abstract in AATA vol. 20 (1983) #20-406.

472

Rodger, William. Forged drawings. *Hobbies* (USA), 80 (February 1976) 152–153.

On the prevalence of forged drawings, techniques of the forger, and tips on identifying forgeries.

473

Rosemberg, Jakob. Ein erfolgreicher Fälscher spätgotischer Zeichnungen. Mehr über den sogenannten Wiener Meister mit den Bandrollen um 1481. *Festschrift Friedr. Winkler*, 1959, pp. 148–153, 7 illus.

A forger of late Gothic sketchings.
For related articles, see RGR #s 545 & 550.

474

Russoli, Franco. Per un catalogo dell' opera di Modigliani. *Scritti Stor. Arte M. Salmi*, 3 (1963) pp. 475–480, 3 illus.

475

Seiberling, Dorothy. Great Rodin, his flagrant faker. *Life* (USA), 58 (4 June 1965) 64–71, illus.

Portrait of Ernst Durig and his fake Rodin drawings and sculptures.

476

Spielman, Heinz. Kokoschka-Fälschungen V. Zu Kokoschkas Kreide-Zeichnungen (Kokoschka-forgeries v. To Kokoschka's chalk-drawings). *Weltkunst* (Germany), 53 no. 4 (1983) 416–417, 14 fig.

French abstract in RAA 1983 #9847.

477

Spielman, Heinz. Kokoschka-Fälschungen VI. Zur Geschichte gefälschter Kokoschka-Zeichnungen (Kokoshka-forgeries VI. On the history of forged Kokoschka drawings). *Weltkunst* (Germany), 53 no. 5 (1983) 559–570, 127 illus.

French abstract in RAA 1983 #9848. This article also includes a catalog of forged drawings, signatures, and incorrect attributions.

478

Spielman, Heinz. Nachtrag zu Kokoschka-Fälschungen VI. (Postscript to Kokoschka-forgeries VI). *Weltkunst* (Germany), 53 no. 7 (1983) 896–898, 24 illus.

French abstract in RAA 1983 #9849. Contains a catalog of forged drawings.

479

Trucco, Terry. The art market. *ARTnews* (USA), 80 no. 2 (February 1981) p. 26.

Forgery of an L.S. Lowry drawing, *Man with walking stick in street*, discovered at Christie's.

480

Unsigned article. [Editorial] The Keating affair. *Burlington Magazine* (England), 119 no. 886 (1977) 3.

481

Unsigned article. [The Vasari diary] Fragonard fakes. *ARTnews* (USA), 77 no. 5 (May 1978)32, 34.

Sculpture

See also Drawings (Periodicals) #475, and Exhibitions #1721, #1765, and #1767.

Books

482

Alscher, Ludger. *Götter vor Gericht. Das Fälschungsproblem des Bostoner "Throns"* (Gods of judgement. The problem of falsification of Boston's "Throne"). Berlin: Deutsch Verlag Wiss., 1963, 138 p., illus.
The *Boston Throne Relief*

483

Ashmole, Bernard. *Forgeries of ancient sculpture: creation and detection.* Oxford: Blackwell, 1962, 15 p., 6 plates. (The J.L. Myres Memorial Lecture Delivered in New College, Oxford, on 9 May 1961).

484

Bieber, Margarete. *Ancient copies: contributions to the history of Greek and Roman art.* New York: New York University Press, 1977, 302 p., 161 plates (911 figures).

Contents: Preface; Introduction; List of abbreviations; List of illustrations; 1. Problems and research in copies (1889–1970); 2. The author's approach to the problem; 3. The importance of clothing in judging Roman copies; 4. Original and copy; 5. Addition of clothing and attributes; 6. Different reasons for denuding in Greek and Roman art; 7. Artemis and the Lares; 8. The fusing of parts of the same or of different dresses; 9. The shoulder-back mantle; 10. The right and wrong ways of draping the himation; 11. Roman men in Greek himation (*Romani Palliati*) and their female counterparts; The copies of the Herculaneum women; Portraits of Roman ladies as Priestesses of Ceres and of Empresses as *Augustae* or *Divae*; 14. Typical mistakes and mannerisms found on Roman copies; 15. An outline of the history of copying; 16. Late antique and early Christian copies; Conclusion; Bibliography; Museums and sites; Index; Plates.

485

Lauter, Hans. *Zur Chronologie römischer Kopien nach Originalen des V. Jahrhundert* (Concerning the chronology of Roman copies after fifth century originals). [Erlangen, Offsetdruck-Fotodruck], 1969?, 186 p., illus., includes bibliographical references.

486

Noble, Joseph Veach and von Bothmer, Dietrich. *An inquiry into the forgery of the Etruscan terracotta warriors in the Metropolitan Museum of Art.* New York: The Metropolitan Museum, 1961, 28 pp. 24 plates, map. (Metropolitan Museum of Art Papers, No. 11.)

For a review of Noble and von Bothmer's book, see P.J. Riis' article in *Gnomon* (Germany), 35 (1963) 711–714.

487

Türr, K. *Fälschungen antiker Plastik seit 1800* (Forged antique sculpture since 1800). Berlin: Mann, 1984, 267 p., illus.

488

Wear, Bruce. *The second bronze world of Frederic Remington.* Ranch Publishing Company, 1976, 185 p., plates, photos.

Contents: List of illustrations; Chapter I, Frederic Remington 1861–1909; Chapter II, Foundries and Remington; Chapter III, Casting processes: French sand casting, cire perdue or the lost wax process as used in Remington bronzes; Chapter IV, Detection of fakes and forgeries: fraudulent bronzes (copies, reproductions, facsimiles, replicas); Addendum; Glossary; A list of Remington bronzes by subject matter; Appendix A: A big business selling fakes and forgeries; Appendix B: Art expert exposes fakes; Appendix C: Trial—a case on Remington bronzes; Appendix D: Bronzes sold at auction; Extensive Remington art collections in public institutions.

Sections of Books

489

Beale, Arthur. "A technical view of nineteenth-century sculpture," in *Metamorphoses in nineteenth-century sculpture*, Jeane L. Wasserman, ed. Cambridge, Mass.: Fogg Art Museum, Harvard University Press, 1975, pp. 28–55, 60 photos, 4 illus.
English abstract in AATA vol. 15 (1978) #15-749.

490

Bloch, Peter. "Original—Kopie—Verfälschung (Original—copy—falsification)," in *Jahrbuch der Stiftung Preussischer Kulturbesitz* (Germany), 16 (1979) 41–72, 18 illus.

491

La Moureyre-Gavoty, Françoise de. *Sculpture italienne* (Italian sculpture). Institut de France. Preface by Julien Cain. Paris: Editions de musées nationaux, Palais du Louvre, 1975, 240 p. (Inventaire des collections publiques françaises, 19). 231 illus., bibliog., index.
English abstract in RILA vol. 2 (1976) #7029.

492

Pope-Hennessy, John. *The study and criticism of Italian sculpture.* New York: Metropolitan Museum of Art, 1980, 244 illus.

This volume contains 10 articles on 15th-century sculpture, one of which deals with forgeries in Italian Renaissance sculpture.
For the complete contents of the book, see English abstract in RILA vol. 8 (1982) #956.

493

Schuyler, Jane. *Florentine busts: sculpted portraiture in the fifteenth century.*
(Ph.D. dissertation, Columbia University, 1972). New York: Garland, 1976.
315 pp. (Outstanding dissertations in the fine arts), 132 illus., bibliog.

The last chapter of this dissertation is concerned with distinguishing
18th and 19th century forgeries from authentic Quattrocento busts.
English abstract in RILA vol. 4 (1978) #5038.

494

Vikan, Gary. "The so-called *Sheikh Ibada Group* of early coptic sculptures,"
in *Byzantine Studies Conference Abstracts of Papers* (USA), 3 (1977)
15–16.

French abstract in RAA 1981 #4514.

Periodicals

495

Amyx, D.A. A forged Corinthian animal frieze. *Bulletin of the Brooklyn Museum*
(USA), 21 no. 2 (Spring 1960) 9–13, 2 illus.

496

Androsov, S.O. Zametki o poddelkah ital'janskoj renesansnoj skul'ptury.
Muzcj (USSR), 2 (1981) 23–30, 8 illus. Summary in English.

On forged Italian Renaissance sculpture. Among the sculptors discussed are Giovanni Bastianini, Antonio Rossellino, and Donatello.
French abstract in RAA 1982 #8203.

497

Appuhn, H. Die schönsten Minnekästchen aus Basel. Fälschungen aus der
Zeit der Romantik. *Zeitschrift für schweizerische Archäeologie und Kunstgeschichte* (Switzerland), 41 no. 3 (1984) 149–166, 14 illus. Summaries
in German, French, Italian and English.

French abstract in RAA 1985 #1202.

498

Banti, Luisa. Osservazioni sulla *Diana di St. Louis. Studi etruschi* (Italy),
26 (1958) 237–241, 2 illus.

499

Berger, Ursel. Zum Problem der 'Originalbronzen' Deutsche Bronzeplastiken
im 19. und 20. Jahrhundert (Observations on the problem of 'original'
bronzes. German bronzes in the 19th and 20th centuries). *Pantheon*
(Germany), 40 no. 3 (July–September 1982) 184–195, 15 illus. Summary
in French and English.

English abstract in RILA vol. 11 (1985) #2718.

500

Berton, Paul. Crimes and connoisseurs. *Macleans* (Canada), 97 no. 43 (22 October 1984) 72, 74, illus.

Three forged Modigliani sculptures found in the Fosso Canal in Livorno, Italy. The article also touches on the problem of fake Salvador Dali prints.

501

Bloch, Peter. Echt oder falsch? Skulpturen und Kunstgewerbe (True or false? Sculpture and applied arts). *Weltkunst* 46 no. 22 (1976) 2234–2236, 6 illus.

502

Bloch, Peter. Sculptures néo-gothiques en Allemagne (Neo-gothic sculpture in Germany). *Revue de l'Art* (France), no. 21 (1973) 70–79, 22 illus. Summary in English.

French abstract in RAA 1975 #10576.

503

Blümel, Carl. Idolino, Apollon Kitharista, Münchner Knabenkopf mit Siegerbinde. *Archäologischer Anzeiger* (Germany), no. 2 (1974) 247–258, illus.

504

Blümel, Carl. Teure Fälschungen (Costly forgeries). *Forschungen und Berichte. Staatliche Museen zu Berlin* (Germany), 3–4 (1961) 13–17, 5 illus.

505

Brommer, Frank. Falsche Köpfe (False heads). *Archäologischer Anzeiger* (Germany), no. 3 (1963) 439–450, 10 illus.

The head of the *kouros* in the Metropolitan Museum of Art, after comparison with others of its kind (both genuine and fake), is discovered to be a fake.

English abstract in AATA vol. 6 (1966–1967) #(6)-G4-13.

506

Brooks, Valerie. A flood of fakes: think twice before spending thousands for that serene antique Buddha from Burma. *Connoisseur* (England), 212 no. 848 (October 1982) 26, 28, 30, 4 illus.

English abstract in ABM vol. 16 (1985) #5631.

507

Buchholz, Hans-Günter. Zu einigen gefälschten Basaltstatuetten aus Syrien (On some forged basalt statues from Syria). *Archäologischer Anzeiger* (Germany), 1963, pp. 112–126, 6 illus.

French abstract in RAA 1963 #3214.

508

Byvanck-Quarles van Ufford, L. F. Baroni: Osservazioni sul *Trono di Boston*. *Bulletin van de Vereeniging tot de Bevordering der Kennis van de antieke Beschaving* (Netherlands), 37 (1962) 89–90.

The *Boston Throne Relief.*

509

Cagiano de Azevedo, Michel-Angelo. Sulla authenticita di alcune terracotte del Metropolitan Museum. *Bolletino dell' Instituto Centrale del Restauro* (Italy), no. 1 (1950) 44.

On the Etruscan warriors in the Metropolitan Museum of Art.

510

Cantera y Burgos, Francisco. Relieves históricos de la Judería de Toledo. *Sefarad* (Spain), 26 (1966) 305–322.

511

Castiglione, L. A recently published forgery. *Acta Archaeologica Academiae Scientiarum Hungaricae* (Hungary), 23 (1971) 231–245, illus.

Castiglione argues that a sculpted marble slab, believed by Edith B. Thomas to be from the late 2nd to early 3rd centuries A.D., depicting King David dancing at the Ark, is a forgery. The article in a carefully reasoned, critical analysis of Thomas' book entitled *King David leaping and dancing. A Jewish marble from the Roman Imperial period.* (Budapest: Akad. Kiado, 1970, 45 p. 10 plates).

512

Cellini, Pico. Storia di una statua fittile. *Paragone* (Italy), no. 81 (1956) 54–58, 2 plates.

On an Etruscan *Diana* believed to be sculpted by forger Aleco Dossena.

513

Chamberlain, Betty. Controlling sculpture fakes. *Sculpture Review* (USA), 31 no. 4 (1982–1983) 7 + .

514

Cook, Brian. A fake porphyry head. *Burlington Magazine* (England), 126 no. 970 (January 1984) 18–20.

515

Corbett, Patricia. The Modigliani affair. *Connoisseur* (England), 215 no. 875 (January 1985) 32, 34, illus.

Three forged sculptures dredged up from the Fosso Canal in Livorno, Italy, where legend has it the young Amedeo Modigliani had thrown some of his work.

516

Davis, Frank. The art of deception. Fakes and forgeries. *Country Life* (England), 161 no. 4170 (2 June 1977), 1535–1536, 6 illus.

A survey of forgeries in sculpture by Giovanni Bastianini and Aleco Dossena, with mention of other famous forgeries.

517

Davis, Frank. Follies and fakes of the art world. *Country Life* (England), 161 (24 February 1977) 444–445, illus.

On a wax statuette of Flora purchased by Dr. von Bode for the Berlin Museum. The statuette was originally thought to be by Leonardo da Vinci.

518

Dixon, K.A. First Tikal-inspired fake: a stone sculpture from west Mexico. *Expedition* (USA), 9 no. 2 (Winter 1967) 36–38 + .

519

Easby, Dudley T., Jr.; and Dockstader, Frederick J. Requiem for Tizoc. *Archaeology* (USA), 17 no. 2 (June 1964) 85–90, illus.

A gold figurine of the Aztec ruler Tizoc is discovered to be a modern forgery.
English abstract in AATA vol. 5 (1964–1965) #4723.

520

Ecke, Gustav. Once again Hui-Hsien: fraud and authenticity of the figurines. *Artibus Asiae* (Switzerland), 15 no. 4 (1952) 305–323, illus.

English abstract in G&U #175.

521

Elbern, Victor H. Drei "koptische" Antikenkopien (Three "coptic" antique copies). *Cahiers Archéologiques* (France), 17 (1967) 237–245, 8 illus.

522

Failing, Patricia. The Degas bronzes Degas never knew. *ARTnews* (USA), 78 no. 4 (April 1979) 38–41, 6 illus.

English abstract in RILA vol. 5 (1979) #7090.
French abstract in RAA 1979 #9848.

523

Fleming, Stuart J.; and Stoneham, D. Thermoluminescent authenticity study and dating of Renaissance terracottas. *Archaeometry* (England), 15 no. 2 (1973) 239–247.

English abstract in AATA vol. 15 (1978) #15-649.

524

Fonti, D. Arrestato per insulti al Duce mentre gli scolpisce il ritratto (Arrested for insulting the Duce while sculpting his portrait). *Bolaffiarte* (Italy), 9 no. 76 (January–February 1978) 26–29, 10 illus.

On forger Aleco Dossena.
English abstract in ABM vol. 9 (1978) #5407.

525

Frankfurter, Alfred. Unhappy warriors. *ARTnews* (USA), 60 no. 1 (March 1961) 25, 65–67, illus.

526

Franzoni, Lanfranco. Bronzetti pseudo-antichi di officine venete. *Instituto veneto di scienze, lettere ed arti. Classe di scienze morali, lettere ed arti* (Italy), 124 (1965–1966) 39–59, 20 illus.

French abstract in RAA 1967 #6357.

527

Frel, Jiří. Miscellanea pontica. II. Fragments antiques de Théodosie au Musée du Louvre. *Sborník Prací filosofické Fakulty brněnské University* (Archeol.), (Czechoslovakia), 12 (1963) 93–96, 3 plates.

528

Fridrich, J.; and Kulka, J. Verification of a prehistoric sculpture from Modiany. *Archeologické Rozhledy* (Czechoslovakia), 19 no. 6 (1967). [In Czech].

English abstract in AATA vol. 7 (1968) #7-458.

529

Garbini, G. Studi di archeologia orientale. *Annali Istituto Orientale di Napoli* (Italy), 33 no. 3 (1973) 365–372, illus.

530

Getz-Preziosi, Patricia. An early Cycladic sculpture. *Antike Kunst* (Germany), 18 no. 2 (1975) 47–50, illus.

The author disputes the contention that an early Cycladic sculpture, in the National Archaeological Museum in Athens, is a forgery. He believes the piece is one of four genuine pieces (two in private collections, the other at the Ashmolean Museum in Oxford), all carved by the same person whom he calls the "Athens Master."

531

Gjodesen, Mogens. Deux ex Machina. *Meddelelser fra Ny Carlsberg Glyptotek* (Denmark), 8 (1951) 12–32, 18 illus.

French abstract in RAA 1950–1951 #4462
On two archaic bronze statuettes, Greek and Syrian.

532

Grunfeld, Frederic V. The crystal skull. *Horizon* (USA), 9 no. 1 (Winter 1972) 72–73, illus.

Controversy surrounding a realistic life-size crystal skull in the British Museum. The official opinion of the museum is that it is Aztec, from Mexico, 15th century.

533

Gwinnett, A. John; and Gorelick, Leonard. Authenticity analysis of two stone statuettes in the Mildenberg collection. *Museum of the Applied Science Center for Archaeology* (USA), 2 no. 3 (December 1983) 88–90, 9 illus.

English abstract in AATA vol. 21 (1984) #21-922.

534

Herzer, H. Ein Relief des Berliner Meisters (A relief of a Berlin Master). *Objets* (Switzerland), 4–5 (1970) 39–46.

535

Hochfield, Sylvia. The Mansoor collection: an insoluble controversy? *ARTnews* (USA), 77 no. 6 (Summer 1978) 50–57, 24 illus.

536

Homann-Wedeking, Ernst. Echtheitsargumente (Authenticity argument). *Archäologischer Anzeiger* (Germany), 1963, 225–231.

537

Johnson, Franklin P. On believing Fioravanti. *American Journal of Archaeology* (USA), 70 no. 4 (October 1966) 373.

On Walter Fioravanti, one of the forgers of the three Etruscan warriors at the Metropolitan Museum in New York.

538

Jucker, Hans. Die Berenike aus Perinth. *Archäologischer Anzeiger* (Germany), no. 4 (1970) 487–492, illus.

A Hellenistic forgery of a Hellenic bust from Perinth, now in the Athens Museum.

539

Kohler, Ellen L. Ultimatum to terracotta forgers. *Expedition* (USA), 9 no. 2 (Winter 1967) 16–21, illus.

English abstract in AATA vol. 8 (1970–1971) #8-909.

540

Kotschenreuther, H. Betrogen nach allen Regein der Kunst. II. Von Fälschen, Kunstlern und Experten. *Artis* (Germany), 27 no. 3 (1975) 12–16, 5 illus.

French abstract in RAA 1975 #7763.

541

Kurz, Otto. The *Bonus eventus* relief in the British Museum. *Journal of the Warburg Courtauld Institutes* (England), 25 (1962) 335–337, 3 illus.

French abstract in RAA 1962 #1706.

542

Lefferts, Kate C.; Majewski, Lawrence J.; Sayre, Edward V.; and Meyers, Pieter. Technical examination of the Classical bronze horse from the Metropolitan Museum of Art. *American Institute for Conservation, Journal* (USA), 21 (1981) 1–42

English abstract in AATA vol. 19 (1982) #19-1853.

543

Lerner, Judith A. Three Achaemenid "fakes": a re-evaluation in the light of 19th century Iranian architectural sculpture. *Expedition* (USA), 22 no. 2 (Winter 1980) 5–16, 12 illus.

544

Lindemann, B.W. Ferdinand Tletz. Probleme des Kleinplastischen Werks. *Zeitschrift des Deutschen Vereins für Kunstwissenschaft* (Germany), 37 no. 1–4 (1983) 73–108, 62 illus.

545

Love, Iris. A stylistic discussion concerning the authenticity of the three Etruscan warriors in the Metropolitan Museum of Art. *Marsyas* (USA), 9 (1960–1961) 14–35, 26 illus.

French abstract in RAA 1960 #4055.

546

Lynes, Russell. Forgery for fun and profit. *Harper's* (USA), 236 no. 1413 (February 1968) 21–22, 24, 26, 28 illus.

Profile of forger Aleco Dossena.

547

Mallon, P. Des imitations des anciennes sculptures chinoises. *Artibus Asiae* (Switzerland), 2 (1927) 41–49, illus.

548

Mazzolai, Aldo. Per un Corpus dei bronzetti etruschi. La collezione del Museo archeologico di Grosseto. *Studi etruschi* (Italy), 26 (1958) 193–223, 39 illus.

French abstract in RAA 1958 #4124.

549

Marguerite, Antoine. Petites histoires de la falsification. *Arts du Monde* (France), no. 6–7 (1951) 10–11.

On forger Aleco Dossena.

550

Moltesen, M. En forfalskningshistorie. *Meddelelser fra Ny Carlsberg Glyptotek* (Denmark), 37 (1981) 51–69, 12 illus. Summary in English.

French abstract in RAA 1982 #9126.

551

Moorey, P.R.S.; and Fleming, Stuart J. Problems in the Study of the anthropomorphic statuary from Syro-Palestine before 330 B.C. *Levant* (England), 16 (1984) 67–90.

English abstract in AATA vol. 22 (1985) #22-2546.

552

Muscarella, Oscar White. An aftercast of an ancient Iranian bronze. *Source: Notes in the History of Art* (USA), 1 no. 2 (Winter 1982) 6–9, 1 illus.

English abstract in AATA vol. 19 (1982) #19-1869.

553

Nagel, Charles. Editor's Letters: St. Louis' *Diana*, a controversy. *ARTnews* (USA), 61 no. 1 (1962) 10.

A reply to an article by Harold W. Parsons, (#561).

554

Natanson, Ann. Three students and a dockworker put their heads together and confound the art world. *People Weekly* (USA), 22 (8 October 1984) 55–56, illus.

Three forged Modigliani sculptures found in the Fosso Canal in Livorno, Italy.

555

Negri Arnoldi, Francesco. Un marmo autentico di Desiderio all' origine di un falso Antonio Rossellino. *Paragone* (Italy), no. 209 (1967) 23–26, 3 plates.

556

Neugass, Fritz. Hochflut von Rodinfälschungen (Surge of Rodin fakes). *Weltkunst* (Germany), 35 (1965) 965.

On forger Ernst Durig and his fake Rodin sculptures.

557

Nguyet, T. [Editorial]. Khmer sculpture. *Arts Asiatiques* (France), 12 (March/April 1982) 4 +, illus.

558

Noble, Joseph Veach. The forgery of our Greek bronze horse. *Metropolitan Museum of Art Bulletin* (USA), 26 no. 6 (1968) 235–236.

559

Parlasca, K.; and Blümel, Carl. Zwei falsche bronzeporträts (K. Parlasca). Zur echtheitsfrage des antiken bronzepferdes im Metropolitan museum in New York (C. Blümel). (Two forged bronze reliefs [K. Parlasca]. The recurring question of the ancient bronze horses in the Metropolitan Museum in New York [C. Blümel]. *Archäologischer Anzeiger* (Germany), no. 2 (1969) 203–216, illus.

560

Parronchi, Alessandro. Une Madone Donatellienne de Jacopo Sansovino (A Donatello-like Madonna of Jacopo Sansovino). *Revue de l'Art* (France), no. 21 (1973) 40–43. Summary in English.

561

Parsons, Harold W. The art of fake Etruscan art. *ARTnews* (USA), 60 no. 10 (February 1962) 34–37, 68, 13 illus. Reply with rejoinder, Charles Nagel, vol. 61 no. 1 (March 1962) 10, 65.

English abstract in AATA vol. 4 (1962–1963) #3677.

562

Peroni, Adriano. Su alcuni falsi della scultura bresciana del Rinascimento. *Arte lombarda* (Italy), 9 (1965) 111–118, 11 illus.

On three sculptors: Pietro Faitini, Aleco Dossena, and Giovanni Bastianini.

563

Perzynski, F. A Chinese sculpture. *Art in America* (USA), 16 (1928) 116–121, illus.

564

Petráček, Karel. Quelques faux sud-arabes (Several false south-arabs). *Annales d'Ethiopie* (Ethiopia), 4 (1961) 125–127, 6 illus.

French abstract in RAA 1962 #1703.

565

Pope-Hennessy, John. The forging of Italian Renaissance sculpture. *Apollo* (England), 99 no. 146 (April 1974) 242–267, 72 illus.

French abstract in RAA 1974 #9527.

Among the many sculptors discussed are: Lorenzo Bartolini, Giovanni Bastianini, Andrea del Verrocchio, Desiderioda Settignano, Mino da Fiesde, and Antonio Rossellino.

566

Prag, A.J.N.W. Athena Mancuniensis. Another copy of the Athena Parthenos. *Journal of Hellenic Studies* (England), 92 (1972) 96–144.

567

Prag, A.J.N.W.; and Bowman, S.G.E. Athena Parthenos: a nineteenth-century forger's workshop. *Journal of Hellenic Studies* (England), 103 (1983) 151–154, illus.

568

Pressouyre, Léon. Sur une tête de roi gothique et sa copie (A gothic head of a king and its copy). *Revue de l'Art* (France), no. 21 (1973) 32–39, 15 illus. Summary in English.

French abstract in RAA 1974 #8841.

569

Radcliff, Anthony. Replicas, copies and counterfeits of early Italian bronzes. *Apollo* (England), 124 no. 295 (September 1986) 183–187, 10 illus.

570

Rostand, André. Le calendrier sculpté de Tour-en-Bessin (The sculpted calendar of Tour-en-Bessin). *Bulletin de la Societe des Antiquaires de Normandie* (France), 50 (1946–1948) 293–297.

French abstract in RAA 1950–1951 #2450.

571

Rizzi, A. Sui falsi erratici di Venezia. *Ateneo veneto* (Italy), 20 no 1–2 (1982) 309–317, 3 illus.

French abstract in RAA 1984 #10977.

572

Rossi, P.A. Breathing fire and smoke: the great bronze casting debate. *Southwest Art* (USA), 11 no. 9 (February 1982) 62–69, 10 illus.

English abstract in ABM vol. 15 (1984) #5563.

It is often difficult to authenticate bronze casts of Western sculptors who are deceased. The work of Frederic Remington is used to illustrate the problems one encounters when authenticating such works.

573

Salzmann, D. Eine verkannte Statuette des Antinoos (A mistaken statue of Antinoos). *Archäologischer Anzeiger* (Germany), no. 1 (1982) 139–142, illus.

574

Sani, Bernardina. Le vrai et le faux dans l'oeuvre de Bastianini (The true and the false in the work of Bastianini). *Revue de l'Art* (France), no. 21 (1973) 102–107, 10 illus. Summary in English.

575

Seeden, Helga. Some old and new bronzes: true or false? *Beytrus (Archae-ological Studies)* (Lebanon), 26 (1978) 5–25, 8 plates.

English abstract in AATA vol. 16 (1979) #16-1753.
On forged metal gods from the 3rd-2nd millennia B.C. in Syria/Lebanon.

576

Seidel, Linda. A romantic forgery: the romanesque "portal" of Saint-Etienne in Toulouse. *Art Bulletin* (USA), 50 no. 1 (March 1968) 33–42, plates.

577

Shapiro, Maurice L. Renaissance or neo-classic? A forgery after the antique reconsidered. *Art Bulletin* (USA), 44 no. 2 (June 1962) 131–135, 8 illus.

French abstract in RAA 1962 #1707.

578

Simpson, C. Cloisters murders. *Art & Artists* (England), 197 (February 1983) 22–23.

On fake medieval sculpture.

579

Sirén, O. Quelques observations sur les imitations des anciennes sculptures chinoises. *Artibus Asiae* (Switzerland), 1 (1925–1926) 64–75, 132–145, illus.

580

Skupinska-Lovset, I; and Fleming, Stuart J. A Scythian figurine from Beth Shean. *Museum of Applied Science Center for Archaeology* (USA), 1 no. 3 (1979) 76–77, 1 illus.

581

Staccioli, R.A. I guerrieri etruschi di New York riconosciuti falsi. *Studi etruschi* (Italy), 29 (1961) 317–318.

582

Strehlke, C.B. A bronze lion and panther in the Wadsworth Atheneum, Hartford. *Esercizi. Arte, musica, spettacolo* (Italy), 1 (1978) 33–37, 2 illus.

French abstract in RAA 1979 #11859.

583

Strom, Deborah. A new identity for the *Dudley Madonna and Child* in the Victoria and Albert Museum. *Antichita viva* (Italy), 23 no. 4–5 (1984) 37–41, 7 illus. Summary in Italian.

584

Strom, D. A new look at the *Mellon Christ Child* in the National Gallery of Art. *Antichità viva* (Italy), 22 no. 3 (1983) 9–12, 8 illus. Summary in Italian.

English abstract in ABM vol. 16 (1985) #7464.

French abstract in RAA 1984 #8473.

585

Tölle, R. Eine Lakonische Göttin des 7, Jahrhunderts? (A Laconian goddess of the 7th century?). *Revue Archéologique* (France), 2 (1964) 105–111.

English abstract in AATA vol. 6 (1966–1967) #(6)-G1-10.

586

Ucko, Peter J., and Hodges, H.W.M. Some pre-Dynastic Egyptian figurines: problems of authenticity. *Journal of the Warburg and Courtauld Institutes* (England), 26 (1963) 205–222, 26 illus.

587

Unsigned article. Fallen warriors. *Time* (USA), 70 (24 February 1961) 60, illus.

The three fake Etruscan warriors at the Metropolitan Museum of Art.

588

Unsigned article. Feat of clay. *Newsweek* (USA), 57 no. 9 (27 February 1961) 57, illus.

New York's Metropolitan Museum of Art announces its three Etruscan warriors (5th century B.C.) are modern forgeries.

589

Unsigned article. Forger unforged. Or the fake unfaked. *Apollo* (England), 88 (December 1968) 497.

Greek bronze statuette horse (5th century B.C.), in the Metropolitan Museum of Art, is declared a forgery.

590

Unsigned article. A masterpiece of fakery. *Life* (USA), 50 no. 10 (10 March 1961) 40A–40B.

On Harold W. Parsons and how he tracked down Walter Fioravanti, forger of the fake Etruscan warriors at the Metropolitan Museum of Art. Forgeries by Aleco Dossena are also mentioned.

591

Unsigned article. Monet and the phoney pony. *Time* (USA), 90 (15 December 1967) 84.

Greek bronze statuette horse (5th century B.C.), in the Metropolitan Museum of Art, is declared a modern forgery.

592

Unsigned article. Of a different color. *Newsweek* (USA), 70 no. 25 (18 December 1967) 94.

Joseph Veach Noble, vice director of the Metropolitan Museum of Art, announces that their famed Greek bronze statuette horse (5th century B.C.) is a twentieth century forgery.

593

Unsigned article. Which horse is a fake? *Ceramics Monthly* (USA), 21 no. 7 (September 1973) 43.

594

Vandersall, Amy L. Five "Romanesque" portals: questions of attribution and ornament. *Metropolitan Museum Journal* (USA), 18 (1983) 129–139.

595

Ward, William. The Modigliani caper. *Art & Antiques* (USA), December 1984, p. 16, 1 illus.

596

Weisburd, S. Science for art's sake: five easy pieces. *Science News* (USA), 126 no. 20 (17 November 1984) 311.

A bust of Antonia Minor, the mother of Claudius Caesar (Fogg Museum, Harvard University), was subjected to scientific analysis and found to be comprised of 5 different, unrelated pieces of marble. The head of the bust is believed to be authentic.

597

Wood, Susan. The bust of Philip the Arab in the Vatican: a case for the defense. *American Journal of Archaeology* (USA), 86 no. 2 (April 1982) 244-247, 2 plates.

Ceramics

See also Hallmarks; Antiquities (Books) #691 and Exhibitions #1757.

Books

598
Becker, Klaus, and Moreno y Moreno, A. *Applications of thermoluminescence measurements in ancient ceramics.* Report, (ORNL-TM-4572, 35 pages). From Nuclear Science Abstracts, 30 no. 7 (1974) #18659.

599
Neuwirth, Waltraud. Wiener Porzellan: Original, Kopie, Verfälschung, Fälschung (Vienna porcelain: originals, copies, forgery, faking), Wien: Neuwirth, 1979, 612 p., 600 illus., bibliog., index. Summaries in English and French.

Sections of Books

600
Battie, David. "Forgeries and other deceptions" (Appendix), in *The history of porcelain.* Paul Atterbury, general editor, New York: William Morrow and Company, Inc., 1982, pp. 228–239, illus.

Appendix includes discussions on porcelain of China and Japan; Worcester; Chelsea and Derby; Sevres; Vienna; Meissen; Capodimonte and Berlin. Numerous photos.

601
Beurdeley, Michel. "Fakes—European enamelling and overpainting; Fakes—Overpainting in the eighteenth century," in his *Porcelain of the east India companies.* Translated by Diana Imber, London: Barrie and Rockliff, 1962, pp. 142–143.

602
Bradshaw, Peter. "Reproductions, fakes, restoration and collecting" (Chapter XIII), in his *18th century English porcelain figures, 1745–1795,* Woodbridge, Suffolk: Baron Publishing, 1981, pp. 270–281.

603
Brunet, Marcelle, and Preaud, Tamara. "Marques et signatures; imitations et faux," in their *Sèvres: des origines à nos jours.* Fribourg, Switzerland: Office du Livre, 1978, pp. 339–340.

604

Feest, Christian F.; Erlach, Rudolf; Pichler, Bernhard; Vendl, Alfred; Vana, Norbert; Bowman, Sheridan G.E.; and Bauer, Wilhelm P. "TL-Unter suchungen an suedamerikanischen Keramiken. 1. Figuralkeramik der Zapoteken. 2. Moche-Keramik (TL study of South American ceramics. Part 1. Effigy pottery of the Zapotecs. Part 2. Moche ceramics)," in *Wiener Berichte ueber Naturwissenschaft in der Kunst*, vol. 1, edited by Alfred Vendl and Bernhard Pichler, pp. 40–48, table, 6 illus. Summary in English.

English abstract in AATA vol. 22 (1985) #22-1155.

605

Des Fontaines, Una. "Identification" (Chapter Six), in her *Wedgwood Fairyland Lustre:* the work of Daisy Makeig-Jones. New York & London: Born-Hawes and Sotheby Parke Bernet, 1975, pp. 55–67, illus.

Contents of chapter six: Marks and backstamps on Wedgwood earthenware and bone china; forgeries; systems of numbering and coding patterns; comprehensive pattern numbers; lustre pattern books; dating; shapes and their sources; illustrations of shapes.

606

Godden, Geoffrey Arthur. *Godden's guide to English porcelain.* London: Hart-Davis, MacGibbon, 1978, 286 pp., 108 illus., bibliog., index.

English abstract in RILA vol. 5 (1979) #5335.

607

Hillier, Bevis. "Repairs, reproductions and fakes," in her *Pottery and porcelain 1700–1914: England, Europe and North America.* London: Weidenfeld and Nicolson, 1968, pp. 298–318.

608

Honey, W.B. *Old English porcelain: a handbook for collectors.* London: G. Bell and Sons, Ltd., 1931, pp. 13, 80, 93, 152 (forged marks); pp. 40, 181, 203, 207, 211, 257 (forgeries).

609

Lehmann, Henry. "Forgeries and principle workshops" (Part 3: Collections and collectors), in his *pre-Columbian ceramics.* Translated by Galway Kinnell. New York: The Viking Press, 1962, pp. 115–116.

610

Mortlock, A. Thermoluminescence: Authentication of ceramic art objects. *The Australasian Antique Collector* (Australia), no. 15 (1974 annual) 44-46.

English abstract in AATA vol. 12 (1975) 12-1116.

611

Neave-Hill, W.B.R. "Copies and fakes," in his *Chinese ceramics*. New York: St. Martin's Press, pp. 134, 138–141, 146, 154, 157, 160–162. Appendix of ceramic form through the ages; reign-names, hall-marks and emblems; glossary; bibliog.; index.

612

Neuwirth, Waltraud. "Wiener Porzellan von 1718 bis heute" (Viennese porcelain from 1718 to today), in *Internationales Symposium anlässlich des 300. Geburtstages Johann Friedrich Böttgers* (5–6 Feb. 1982), Dresden-Meissen. Freiberg: Bergakad, 1983, pp. 118–121, 6 illus.

French abstract in RAA 1985 #10979.

613

Rice, D.G. "Introduction: the identification of Rockingham porcelain" (Chapter I), in his *Rockingham ornamental porcelain*. London: The Adam Publishing Company, 1965, pp. 1–5.

614

Röntgen, Robert E. "Outside painting, imitations and copies of Meissen porcelain," and "Imitations of Meissen marks," in his *The book of Meissen*. Pennsylvania: Schiffer Publishing Ltd., 1984, pp. 223–232; 287–300, illus.

615

Satō, Masahiko. "Authenticating Kyō Ware," in *Kyoto ceramics*. Translated and adapted by Anne Ono Towle, and Usher P. Coolidge. New York & Tokyo: Weatherhill/Shibundo, 1973, pp. 122–125.

616

Savage, George. "Forgeries," in his *18th century German porcelain*. London: Rockliff, 1958, pp. 216–219, passim. Contains an index of marks; bibliog.; index of places; index of subjects; index of persons.

617

Thiel, Albert Willem Rudolf. "Advice to collectors," in his *Chinese pottery and stoneware*. Los Angeles: Borden Publishing Company, 1953, pp. 99–106, illus.

618

Wills, G. *Wedgwood*. London: Country Life Books; distributed by Hamlyn, 1980, 128 pp. (The Country Life Library of Antiques Series), 99 illus., bibliog.

Contains a short section offering information on forgeries. Also contains a list of Wedgwood marks.

English abstract in ABM vol. 12 (1981) #1078.

Periodicals

619

Aitken, Martin; Moorey, P.R.S.; and Ucko, P.J. The authenticity of vessels and figurines in the Hacilar style. *Archaeometry* (England), 13 no. 2 (August 1971) 89–142, illus., bibliography, 5 appendices.

English abstract in AATA vol. 18 (1981) #18-505.

620

Anscombe, Isabelle, From admiration to imitation: faking Bernard Leach's pottery. *Connoisseur* (England), 206 no. 828 (February 1981) 152–153, 3 illus.

English abstract in ABM vol. 12 (1981) #5619.

621

Arias, C. and Bigazzi, G. Thermoluminscenza: test di autenticità per le ceramiche. *Faenza* (Italy), 61 nos. 1–3 (1975) 33–41, 7 illus., 1 plate. Summaries in French, English and German.

622

Bailey, D.M. A false Roman lamp. *Archaeology* (USA), 11 (June 1958) 126, illus.

Purchased in Cyprus, this forged lamp is made of a light buff clay. A relief of a plowing scene appears on the discus. The scene was evidently taken from an engraving dating back to 400 B.C. which is now in the Villa Guilia Museum, Rome.

623

Bailey, D.M. A giant Roman lamp. *Museums Journal* (England), 59 (February 1960) 265–267.

English abstract in AATA vol. 3 (1960) #2766.

624

Bailey, D.M. A group of false Roman lamps. *British Museum Quarterly* (England), 29 no. 3–4 (1965) 94–98.

625

Bailey, D.M. A rehabilitated forgery. *British Museum Quarterly* (England), 33 (Spring 1969) 113–117.

A small piece of pottery, believed to be a forgery, was discovered to be authentic after further tests.

English abstract in AATA vol. 8 (1970–1971) #8-247.

626

Bailey, D.M. Roman lamps—reproductions and forgeries. *Museums Journal* (England), 60 (May 1960) 39–46.

English abstract in AATA vol. 3 (1960) #2767.

627

Bailly, Robert. Un fabricant de lampes romaines au XXᵉ siècle. *Cahiers ligures de Préhistoire et d'Archéologie* (France), 3 (1954) 114–118, 1 illus.

French abstract in RAA 1954 #1313.

628

Becker, Klaus and Goedicke, Christian. A quick method for authentication of ceramic art objects. *Nuclear Instruments and Methods* (Netherlands), 151 nos. 1–2 (1978) 313–316.

English abstract in AATA vol. 15 (1978) #15-1513.

629

Becker, Klaus, and Moreno y Moreno, A. Applications of thermoluminescence measurements in ancient ceramics. *Proc. Int. Conf. Lumin, Dosim,* 4th, 3 (1974) 1021–1041.

English abstract in AATA vol. 12 (1975) #12-1072.

630

Baumann, Peter, Bei Keramikfaelschern in Ekuador (At the ceramic forgers of Ecuador). *Keramik Magazin* (Germany), 2 no. 2 (1980) 124–127, 5 photos.

English abstract in AATA vol. 17 (1980) #17-1390.
On forged pre-Columbian potteries.

631

Boden, G. Lumineszenzautoradiographie an Kieselkeramiken (Luminescence autoradiography of silica ceramics). *Berliner Beitraege zur Archaeometrie* no. 5 (1980) 85–88, 2 photos.

632

Di Peso, C. C. Clay figurines of Acambaro Guanajuanto, Mexico. *American Antiquity* (USA), 18 (April 1953) 388.

633

Dow, Sterling. A new copy of a forged Celtiberian plate. *Archaeology* (USA), 4 no. 4 (December 1951) 194–198, 2 illus.

French abstract in RAA 1950–1951 #2460.

634

Ducret, S. Echt oder falsch (True or false). *Keramik-Freunde der Schweiz* (Switzerland), no. 15 (1950) 13, 2 illus.

An earthenware plate reproduction found to be a mid-18th century forgery that carries the mark "Z" for the manufacturer of Zurich.
French abstract in RAA 1950–1951 #2463.

635

Editorial. [Thermoluminescence dating of the Monsters of Acambro]. *Antiquity* (England), 52 no. 204 (March 1978) 3-4.

636

Ehret, G. Porzellan hat seinen Preis (Porcelain has its price). *Artis* (Germany), 31 no. 11 (November 1979) 19, 2 illus.

The problems involved in collecting authentic porcelain dating from the 18th century onward.

637

Fleming, Stuart J. Authenticity of figurines, animals, and pottery facsimilies of bronzes in the Hui Hsien style. *Archaeometry* (England), 14 no. 2 (1972) 237–244.

English abstract in AATA vol. 9, (1972) #9-776.

638

Fleming, Stuart J. Scientific scrutiny. *National Antiques Review*, 7 no. 1 (July 1975) p. 3.

Thermoluminescent dating of T'ang Dynasty pottery revealed their age to be about 50 years.
English abstract in AATA vol. 15 (1978) #15-646.

639

Fleming, Stuart J. Thermoluminescent and glaze studies of a group of T'ang Dynasty ceramics. *Archaeometry* (England), 15 no. 1 (1973), pp. 31–52.

English abstract in AATA vol. 15 (1978) #15-648.

640

Freeman, Kenneth A. and Graichen, Charles. False vermilion on two Chinese ceramic objects. *Far East Ceramic Bulletin* (USA), 6 no. 2 (June 1954), pp. 5–8.

English abstract in AATA vol. 1 (1955–1957) #348.

641

Gettens, Rutherford J. True and false vermilion on early Chinese ceramics. *Far East Ceramic Bulletin* (USA), 6 no. 1 (March 1954), pp. 16–27.

English abstract in AATA vol. I (1955–1957) #349.

642

Hayward, J.F. Some spurious antique vase designs of the sixteenth century. *Burlington Magazine* (England), 114 (June 1972) 378–386, illus.

643

Holm, Knud. Et persisk fad—eller flere (A Persian dish—or several). *Nationalmuseets Arbejdsmark* (Denmark), 1969, pp. 131–140.

A forged Persian dish made from 7 different dishes.
English abstract in AATA vol. 8 (1970–1971) #8-253.

644

Howard, Davis S. The milanese connection: a faker of oriental export porcelain unmasked. *Connoisseur* (England), 206 no. 830 (April 1981) 289–291, 8 illus.

French abstract in RAA 1981 #9191.
English abstract in AATA vol. 19 (1982) #19-1696.

645

Mackenna, F. Severne. Reproductions and fakes of Chelsea, Cookworthy, Champion and Worcester. *Apollo* (England), 55 no. 323 (1952) 21–22.

646

Markbreiter, S. China art ceramics: new or antique? *Arts of Asia* (Hong Kong), 10 no. 5 (September–October 1980) 148–154, 30 illus.

On reproductions from the China Art Ceramic Company of Taipei.
English abstract in ABM vol. 14 (1983) #0972.

647

Moraes-Passos, Alfonso de. O camafeu de Dourados (Mato Grosso). *Revista de Historia* (Brazil), 11 (1960) 477–488, 4 illus.

A ceramic Egyptian amulet believed to be a forgery.

648

Muscarella, Oscar White. Hacilar ladies: old and new. *The Metropolitan Museum of Art Bulletin* (USA), October/November 1971, pp. 74-79, 9 illus.

English abstract in AATA vol. 9 (1972) #9-288.

649

Neuwirth, Waltraud. Michael Powolnys 'Springendes Pferd' (Michael Powolny's 'Jumping Horse'). *Weltkunst* (Germany), 50 no. 21 (1 November 1983) 3077–3080, 14 illus.

English abstract in ABM vol. 14 (1983) #7330

650

Neuwirth, Waltraud. Thüringische Porzellanfiguren nach J. Callot, Bettler und Zwerge mit echten und gefälschten Marken (Thuringian porcelain figures after Callot, Bettler and Zwerge with etchings and forged marks). *Weltkunst* (Germany), 49 no. 10 (1979) 1258–1261, 19 illus.

French abstract in RAA 1979 #13738.

651

Neuwirth, Waltraud. Wiener Porzellan echt oder gefälscht (Viennese porcelain true or false). *Kunst* (Germany), 80 no. 3 (1977) 148–152, 10 illus.

652

Neuwirth, Waltraud. Wiener Porzellan, echt oder gefälscht? (Viennese porcelain true or false?). *Alte und moderne Kunst* (Austria), 20 no. 141 (1975) 52–53, 6 illus.

653

Neuwirth, Waltraud. Wiener Porzellan, echt oder gefälscht (Viennese porcelain, true or false?). *Weltkunst* (Germany), 45 no. 9 (1975) 744–777, illus.

654

Oliver, A. Victorian Staffordshire pottery fakes. *Antique Collector* (England), 46 no. 3 (March 1975) 46–49, 8 illus.
English abstract in ABM vol. 6 (1975) #4343.

655

Payne, Joan Crowfoot; Kaczmarczyk, Alex; and Fleming, Stuart J. Forged decoration on predynastic pots. *Journal of Egyptian Archaeology* (England), 63 (1977) 5–12, illus. (Drawings).

Contents: I. Suspected vessels and their decoration (Payne); II. Investigation of pigment (Kaczmarczyk); III. Thermoluminescence dating of the fabrics (Fleming).

656

Pei, W.C. and Eierhoff, J. On a collection of prehistoric pottery at the Catholic mission in Lanchow. *Monum. serica.* 13 (1948) 376–384, 11 illus.
French abstract in RAA 1953 #12766.

657

Piatkiewicz Dereniowa, M. Dwie wazy majolikowe z dekoracą a istoriato w zbiorach wawelskich. *Stud. Dziejów Wawelu* (Poland), 4 (1978) 418–433, 15 illus. Summary in French.

Two majolica vases, purchased in 1938 and thought to be of the 16th century, are in fact 19th century forgeries from Doccia, Italy.
French abstract in RAA 1979 #2165.

658

Plenderleith, H.J. Further notes on the Hui-Hsien problem. *Far East Ceramic Bulletin* (USA), 6 (September 1954) 1–5.
English abstract in AATA vol. 1 (1955–1957) #352.

659

Radford, C.A. Raleigh; Jope, E.M.: and Hurst, J.G. The Crickdale bowl. *Antiquity* (England), 51 no. 201 (March 1977) 51–52.

Publication of a note by Mr. C.A. Raleigh Radford regarding a recently manufactured bowl discovered by excavators in 1954. The bowl was planted by Mr. Ivan Martin "to cheer up and encourage archaeologists on a dig."

660

Ross, M.C. Method for detecting false Limoges painted enamels by use of enlarged photographs. *Journal of the Walters Art Gallery* (USA), 12 (1949) 40–53.

661

Sainsbury, W.J. Rogue's gallery of continental soft paste porcelain. *Apollo* (England), 53 (January 1951) 11–12.

662

Saville, Marshall H. Fraudulent blackware pottery of Colombia. *Indian Notes*, 5 no. 2 (April 1928) 144–154, photos.

663

Schultze-Frentzel, Ulrich. Keramische Antiquitaeten im Roentgenbild (Ceramic antiquities in the x-ray picture). *Arbeitsblaetter fuer Restauratoren* (Germany), Jahrgang 5, no. 1, Gruppe 19 (1972) 13–22.

On the use of x-rays in restoration work and in the detection of falsifications.

English abstract in AATA vol. 9 (1972) #9-456.

664

Schultze-Frentzel, Ulrich. Rontgen-Grobstrukturuntersuchung keramischer Antiquitaten (Investigation of the macro-structure of ceramic antiquities by x-rays). *Ber. Deut. Ker. Gesel.* (Germany), 45 no. 12 (1968) 601–606.

English abstract in AATA vol. 8 (1970–1971) #8-14.

665

Shaplin, P.D. Thermoluminescence and style in the authentication of ceramic sculpture from Oaxaca, Mexico. *Archaeometry* (England), 20 no. 1 (1978), pp. 47–54.

English abstract in AATA vol. 15 (1978) #15-1569.

666

Smeets, R. The wonderful Delft Black. *Klei en Keramiek* (Netherlands), 13 no. 3 (1963) 63–68.

English abstract in AATA vol. 5 (1964–1965) #4848.

667

Sterba, Günter. Porzellanfiguren aus Pfalz-Zweibrücken mit Höchster Radmarke (Porcelain figures from Pfalz-Zweibrücken with the wheel mark of the Höchst factory). *Keramos* (Germany) 53–54 (July–October 1971) 52–56, 3 illus., 2 text figs.

English abstract in RILA 1973 Demonstration Issue, #640.

668

Šujan, V. O falšování lidové keramiky. *Muzejní a vlastivědní Práce* (Czechoslovakia), 8 nos. 1–4 (1970) 40–58, 25 illus., 3 plates.
Ceramic forgeries of the 17th–18th centuries.

669

Unsigned article. Bernard Leach forgeries. *Ceramic Review* (England), 82 (July/August 1983) 34, illus.

670

Unsigned article. Fakes of Hacilar. *Time* (USA), 98 (6 September 1971) 40, illus.

671

Unsigned article. Heat treatment unmasks a sham Zapotec. *The Unesco Courier* (France), 34 (March 1981) 15, 2 photos.

672

Unsigned article. L'expertise scientifique provoque une hécatombe de fausses poteries préhistoriques dans les musées. *Connaissance Arts* (France), no. 235 (September 1971) 11.

673

Unsigned article. Time of the forgers. *Newsweek* (USA), April 23, 1975, p. 69, illus.
General article on the lucrative trade in pre-Columbian artifact forgeries. Covers ceramic sculpture, methods used in their creation, and difficulty in detection.

674

Unsigned article. Tough time for pottery: thermoluminescent dating. *Science Digest* (USA), 64 (September 1968) 38–39, illus.

675

Vergnet-Ruiz, Jean. Le plat de la Passion. *Revue du Louvre et des Musées de France* (France), 14 (1964) 75–84, 5 illus.
French abstract in RAA 1964 #6571.

676

Von Faber Castell, C. Vier falsche Gallé-Vasen (Four forged Gallé vases). *Weltkunst* (Germany), 53 no. 12 (1983) 1644–1646, 7 illus.

677

Wagner, Guenther A.; and Bischof, H. Echtheitstests mittels Thermolumi-
neszenz an altchinesischen Keramikplastiken (Authenticity tests by
thermoluminescence on ancient Chinese ceramic sculptures).
Archaeologie und Naturwissenschaften (Germany) 1 (1977) 20–41, 24
photos, 2 illus., 35 refs.

The results of thermoluminescence testing on pieces from a collection
of ancient Chinese ceramics. Two pieces proved to be made some 50–80
years ago.

English abstract in AATA vol. 16 (1979) #16-1605.

678

Yap, C.T., and Tang, S.M. X-ray fluorescence analysis of Chinese porcelains
from K'ang Hsi to modern times using ^{109}Cd source. *Applied Spectroscopy* (USA), 38 no. 4 (1984) 527–529.

English abstract in AATA vol. 21 (1984) #21-2036.

679

Yap, C.T., and Tang, S.M. X-ray fluorescence analysis of modern and recent
Chinese porcelains. *Archaeometry* (England), 26 no. 1 (February 1984)
78–81, table, illus., appendix.

English abstract in AATA vol. 21 (1984) #21-2035.

Hallmarks

See also Ceramics (Sections of Books) #603, #614, (Periodicals) #650, and Exhibitions #1757.

Books

680

Boucaud, Philippe. *250 poinçons d'étain, faux, copies, imitations, truquages.* Paris (6ᵉ), l'auteur, 51, Rue Bonaparte, 1971, 122 p., illus.

681

Citroen, K.A. *Valse zilvermerken in Nederland.* Amsterdam: Noord-Hollandsche U.M., 1977, 81 p., illus.

682

Citroen, K.A. *Faked silver marks in the Netherlands.* Amsterdam; New York, 1976.

683

Helft, Jacques. *Nouveaux poinçons: suivis de, Recherches techniques et historiques sur l'orfevrerie sous l'Ancien Régime.* Preface by Pierre Dehaye. Paris: Berger-Levrault, 1980, 418 p., illus., includes bibliographical references.

Periodicals

684

Barends, F. Naar aanleiding van een Sèvres merk (On a Sèvres mark). *Antiek* (Netherlands), 12 no. 7 (Feb. 1978) 488–490, 4 illus. Summary in English.

English abstract in RILA vol. 5 (1979) #2413.
French abstract in RAA 1978 #9815.

685

Gans, L.B. Ongeldige kleureen op antiek Engels zilver (Non-valid hallmarks on English antique silver). *Antiek* (Netherlands), 8 no. 7 (1974) 562–567.

English abstract in AATA vol. 13 (1976) #13-555.

686

Jackson, Betty. Collecting antique English silver: pleasures and pitfalls. *National Antiques Review*, 5 no. 3 (September 1973) 10–11.

687

Neuwirth, Waltraud. Sèvres oder Samson oder? (Sèvres or else Samson).
Weltkunst (Germany), 47 no. 22 (1977) 2453, 2 illus.

Imitations of the Sèvres trademark in the 19th century, especially that
of the Samson firm in Paris.
French abstract in RAA 1978 #7198.

688

Pieper Lippe, M. Pauluskopf und Engelmarke. Zur Frage der Kombination
von Zinnmarken (Paul's head and angel's marks. On the question of
their combination in pewter). *Kunst und Antiquitäten (Germany), no. 3
(1980) 49–50, 6 illus.*

French abstract in RAA 1981 #2322.

Antiquities

Books

689

Andren, Arvid. *Arkeologins marodörer* (The marauders of Archaeology). (Studies in Mediterranean Archaeology Pocket-Book 19). Paul Åströms Förlag, 1983, 122 p., 19 illus.

English abstract in AATA vol. 20 (1983), #20-150.

690

Blegen, Theodore C. *The Kensington rune stone: new light on an old riddle.* St. Paul, Minnesota: Minnesota Historical Society Press, 1968, 212 p., illus.

691

Boone, Elizabeth H. (Ed.) *Falsifications and misreconstructions of pre-Columbian art.* (A Conference at Dumbarton Oaks, October 14 and 15, 1978). Washington, D.C.: Trustees for Harvard University, 1982, 142 p., illus.

Contents: the art historian's dilemma: with remarks upon the state of art falsification in the central and north Andean regions, by Robert Sonin; The falsification of ancient Peruvian slip-decorated ceramics, by Alan R. Sawyer; The identification of a Moche fake through iconographic analysis, by Christopher B. Donnan; A counterfeit Moche-Recuay vessel and its origins, by Raphael X. Reichert; On faked Peruvian silver head jars distributed as pre-Columbian, by S. Henry Wassén; Three Aztec masks of the God Xipe, by Esther Pasztory; Problems in the study of narrative scenes on classic Maya vases, by Dicey Taylor: Archaeological buildings: Restoration or misrepresentation, by Agusto Molina-Montes.

692

De Pradenne, A. Vayson. *L'affaire de Glozel: historique de l'affaire.* Paris: Paul Catin, 1928, 76 p., illus.

693

Dupont-Sommer, A. *Un dépisteur de fraudes archéologiques, Charles Clermont-Ganneau 1846–1923, membre de l'académie des Inscriptions et Belles-Lettres.* Paris: Institut de France, 1975, 20 p.

694

Fontander, Björn. *Antikfynd eller bluff? En bok om förfalskningar och kopior av antikviteter? (The antique finds or bluff? A book on the falsifications and copies of antiquities).* Västeras: Icaförl., 1971, 120 p., illus.

695

Jahn, M. E.; and Woolf, D. J. *The lying stones of Dr. Beringer, being his Lithographiae Wirceburgensis.* Berkeley: University of California Press, 1963.

696

Jensen, Carl Christian. *Again the Kensington stone.* La Crosse: Sumac Press, 1969, 1 vol. (unpaged), illus.

697

Muscarella, Oscar White. Unexcavated objects and ancient Near Eastern art: addenda. Malibu, California: Undena Publications, 1979, 19 p., illus. (Monographic journals of the Near East. Occasional papers on the Near East; vol. 1, issue 1 (October 1979). Addenda to the author's article published in: *Mountains and lowlands,* edited by Louis D. Levine and T. Cuyler Young, Jr. 1977. (See # 707).

698

Paul, Eberhard. *Die Falsche Göttin. Geschichte der Antikenfälschung* (The false Goddess. History of antique forgeries). Heidelberg: L. Schneider; Leipzig: Koehler, 1962, 208 p., illus., index.

699

Paul, Eberhard. *Gefälschte Antike: von der Renaissance bis zur Gegenwart* (Antique forgery: from the Renaissance to today). Leipzig: Koehlen und Amelang, 1981, 283 p., illus., bibliographical refs.

700

Paul, Eberhard. *Studien zur Problematik der Antikerfälschungen* (Studies concerning the problem of antique forgery). Leipzig, 1963, 253 p., index (Phil. Diss., Leipzig, 1963).

701

Reith, Adolf. *Archaeological fakes.* Translated from the German by Diana Imber. London: Barrie & Jenkins; New York: Praeger Publishers, 1970, 183 p., illus., facsims., bibliog (pp. 181-183).

702

Reith, Adolf. *Vorzeit gefälscht* (Antiquity falsified). Tubingen, Germany: Ernst Wasmuth, 1967, 156 p., illus.

English abstract in AATA vol. 7 (1968–1969) #7-1119.

703

Sklenář, Karel. *SLepé uličky archeologie.* Prague: Prague: Čs. spis., 1977, 279 p., illus., bibliography (pp. 272–276).

Sections of Books

704

Burke, J. and Megaw, J.V.S. "British decorated axes: a footnote on fakes," in *The Proceedings of the Prehistoric Society, Great Britain,* 32 (1966) 343–346, illus.

705

Fraser, Peter Marshall. "Some Alexandrian forgeries," in *Proceedings of the British Academy London* (England) 47 (1962) 243—250, 7 illus.

706

Hume, Ivor Noël. "Of mermaids, fakes and other grave matters", in his *All the best rubbish*. New York: Harper & Row, 1974, pp. 97–106; 261–289, passim, illus.

707

Muscarella, Ocsar White. "Unexcavated objects and ancient Near Eastern art," in *Mountains and Lowlands: essays in the archaeology of Greater Mesopotamia*, edited by Louis D. Levine, and T. Cuyler Young. Malibu, CA: Undena, 1977.

See also #697.

708

Muscarella, Oscar White. "Unexcavated objects and ancient Near Eastern art," in *Bibliotheca Mesomopotamica*, vol. 7 (1977) 153–207, 9 illus. Malibu, CA: Undena, 1977.

See also #697

709

Strommenger, E. Rollsiegelfälschungen. *Berliner Jahrbuch für Vor- und Frühgeschichte*, 1 (1961) 196–200, 4 illus.

Periodicals

710

Aitken, Martin, and Huxtable, Joan. Thermoluminescence and Glozel; a plea for caution. *Antiquity* (England) 49 no. 195 (September 1975) 223–226.

711

Bahn, Paul G. How to spot a fake azilian pebble. *Nature* (England), 308 no. 5956 (15 March 1984) 229, b/w photo., 14 refs.

English abstract in AATA vol. 22 (1985) #22-1220.

712

Blacking, John. Edward Simpson, alias Flint Jack: a Victorian craftsman. *Antiquity* (England) 27 no. 108 (December 1953) 207–211, illus.

713

Bogucki, Peter I. The Mnikow bone artifacts: a nineteenth-century archaeological forgery. *Polish Review* (USA) 24 no. 4, (1979) 92–102.

714

Borsos, B. Hamisított régiségek. I. (Forged antiquities. I.) *Művészettörténeti Értesito* (Budapest), 21 no. 3 (1972) 200–205, 6 illus. Summary in German.

715

Breuil, Abbé. Stories about fakes. *Antiquity* (USA) 29 no. 116 (December 1955) 196–198.

716

Cooney, John D. Assorted errors in art collecting. *Expedition* (USA) 6 no. 1 (Fall 1963) 20–27, 8 illus.

Examples of forgeries of antiquities with special emphasis on Egyptian antiquities.

717

Cooney, John D. A reexamination of some Egyptian Antiquities. *Bulletin of the Brooklyn Museum* (USA), 11 no. 3 (1950) 11-26, 10 illus.

718

Crawley, G. The archaeopteryx caper and the intelligent universe. *British Journal of Photography* (England), 132 (20 December 1985) 1430—1435, illus.; 132 (27 December 1985) 1460–1461 +, illus.

719

Editorial. An archaeological fake in the Netherlands. *Antiquity* (England) 50 (March 1976) 2–3.

Concerning several fake early and late paleolithic artifacts being sold to museums in the Netherlands.

720

Editorial. [The Glozel controversy]. *Antiquity* (England) 51 no. 202, (July 1977) 89–91.

721

Editorial. [The Kensington Runestone]. *Antiquity* (England), 48 no. 190 (June 1974) 82–83.

722

Editorial. [The plundering of archaeological sites, illegal export and import of antiquities, and fake antiquities being sold to museums in Europe and America]. *Antiquity* (England) 45 (December 1971) 246–247.

723

Editorial. [The Glozel controversy]. *Antiquity* (England) 50 no. 197 (March 1976) 2.

724

Ekholm, Gordon. The problem of fakes in pre-Columbian art. *Curator,* 7 (1964) 19–32.

This article is especially valuable for references to previous published studies on pre-Columbian fakes.

725

Farrar, R.A.H. The Sherborne controversy. *Antiquity* (England), 53 no. 209 (November 1979) 211–216; Discussion, 60 no. 213 (March 1981), 44–46, illus, (R.A.H. Farrar); 60 no. 215 (November 1981) 219–220, (Ann de G. Sieveking).

726

Fulford, Michael and Sellwood, Bruce. The Silchester Ogham Stone: a reconsideration. *Antiquity* (England) 54 (July 1980) 95–99, illus., bibliography.

Contents of the article: Introduction; circumstances of the find; Description of the stone; The Ogham; Petrographic analysis, (A) Thin section, (B) X-ray diffraction of the whole rock and clay fraction, Whole rock, Clay fraction, Origin of the sandstone; Discussion.

727

Fúster, Luis Fernández. Una estela hispanorromana falsificada en el Museo de Granada. *Archivo Español Arqueologia* (Spain), 23 no. 78 (January–March 1950) 102–105, illus.

728

Garrod, Dorothy. Recollections of Glozel. *Antiquity* (England), 42 (September 1968) 172–178.

729

Gerasimov, Todor. Falšivi pečati na bălgarski care ot 10, 13 i 14 v. *Arkheologija* (Bulgaria), 12 no. 2 (1970) 32–43, 8 illus. Summary in French.

Fake seals of the Bulgarian Kings of the 10th, 13th and 14th centuries.

730

Golvin, J.C. Le site antique, découverte et renaissance. *Dossiers (Les) de l'Archéologie* (France), no. 25 (1977) 121–129.

731

Hall E. T. The Glozel affair. *Nature* (England), 257 no. 5525 (2 October 1975) 355–356.

English abstract in AATA vol. 13 (1976) #13–421.

732

Jahn, Melvin E. Dr. Beringer and the Würzburg "Lugensteine." *Journal for the Bibliography of Natural History*, 4 (1963) 138–146.

733

La Dassor, Gray. Genuine versus fraudulent flint. *Central States Archaeological Journal* (USA), 6 no. 1 (1959) 12; *Abstracts of New World Archaeology*, 1 (1959) 13.

English abstract in AATA vol. 3 (1960–1961) #3347.

734

Leichty, Erle. A remarkable forger, *Expedition* (USA) 12 no. 3 (Spring 1970) 17–21, illus., port.

On forged cuneiform tablets at the University Museum, University of Pennsylvania.

735

Lizardi, Ramos Cesar. Las falsificaciones de inundan a Mexico. *Katunob* (USA), 7 no. 2 (1970) 19–22.

On the abundance of forgeries from Mexico.

736

Mallat, Jon M. Dr. Berlinger's fossils: a study in the evolution of scientific world view. *Annals of Science* (England) 39 (July 1982), 371–380, illus.

737

Mayer, A.W. Joh. Archeologie en chemie (Archaeology and chemistry). *Chemisch Weekblad* (Netherlands), 59 (1963) 549—559.

English abstract in AATA vol. 5 (1964–1965) #4476.

The cases of Glozel, Lascaux and Rouffignac are discussed, and the scientific methods used to differentiate authentic from inauthentic archaeological discoveries.

738

McKerrell, H.V.; Mejdahl, V.; François, H.; and Portal, G. Thermoluminescence and Glozel: a plea for patience. *Antiquity* (England), 49 no. 196 (December 1975) 267–272, illus., diags.

739

McKerrell, H.V.; Mejdahl, V.; François, H.; and Portal, G. Thermoluminescence and Glozel. *Antiquity* (England), 48 (December 1974) 265–272, illus; Reply. 49 (March 1975) 2–3, illus., tabs., diags.

740

McKusick, Marshall. The North American periphery of antique Vermont. *Antiquity* (England), 53 (July 1979) 121–123.

A biting commentary on speculative fictional books on American prehistory, and on the need to critically evaluate such works by competent archaeologists. Numerous books and theories are cited as well as archaeological frauds.

741

McKusick, Marshall. Psychic archaeology from Atlantis to Oz. *Archaeology* (USA), 37 (September/October 1984) 48–52; illus, map; 38 (January/February 1985) 75.

742

Miles, Charles. Indian relics: aspects of fake artifacts. *Hobbies* (USA), 75 (August 1970) 114–115, illus.

On the abundance of fake Indian relics and the difficulty in discerning genuine from fake, such as a notched hoe made of obsidian found in California. Judging authenticity from where the artifact was found can lead to mistakes in distinguishing the authentic from the inauthentic.

743

Naveh, Joseph. An ancient amulet or a modern forgery? *Catholic Biblical Quarterly* (USA), 44 no.2 (April 1982) 282–284.

744

Nougayrol, J. Du bon usage des faux. (Good usage of forgeries). *Syria* (France), 42 nos. 3–4 (1965) 3–4, 1 photo.

A forged neo-Assyrian brick with the inscription of the seal of Urzana, King of Musasir.

745

Peacock, D.P.S. Forged brick-stamps from Pevensey (Sussex). *Antiquity (England)*, 47 (June 1973) 138–140, illus.

746

Porda, Edith. Forged north Syrian seals. *Archaeology* (USA), 10 no. 2 (June 1957) 143.

747

Renfrew, Colin. Glozel and the two cultures. *Antiquity* (England), 49 no. 195 (September 1975) 219–222.

748

Rowe, John H.; and Guadagno, Jimmy. Forged Tiahuanaco-style keros. *American Antiquity* (USA), 20 (1955) 392–393, 1 illus.

English abstract in AATA vol. 1 (1955-1957) #970.

749

Sakař, V. Některé sporné nálezy se Severozápádních Čech, datované do doby římské. *Archeologické Rozhledy* (Czechoslovakia), 14 (1962) 108–110. Summary in German.

A study of several forged objects from the Roman period.

750

Schaffer, Simon. Forging the past: a spectre which haunts many historians, whether of art or of science, is the forgery. *History Today* (England), 35 (July 1985) 3–4, illus.

On forgeries in paleontology, especially the controversy surrounding the fossil bird archaeopteryx.

751

Schoske, S. Die wundersame Vermehrung aegyptischer Antiken (The miraculous increase of Egyptian antiquities). *Die Waage* (Germany), 23 no. 3 (1984) 97–103, 10 photos.

English abstract in AATA vol. 22 (1985) #22-266.

752

Sieveking, Ann G. A new look at the Sherborne bone. *Nature* (England) 283 (February 1980) 719–720.

753

Snow, Dean R. Martians & Vikings, Madoc & Runes: a seasoned campaigner's look at the never-ending war between archaeological fact and archaeological fraud. *American Heritage* (USA), 32 no. 6 (October/November 1981) 102–108.

754

Strommenger, E. Die gefälschte Kunstgeschichte Ein Hausputz in der Vorderasiatischen Altertumskunde? *Acta Praehistorica et Archaeologica* (Germany), no. 7–8 (1976–1977) 319–322.

755

Warren, S.E. A second "affaire Glozel?" *Antiquity* (England) 49 no. 195 (September 1975) 222–223.

756

Wilson, John A. Crackpots and forgeries in art and science. *Science Digest* (USA) 66 no. 5 (November 1969) 40–44.

General interest article on the forging of antiquities.

757

Yule, Paul. Zwei minoisch-griechische bilinguische siegel. *Archäologischer Anzieger* (Germany) no. 2 (1977) 141–149, illus.

Media

758

Editoral [Comments on the BBC program "Science Now" on the Glozel controversy]. *Antiquity* (England), 51 no. 201 (March 1977) 7.

Inscriptions

See also Antiquities (Periodicals) #726 and Bronzes (Periodicals) #987.

Books

759

Gordon Arthur Ernest. *The inscribed fibula Praenestina: problems of authenticity.* Berkeley: University of California Press, 1975, xi, 84 p., bibliography, pp. viii–xi, index. (University of California Publications: Classical Studies; vol. 16).

760

Guarducci, Margherita. *La cosiddetta fibula prenestina.* Rome: Memorie della Accademia Nazionale dei Lincei, vol. xxiv, 159 p.

Guarducci concludes that the fibula Praenestina was manufactured after 1876 and inscribed between 1880-1887. For a review of Guarducci's book see David Ridgeway's "The forgers and the fibula", *Times Literary Supplement* (England), 19 June 81, p. 691.

761

Panciera, Silvio. *Un falsario del primo Ottocento. Girolamo Asquini e l'epigrafia antica delle Venezie.* Rome: Edizioni di storia e letteratura, 1970, 209 p., plates, port. (Note e discussioni erudite, 13)

Sections of Books

762

Corbett, P.; and Woodhead, G. "A forger of graffiti." *The Annual of the British School at Athens* (England), no. 50 (1955) 251–265, plates 50–53.

763

Ferrua, Antonio. "Di un 'iscrizione pseudocristiana e pseudoantica," in *Festschrift Engelbert Kirschbaum,* edited by A.M. Amman, et al., 1963, pp. 104–108.

Periodicals

764

Frankis, P.J.; and Bailey, Richard N. A runic forgery from Cullercoats. *Archaeologia Aeliana* (England), 47 (1969) 43–46, plate.

765

Hamp, E.P. Is the fibula a fake? *American Journal of Philology* (USA), 102 (Summer 1981) 151-153

766

Levenson, J.D. Spindle whorl inscription from Chatal Hüyük: a forgery. *American Schools of Oriental Research Bulletin* (USA), no. 209 (February 1973) 37–40.

767

Naveh, Joseph. Some recently forged inscriptions. *American Schools of Oriental Research Bulletin* (USA), no. 247 (Summer 1982) 53–58, illus.

On "eight Carian leather manuscripts found in 1966 in the Hebron area."

768

Unsigned Article. Clumsy forger fools the scholars—but only for a time: fake inscriptions debated in scholarly journals. *Biblical Archaeology Review* (USA) 10 no. 3 (May/June 1984) 66–72. illus.

The "Philistine" mss from Hebron.

Coins

Books

769

Akerman, John Yonge. *Fourres and forgeries: general observations on the coins and coinage of the Romans.* New York: Numismatic Communications, 1970, XIXp., illus.

770

Dieffenbacher, Alfred. *Counterfeit gold coins nineteenth and twentieth centuries. Fully illustrated.* Montreal: Dieffenbacher Coin LTD., c1963, unpaged, illus.

771

Gamberini di Scarfèa, Cesare. *Le imitazioni e le contraffazioni monetarie nel mondo. III: Le principali imitazioni e contraffazioni italiane e straniere di monete di zecche italiane medioevali e moderne.* Bologna: La Grafica moderna, 1956, 347 p.

772

Gamberini di Scarfèa, Cesare. *Le imitazioni e le contraffazioni monetarie nel mondo. IV: Le principali imitazioni e contraffazioni italiane e straniere di monete di zecche estere medioevali e moderne. I: Svizzera Francia, Paesi Bassi, Ungheria, Polonia.* Bologna: La Grafica emiliana, 1959, 243 p., illus.

773

Hill, Philip. *Barbarous radiates: imitations of third-century Roman coins.* New York: American Numismatic Society, 1949, 44 p., 4 plates, map, Numismatic Notes and Monographs no. 112.

774

International Association of Professional Numismatists. *First International Congress for the Study of and the Defense Against Coin Forgery.* Paris: Publications of I.A.P.N. no. 2, analytical report, c1967. In French and English.

775

Scott Kenneth. *Counterfeiting in Colonial Connecticut.* New York: American Numismatic Society, 1957, 243 p., 46 plates, Numismatic Notes and Monograph no. 140.

776

Short, Hugh de S. *Detection of coin forgeries in northwest India.* London: L.S. Forrer, 1950, 11 p.

On the difficulty of detecting forged Indo-Greek coins.
English Abstract in G&U #203.

777

Taxay, Don. *Counterfeit, mis-struck, and unofficial U.S. coins: a guide for the detection of cast and struck counterfeits, electrotypes, and altered coins.* Introduction by John J. Ford, Jr. New York: Arco, 1963, 221 p., illus., index.

English abstract in AATA vol. 5 (1964–1965) #4728.

778

Voigtlaender, H. *Falschmünzer und Münzfalscher: Geschichte der Geldfälschung aus 2½ Jahrtausenden.* (Forged coins and counterfeiters: a history of counterfeit money from 2½ thousand years.) Munster: Numism. Verlag Dombrowski, 1976, 168 p., index.

779

Windler, F.J., Jr. *A description of late Roman Imperial coins (350–478 A.D) . . . and the Becker forgeries of this period.* Nashville, TN: F.J. Windler, 1960, 57 p., [Mimeograph].

Sections of Books

780

Balog, Paul."Fausses monnaies islamiques," in *Congrès Intern. Numism.* Paris, 2 (1953) 469–471, 3 illus.

781

Bendall, Simon. "The forgery of ancient coins," in *The Year Book of the British Association of Numismatic Societies,* no. 16, (1971) 10–14.

782

Bernareggi, E. "I falsi nella serie monetale dei Longobardi in Italia," in *Mélanges de numismatique, d'archéologie et d'histoire offerts à Jean Lafaurie,* edited by P. Bastien, et al. Paris: Société Française de Numismatique, 1980, 175–179, 8 illus., 1 plate.

French abstract in RAA 1984 #11154.

783

Challis, C.E. *The Tudor coinage.* Manchester: Manchester University Press, 1978, xii + 348 p., 53 illus., index.

English abstract in RILA vol. 5 (1979) #5319.

784

Doty, Richard G. "Forgery," in his *The Macmillan encyclopedic dictionary of numismatics.* New York; Macmillan Publishing Co., 1982, p. 141–143.

Related articles in Doty's dictionary are: 1. Authentication; 2. Cast counterfeit; 3. Counterfeit; 4. Counterfeit and forgery detection; 5. Die-struck counterfeit.

785

Gilles, K.J. "Funde und Ausgrabungen im Bezirk Trier. Aus der Arbeit des Rheinischen Landesmuseums Trier: Eine karolingisch ottonische Münzfälscherwerstatt in Trier? Nachträge bzw. Ergänzungen zum Katalog der merowingischen und karolingischen Fundmünzen," in *Kurtrierisches Jahrbuch*, (Germany), 23 (1983), 35–42, 4 illus.

786

Gordus, Adon A., and Gordus, Jeanne P. "Neutron activation analysis of gold impurity levels in silver coins and art objects," in *Archaeological Chemistry* (Advances in chemistry), American Chemical Society, Washington, D.C., 138, pp. 124–147, 1974.

English abstract in AATA vol. 12 (1975) #12-520.

787

Grierson, Philip. "Imitations, ornements monetaires et faux," in his *Bibliographie Numismatic*, 2nd ed. Bruxelles: 4, Bd. l'empereur, 1979, pp. 27–28.

788

Hope, Donald J. "Counterfeits, fakes and forgeries," in his *How to invest in gold coins*. New Rochelle, NY: Arlington House, pp. 242–251, illus., index.

789

Hoyt, Edwin P. "Counterfeit" and " . . . and more counterfeit," in his *Coins, collectors, and counterfeiters*. New York: Thomas Nelson, Inc., 1977, pp. 105–110; 111–123, index.

790

Ilisch, P. "Zur ältesten Fundmünze aus St. Ida zu Herzfeld," in *Heilige Ida von Herzfeld. Festschrift zur tausendjährigen Wiederkehr ihrer Heiligsprechung*. Münster: Aschendorff, 1980, pp. 153–154, 2 illus.

791

Klüssendorf, N. "Falsche Münzen als Beilagen von Archivalien. Numismatische und archivische Probleme," in *Hessisches Jahrbuch für Landesgeschichte* (Germany), 27 (1977) 161–179, 12 illus.

792

Klüssendorf, N. "Falsche Münzen und Scheine aus dem Geldumlauf der kurhessischen Provinz Hanau 1841–67," in *Beiträge zur süddeutschen Münzgeschichte. Festschrift zum 75 jährigen Bestehen des Württembergischen Vereins für Münzkunde*. Stuttgart: Württembergischen Vereins für Münzkunde, 1976, 296–336, 12 illus.

793

Kraft, Konrad. "Zu einigen Fälschungen griechischer Gold-und Silbermünzen," in *Jahrbuch für Numismatik und Geldgeschichte* (Germany), 8 (1957) 51–56, 28 illus.

794

Lafaurie, J. "L'article XI de l'Edit de Pitres du 25 juin 864," in LAGOM. Festschrift für Peter Berghaus. Münster: Numismatischer Verlag der Münzhandlung Dombrowski, 1981, 113–117, 1 illus.

795

Mayer, L.A. A bibliography of Jewish numismatics. Jerusalem: The Magnes Press, The Hebrew University, 1966.

This specialized bibliography contains 15 references, in numerous languages, to fictitious coins, forgeries and counterfeits dating from 1699 to 1959.

796

Mommsen, H.; Bauer, K.G.; and Fazly, Q. "PIXIE analysis of Klippen and coins from Bonn and Jülich." in *International symposium on archaeometry and archaeological prospection, 18.* Proceedings (14–17 March 1978), Bonn. Köln, Rheinland—Bonn: Habelt, 1979, (Archaeo-Physika 10), 348–359, 5 illus.

French abstract in RAA 1981 #5533.

797

Nercessian, Y.T. *Armenian numismatic bibliography and literature.* Los Angeles: Armenian Numismatic Society (Special Publication no. 3), 1984, 729 p.

An outstanding scholarly work, this bibliography contains 12 references to articles on forgeries. In Armenian and English, with lengthy annotations.

798

Oddy, W.A.; and Archibald, M.M. "The technique of some forged medieval silver pennies," in *Scientific Studies in Numismatics* (British Museum Occasional Paper No. 18), British Museum, London, 1980, pp. 81–90.

English abstract in AATA vol. 17 (1980) #17-771.

799

Potin, V. "Ein Münzfund des 11. Jahrhunderts aus dem Leningrader Gebiet," in *LAGOM. Festschrift für Peter Berghaus.* Münster: Numismatischer Verlag der Münzhandlung Dombrowski, 1981, 131–140, illus.

French abstract in RAA 1984 #1328.

800

Probszt, Günther. "Die Linzer Jahrmärkte im Spiegel der Reichs-Munzgesetzgebung," in *Hist. Jahrbuch Stadt Linz* (Austria), 1965, pp. 43–83, 2 plates.

801

Van der Wiel, A. "Valse nederlandse dukaten," in *Jaarboekje kon neder. Genoots. Munt Penningkunde* (Netherlands), 39 (1952) 41–59, 9 illus.

Forged Dutch ducats.

802

Van der Wiel, A. "Valse nederlandse dukaten, II," in *Jaarboekje kon nederl.* *Genoots. Munt Penningkunde* (Netherlands), 43 (1956), 58–67, 17 illus., 1 plate. Summary in English.

Forged Dutch ducats from the 18th and 19th centuries.

803

Weiller, Raymond. *Les monnaies luxembourgeoises.* The coins of Luxembourg Louvain-la-Neuve: Institut supérieur d'archéologie et d'histoire de l'art, Séminaire de numismatique Marcel Hoc, 1977, 311 p., illus., index. (Publications d'histoire de l'art et d'archéologie de l'Université catholique de Louvain, 9; Numismatica Lovaniensie, 2).

The coins of Luxembourg from the middle ages to the present. English abstract in RILA vol. 5 (1979) #4695.

804

Zedelius, V. "Analysis of Klippen from Bonn," in *International Symposium on Archaeometry and Archaeological Prospection, 18.* Proceedings (14–17 March 1978) Bonn. Köln, Reinland-Bonn: Habelt, 1979 (Archaeo-Physika 10), 342–347, 1 illus.

French abstract in RAA 1981 #5536.

805

Zedelius, V. "Die Goldmünze von Niederkassel-Rheidt," in *Bonner Jarhbücher* (Germany), 183 (1983) 587–590, 2 illus.

806

Zedelius, V. "Jülicher Klippen von 1610. Ein Beitrag zur Geschichte und Problematik von Original und Fälschung," in *Bonner Jahrbücher* (Germany), 184 (1984) 561–572, 6 illus.

French abstract in RAA 1985 #7700.

Periodicals

807

Alvey, R.C. A Roman coin forgery from Nottinghamshire. *Thoroton Society Transactions* (England), 86 (1982) 111, illus.

808

Archibald, M.M. The Queenhithe hoard of late fifteenth-century . . . forgeries. *British Numismatic Journal* (England), 50 no. 3, (1980) 61–66, 8 illus.

809

Arnold, Paul. Die braunschweigschen Fälschungen sächsischer Groschen im 15. Jahrhundert. (Braunschweig forgeries of Saxon groschen in the 15th century) *Beiträge und Berichte der Staatlichen Kunstsammlungen Dresden* (Germany), (1976–1977), 183–192, 17 illus.

810

Aubert, Fritz. Fausses monnaies fabriquées à Genève. *Schweizerische Münz-blätter* (Switzerland) no. 84 (1971) 90–100, 14 illus.

811

Babelon, Jean. La fausse monnaie pendant la guerre de Cent Ans. *Bulletin de la Société française de Numismatique* (France), 1951, p. 66.

812

Balan, Ernst-Henri. Kleiner Beitrag zu den Kippermünzen von Mansfeld und Braunschweig-Lüneburg. *Berliner numismatische Zeitschrift* (Germany), no. 30 (1969) pp. 126–130, 6 illus.

French abstract in RAA 1970 #8919.

813

Becker, C.J. Nogle danske imitationer med elementer fra Knud den Stores engelske type Short Cross. *Nordisk numismatisk Årsskrift* (Sweden), 1979–1980, pp. 81–92, 8 illus. Summary in English.

814

Behrens, Gustav. Römische Falschmünzerformen. *Berliner Numismatische Zeitschrift* (Germany), 1949, pp. 42–50, 4 illus.

French abstract in RAA 1952 #5785.

815

Bharadwaj, H.C. and Misra, S. On the authenticity of an alleged gold punch-marked coin. *Journal of the Numismatic Society of India* (India), 34 part 1 (1972) 101–105.

English abstract in AATA vol. 17 (1980) #17-1526.

816

Blunt, C.E. and Thompson, J.D.A. Forgery in the Anglo-Saxon series. *British Numismatic Journal* (England), 28 no. 1 (1956) 18–25, 15 illus.

817

Bonci, Attilio. Sui falsi d'epoca di Casa Savoia. *Bollettino numismatico* (Italy), 9 no. 1 (1972) 4–19, 11 illus.

818

Boon, George C. An early Tudor coiner's mould and the working of Borrowdale graphite. *Transactions of the Cumberland and Westmorland Antiquarian and Archaeological Society.* (England), no. 76 (1976) 97–132, 6 illus.

819

Boone, George C. Counterfeiting in Roman Britain. *Scientific American* (USA), 231 no. 6 (December 1974) 121–130, illus.

820

Boon, George C., and Rahtz, P.A. Third-century counterfeiting at Whitchurch, Somerset. *Archaeological Journal* (England), 122 (1965) 13–51, illus.

821

Bovi, Giovanni. Un processo per falsificazione di monete nella Zecca di Napoli. *Archivio storici per le Provincie napoletane* (Italy), 38 (1958) 206–214, 7 illus.

822

Brunetti, L. Di un' azione di difesa contro i falsificatori. *Italia Numism.* (Italy), 1952, pp. 4–5, 36–37, 2 plates.

823

Buttrey, T.V. The Tubac Ingot. *The Numismatic Chronicle* (England), 21 (1981) 136–142, 3 illus., 1 plate.

824

Calico, F. Xavier. Sobre una falsificacion de las monedas de 8 reales o duros con el nombre de los Reyes catolicos, Fernando e Isabel. *B. ibero-amer. Numism.* (USA), 1 no. 9 (1950) 1–3, 1 illus.

825

Carson, R.A.G. The Geneva forgeries. *The Numismatic Chronicle* (England), 1958, pp. 47–58, 24 illus.

French abstract in RAA 1958 #1802.

826

Castelin, Karel. O chebských falešných mincích. *Numismatické Listy* (Czechoslovakia), 9 (1954), 142–149, 20 illus.

827

Cesano, S.L. Di Uranio Antonio e di altre falsificazioni de monete Romane piu' o meno note. About Uranio Antonino and about other forgeries of more or less known Roman coins). *Revista italiana di numismatica,* (Italy), 1955, pp. 35–69, illus.

828

Collis, J. Coin of Ptolemy V from Winchester. *Antiquity* (England), 49 (March 1975) 47–48.

829

Cope, L.H. A metallurgical examination of the four false dirhams from the Iranian hoard. *Numismatic Chronicle* (England), 15, 7th series (1975) 165–168.

English abstract in AATA vol. 13 (1976) #13-547.

830

Cope, L.H. A silvered bronze false antoninianus ascribed to the Roman Emperor Gordian III A.D. 238–244. *Metallurgia* (England), 75 no. 447 (1967) 15–20.

English abstract in AATA vol. 6 (1966–1967) #(6)-H1-182.

831

Cremaschi, L. Compte rendu analytique du Ier Congrès international d'étude et de dèfense contre les falsifications monétaires. *Rivista italiana di Numismatica* (Italy), 16 (1968) 276–287.

832

Dimitrijevic, S. Savremene kovane i presovane imitacije srednjovekovnog srpskog srebrnog noveca. *Starinar* (Yugoslavia), 26 (1975) 111–122, illus. Summary in French.

833

d'Incerti, Vico. La fotografia al servizio della numismatica. *Italia Numism.* (Italy), 7 (1956) 69–72, 79–81, 15 illus.

834

Dolley, R.H.M. An eighteenth-century forgery of an Anglo-Irish groat or half groat of Edward IV. *British Numismatic Journal* (England), 35 (1966) 148–151, 1 illus.

835

Dolley, R.H.M. Modern forgeries of the post-Brunanburgh Viking coins of York and Derby. *Numismatic Chronicle* (England), 1958, pp. 131–134, 5 illus.

836

Duplessy, Jean. Contrefaçon inédite du 3 patards des Pays-Bas frappée à Lixheim. *Bulletin de la Société française de Numismatique,* (France), 20 (1965) 514.

837

Duplessy, Jean. Douzain hybride inédit au nom de Charles X, roi de la Ligue. *Bulletin de la Société française de Numismatique,* (France), 21 (1966) 97.

838

Ebeling, H.J.M. Muntvervalsing in de XVIIIe eeuw. *Geuzenpenning* (Netherlands), 2 (1952) 58–59, 2 illus.

839

Evers, J.H. Valse gouden nederlandse munten. *Geuzenpenning* (Netherlands), 18 (1968) 27–29, 10 illus.

840

Evers, J.H. Valse munten. *Geuzenpenning* (Netherlands) 13 (1963) 13–18, 5 illus.

841

Galster, Georg. To falske shekler. *Nordisk Numismatisk Unions Medlemsblad* (Sweden), 1955, pp. 89–91, 3 illus.

842

Gedai, I. Árpádkori pénzek hamisitása. *Érem* (Hungary), 28 no. 1, (1972) 16–17, 5 illus.

843

Geiger, Hans-Ulrich. Numismatische Miszellen, RICETORIX—Neuschöpfung eines keltischen Goldstaters. (RICETORIX—A modern creation of a Celtic Gold stater. *Schweizerische Münzblätter* (Switzerland), no. 70 (1968) 48–50.
English abstract in AATA vol. 7 (1968–1969) #7-1790.

844

Gerasimov, T. Fausses monnaies antiques de l'empereur byzantin Jean Zimiscès. *B. Inst. archéol. bulgare* (Bulgaria), 17 (1950), 313–315, 6 illus.

845

Göbl, Robert. Der gute Klang ein Echtheitskriterium? *Mitteilungen der Österreichischen Numismatischen Gesellschaft* (Austria), 10 (1957–1958) 82–83, 4 illus.

846

Göbl, Robert. Zu einigen Fälschungen vorislamischer orientalisher Münzen. *Mitteilungen der Österreichischen numismatischen Gesellschaft* (Austria), 11 (1959–1960), 1–4, 6 illus.

847

Hejna, Antonín, and Radoměrský, Pavel. Penězokazecká dílna v jeskyni Mincovna na Zlatém Koni u Koněprus. *Památky archeologické* (Czechoslovakia), 49 (1958) 513–558, 53 illus. Summary in German.

848

Hepper, F.N. A late eighteenth-century forger's pegged die. *British Numismatic Journal* (England), 28 no. 2 (1957) 422–423, 1 illus.

849

Hofrat, Becker, der Münzfalscher. (Hofrat Becker, the coin forger) *Aureus* (Germany), no. 3 (1960), 4–10, 9 illus.

850

Högberg, Th. Sakuppgifter rörande myntförfalskaren C.N. Svensson. *Nordisk numismatisk Unions Medlemsblad.* (Sweden), 1959, pp. 3–6, 3 illus.

851

Högye, István. 18. sz. hamis pénzek leírása. *Numizmatikai Közlemények* (Hungary), 68–69 (1969–1970) 76–77. Summary in German.

852

Holzmair, E. Eine Purkersdorfer Münzschmuggelaffäre vom Jahre 1773. *Numismatische Zeitschrift* (Austria), 90 (1975) 45–50, 1 plate.

853

Huarte, José María de. Sobre falsificaciones de moneda española en el siglo xix. *Numisma* (Spain), no. 84–89 (1967) 143–157, 1 illus.

854

Hubbard, Clyde. Algunos apuntes sobre falsificación de monedas. *B. Soc. numism.* (Mexico), no. 51 (1966) 109–114, 1 illus. Summary in English.

855

Huszár, Lajos. Magyar várak, mint pénzhamisító műhelyek a 16 sz. *Műemlékvédelem* (Hungary), 13 (1969) 80–87, 9 illus. Summary in French.

856

Jaeckel, Peter. Eine Falschmünzerform des 19. Jahrhunderts. *Schweizerische Münzblätter* (Switzerland), no. 63 (1966) 124–126, 3 illus.

857

Jenkins, G.K. Numismatic forgeries of Pyrrhus. *British Museum Quarterly* (England), 25 (1962) 26–28, 5 illus.

858

Jurukova, Jordanka. Barbarski podgražanija na bizantijski bronzovi moneti ot viv. *Arkheologija* (Bulgaria), 7 no. 1 (1965) 21–23, 4 illus.

859

Kallfass, Monika; Jehn, Hermann; and Heid, Ulrich. Examination of an "Antique copper coin." *Praktische Metallographie* (Germany), 19 no. 5 (1982) 256–265. Summaries in English and German.

English abstract in AATA vol. 20 (1983) #20-999.

860

Káplár, L. and Kahler, F. Adatok a magyarországi pénzhamisitas kérdéseihez; a pénzhamisítás technikájának alakulása az újkorban. *Debreceni Déri Múzeum Évkönyve* (Hungary), 1976, pp. 137–149, 10 illus. Summary in German.

861

Kaplar, L. and Kahler, F. Adatok a 16. századi pénzhamisítás kérdéséhez. *Érem* (Hungary), 29 no. 1 (1973) 17–21, 2 illus.

862

Kiersnowski, Ryszard. Barkwald-jeszcze jedna mennica falszerska z XV w. (Barkwald—one more 15th century forgers' mint) *Wiadomosci Numizmatyczne* (Poland), 19 no. 1 (1975) 1–13. Summary in English.

English abstract in AATA vol. 14 (1977) #14-547.

863

Kiersnowski, Ryszard. Sympozjum numizmatyczne w Warszawie i w Budapest. *Wiadomości numizmatyczne* (Poland), 20 no. 3 (1976) 188–192.

864

Király, Ferene. Baracsai Ákos pénzének szánt koholt dénár. *Numismatikai Közlemények* (Hungary), 54–55 (1955–1956) 55–57, 2 illus.

865

Koch, Bernhard. Falschmünzer auf der Pottenburg bei Hainburg. *Mitteilungen der Österreichischen numismatischen Gesellschaft.* (Austria), 15 (1967)   11–13, 9 illus.

866

Korski, Witold. Falsyfikat grosza krakowskiego Kazimierza Wielkiego. *Wiadmości numizmatyczne* (Poland), 6 (1962) 273–276, 5 illus.

867

Kotljar, N. O monetah Dmitrija-Koributa Ol'gerdoviča. (Two coins attributed to Dmitrij-Koribut Olgerdovic) *Soobščenija Gosudarsvennogo ordena Lenina Ermitaža* (USSR), 40 (1975), 72–75, 1 illus. Summary in English.

English abstract in RILA vol. 5 (1979) #475.
French abstract in RAA 1976 #12882.

868

Kowalski, H. Radiazioni nucleari contro i falsari di monete. *Bollettino numismatico* (Italy), 10 no. 4 (1973) 4–18, 19 illus.

869

Kraay, Colin M. Cast sestertii of Titus. *Numismatic Chronicle* (England), 14 (1954) 199–201, 6 illus.

870

Kraumann, František. Falešné a znehodnocené mince a nové odražky. *Numismatické Listy* (Czechoslovakia), 8 (1953) 140–145.

871

Lagerqvist, Lars O. En sedelförfalskning från 1829. *Nordisk numismatisk Unions Medlemsblad.* (Sweden), 1956, pp. 88–95, 5 illus.

872

Lavanchy, Charles. Le faux monnayage officiel du xviiie au xxe siècle. *Schweizerische Münzblätter* (Switzerland), no. 20 (1955) 85–87.

Forgeries of coins from the Netherlands, France and England, 19th and 20th centuries.

873

Lhotka, J. F. Jr. Falsifications of ancient Coins. *Numismatist* (USA), 71 (February 1958) 131–140; reply with rejoinder. C.H. Subak, 71 (April 1958) 409–410.

874

Lindgren, Torgny. Svensk-dansk avtal om ömesesidig utlämning av Falskmyntare och sedeferapare. *Nordisk numismatisk Unions Medlemsblad.* (Sweden), 1969, pp. 157–160.

875

Lluis y Navas-Brusi, Jaime. La falsificación de moneda ante las leyes de India. *Numisma* (Spain), no. 27 (1957) 41–70, 2 plates.

876

Lluis y Navas-Brusi, Jaime. Las falsificaciónes estatales de moneda. *Nummus* (Portugal), 4 (1956–1957) 71–88.

877

Lluis y Navas-Brusi, Jaime. Los conceptos generales sobre la represión del delito de falsificación de moneda en el Derecho romano. *Numisma* (Spain), no. 30 (1958) 91–97, 7 illus.

878

Lluis y Navas-Brusi, Jaime. Las penas y castigo de los falsarios en el Derecho romano. *Numisma* (Spain), no. 32 (1958) 35–38, 12 illus.

879

Lluis y Navas-Brusi, Jaime. Una falsificación de moneda cristiana en el Reino moro de Granada. *Numario hispánico* (Spain), 2, (1953) 219–224.

880

Love, L.J. Cline; Soto, Louis; and Reagor, B.T. Surface studies of ancient gold coins and modern copies by x-ray fluorescence, scanning electron microscopy and scanning Auger spectroscopy. *Applied Spectroscopy* (USA), 34 no. 2 (1980) 131–139.

English abstract in AATA vol. 17 (1980) #17-1577.

881

Lucheschi, Dino. A propos de deux fausses monnaies vénitiennes. *Schweizerische Münzblätter* (Switzerland), no. 20 (1955) 87–88.

882

MacLeod, Ian D., and Ritchie, I.M. Detection of debasement in (forged) silver coins by means of corrosion potential measurements. *Archaeometry* (England), 23 no. 1 (1981) 65–70, 3 refs.

English abstract in AATA vol. 18 (1981) #18-1671.

883

MacLeod, Ian D. A study of some forged silver coins recovered from 17th century and 19th century shipwrecks. *Chemistry in Australia* (Australia), 49 no. 8 (August 1982) 317–320, 4 photos, 2 illus., 7 refs.

English abstract in AATA vol. 19 (1982) #19-1859.

884

Makomaski, Wacław. Nummi subaerati. *Wiadmosci numizmatyczne* (Poland), 2 no. 2 (1958) 14–22. Summary in English.

885

Marsh, John. The countryside of the coiners. *Country Life* (England), 151 (8 June 1972) 1464, 1466, illus.

An illustrated article on the Cragg Vale Coiners, British counterfeiters of the mid-eighteenth century. The article centers on the district they lived in and how it has changed through the years.

886

Matthys, A. De motte van Kessenich. *Archaeologia Belgica* (Belgium), no. 240 (1981) 3–24, 12 illus. Summary in French.

887

Mattingley, Harold B. A hoard of 'barbarous radiates' from Goring-on-Sea. *Sussex Archaeological Collections* (England), 105 (1967) 56–61, illus., refs.

888

Mayhew, N.J. Imitative sterlings in the Aberdeen and Montraive hoards. *Numismatic Chronicle* (England), 16 (1976) 85–97, illus., refs.

889

Metcalf, D.M., and Schweizer, F. Metal contents of the silver pennies of William II and Henry I (1087–1135). *Archaeometry* (England), 13 no. 2 (August 1971) 177–190.

English abstract in AATA vol. 9 (1972) #9-350.

890

Metcalf, D.M. Another modern forgery of a sceat. *British Numismatic Journal* (England), 48 (1978) 107.

891

Michálek, Miroslav. Soud s padělateli mincí v Chrudimi roku 1884. *Numismatické Listy* (Czechoslovakia), 24 (1969) 56–57. Summary in German.

892

Mikołajczyk, A. Fałszerska mennica w Suczawie. *Wiadmości numizmatyczne* (Poland), 24 no. 4 (1980) 197–224, 7 illus. Summary in English.

893

Millán, Clarisa. Sobre falsificaciones de monedas. *Revista de Archivos, Bibliotecas y Museos* (Spain), 63 (1957) 347–349, 6 plates.

894

Morgenstern, R. Comentario sobre algunas monedas orientales de la época de transición. *Gaceta numismatica* (Spain), no. 49 (1978) 54–62, 40 illus.

895

Morton, A.H. An Iranian hoard of forged dirhams. *Numismatic Chronicle* (England), 15, 7th series (1975) 155–164.

896

Münzfälschungen (coin forgers). *Numismatische Nachrichtenblatt.* (Germany), 16 (1967) 321–323; 17 (1968) 31, 67–68, 138–139, 175–176, 212, 255, 291–292, 320–323, 356, 359, 34 illus.

897

Münzfälschungen (coin forgeries). *Numismatische Nachrichtenblatt.* (Germany), 18 (1969), 288–289, 333–334, 422; 19 (1970) 40–42, 44, 79–88, 180–181, 184, 233, 235, 262–265, 327, 332, 373–375, 427–429, 472, 475, 49 illus.

898

Murari, Ottorino. Un ripostiglio di falsi denari aquilini grossi di Padova nel Museo Civico di Verona. *Italia numism.* (Italy), 16 (1965) 27–28, illus.

899

Novello, E. Moneta falsa in Sicilia nel 1697. *Rivista italiana di Numismatica* (Italy), 22 (1974) 295–301. Summaries in French and English.

900

Oddy, W.A. Coin forgers at work. *Museum of Applied Science Center for Archaeology* (USA), 1 no. 3 (December 1979) 80–81.

English abstract in AATA vol. 17 (1980) #17-768.

901

Pesce, G. Falsificazione e contraffazione di madonnine genovesi (1745–1750). *Quad. ticinesi. Numismatica e antichità classiche* (Switzerland), 2 (1973) 225–231, 4 illus.

902

Peukert, Karel. Falešná mince v Turnově. *Numismatické Listy* (Czechoslovakia), 21 (1966) 80–81. Summary in German.

903

Peukert, Karel. Penězokazecká dílna v jeskyni Babí pec na vrchu Kozákově. *Numismatické Listy* (Czechoslovakia), 22 (1967), 153–157, 2 illus. Summary in German.

904

Piniński, J. Pojeçie monety fałszywej w późnym średniowieczu. *Wiadmości numizmatyczne* (Poland), 20 no. 4 (1976) 239–242. Summary in English.

905

Powell, John S. The forgery of cartwheel pennies. *Seaby's Coin and Medal Bulletin* (England), 731 (July 1979) 217–221.
English abstract in RILA vol. 7 (1981) #5549.

906

Premier congrès international d'étude et de défense contre les falsifications monétaires. *Numário hispánico* (Spain), 11 (1967) 75–81.

907

Probszt, Günther. Nachahmungen von Talern Ferdinands von Tirol. *Mitteilungen der Österreichischen numismatischen, Gesellschaft* (Austria), 13 no. 1 (1963) 3–7, illus.

908

Probszt, Günther. Ungarische Münzfälschungen des 16. Jh. *Mitteilungen der Österreichischen numismatischen Gesellschaft* (Austria), 13 (1963–1964) 52–58.

909

Rancoule, G.; Nouvian, S.; Soulères, A. and Soulères, N. La grotte Nord de Lauradieu (commune d'Auriac, Aude). Un atelier de faux monnayeur du 15ᵉ siecle. *Bulletin de la Société d'Etude scientifique de l'Aude* (France), 74 (1974) 171–176, 3 illus.

910

Reyman, Janusz. O monetach fałszywych i nieprawidłowych. *Otchlani Wieków* (Poland), 32 (1966) 36–40, 6 illus.

911

Robinson, E.S.G. Some early nineteenth-century forgeries of Greek coins. *Numismatic Chronicle* (England), 16 (1956) 15–18, 12 illus.

912

Schneider, H. Modern sovereign forgeries. *Numismatic Circular*, (England), 48 (1950), col. 731–732.

913

Seaby, W.A. and Brady, G. The extant Ormonde pistoles and double pistoles of 1646. *British Numismatic Journal* (England), 43, (1973) 80–95, illus., refs.

914

Sejbal, Jiři. Znalezisko fałszywych monet polskich z Sučan (Czechosłowacja). *Wiadmości numizmatyczne* (Poland), 11 no. 3 (1958) 15–17, 1 illus. Summary in English.

915

Severova, M. Tureckie monety, čekannye na peterburgskom Monetnom Dvorce. *Soobščenija Gosudarsvennogo ordena Lenina Ermitaža* (USSR), 40 (1975) 77–82, 2 illus. Summary in English.

French abstract in RAA 1976 #14573.

916

Shelton, K.J. Usurpers' coins: the case of Magnentius. Byzantinische Forschungen. Internationale Zeitschrift für Byzantinistik. (Netherlands), 8 (1982) 211–235, 11 illus.

917

Shiel, N. A group of forged early imperial coins. *Numismatic Circular* (England), 79 (1971) 451, 1 illus.

918

Shortt, H. de. The detection of coin forgeries in N.W. India. *Journal of the Numismatic Society of India* (India), 23 (1961), 166–174.

919

Sigue la juerga. *Gaceta numismatica* (Spain), 36 (1975) 75–80, 11 illus.

Forgeries of Spanish coins, 17–18th centuries.

920

Skutil, Josef. Falschmünzenwerkstätten in Höhlen. *Mitteilungen der Österreichischen numismatischen Gesellschaft* (Austria), 13 (1963–1964) 91–93.

921

Spencer, J.R. Fifteenth century forgery of a Roman coin. *Oberlin College Art Bulletin* (USA), 28 no. 3 (Spring 1971) 133–140, illus.

922

Stein, Harry J. An unpublished imitation of a coin of Pontius Pilate and other ancient imitations of Jewish coins. *Numismatic Review*, 2 (January–March 1945) 14–16, 1 plate.

923

Steinke, Richard. Nachprägungen und Fälschungen von Goldmünzen. (Minting and forgery of gold coins). Numismatische Nachrichtenblatt (Germany), 12 (1963) 198–202, 225–228; 13 (1964) 88–91, 140–141.

924

Terry, K.W., and De Laeter, J.R. X-ray diffraction analysis of grain size as a method of detection of reproductions among seventeenth-century Spanish silver reales. *Numismatic Chronicle* (England), 14 (1974) 198–202.

English abstract in AATA vol. 12 (1975) #12-1291.

925

Thompson, J.D.A. Documents illustrating the export of counterfeit currency to the West Indies. *British Numismatic Journal* (England), 27 no. 1 (1952) 80–87, 7 illus.

French abstract in RAA 1953 #9891.

926

Tobler, Edwin. Fälschungen von Schweizer Münzen (Forgeries of Swiss coins). *Helvetische Münz. Z.* (Switzerland), 7 (1972) 1–6, 49–54, 105–110, 183–187, 92 illus.

927

Falsificaciones. *Gaceta numismatica* (Spain), no. 30 (1973) 7, 6 illus.

Six forged coins, Spanish and Portuguese, 18th century.

928

Van Dalen, A.; Das, H.A.; and Zonderhuis, J. Nondestructive examination of Roman silver coins by neutron activation analysis. J. Radioanal Chem. 15 no. 1 (1973) 143–149.

English abstract in AATA vol. 11 (1974) #11-826.

929

Vaulter, Roger. La fausse monnaie à travers les âges. *R. française* (France), no. 58 (1954) 23–27, 23 illus.

930

Velter, A.M. Date privitoare la un tezaur din sec. al 15-lea descoperit la Turda. *Cercetari numismatice* (Romania), 1 (1978), 32–41, 1 illus. Summary in French.

French abstract in RAA 1977 #12086.

931

Zakrzewska Kleczkowska, J. Monety fałszywe znalezione w skarbie z 11 wieku w Sochaczewie. *Sprawozdania z Posiedzeń Komisji Naukowych P.A.N.* (Poland), 21 no. 1 (1977) 2–4.

French abstract in RAA 1980 #1564.

Medallions

Sections of Books

932

Amandry, Pierre. *Collection Hélène Stathatos. Les Bijoux antiques.* Strasbourg: University Institute of Archaeology, 1953, pp. 104–105.

For a review of Amandry's book see *Journal of Hellenic Studies* 75 (1955) 174–175, by Sylvia Benton.

Periodicals

933

Amandry, Pierre. Médaillon en or du Musée de Providence. *American Journal of Archaeology* (USA), 59 (1955) 219–222, 2 plates, 19 refs.

934

Cannoo, Jean-Marie. Sur les traces de Garapon, médailleur ou faussaire? *Helvetische Münz. Z.* (Switzerland), 5 (1970) 388–393, 2 illus.

935

Chapman, B. How Billie and Charley left their mark. *Everything Has its Value,* 2 no. 16 (January 1982) 20, 1 illus.

On fake medieval medallions made by William 'Billie' Smith and Charles 'Charley' Eaton.

936

Grotemeyer, Paul. Fälschungen nach habsburgischen Medaillen (Forgeries of Habsburg medallians). *Schweizerische Münzblätter* (Switzerland), no. 37 (1960) 10–13, 7 illus.

937

Guerassimov, T. Médaillon, falsifié, portant le nom de ville de Deultum (Medallion, forged, carrying the name of the town of Deultum [in Bulgaria]). *Izvestija na arkheologičeskija Institut* (Bulgaria), 26 (1963) 275–277, 2 illus.

938

Kisch, Guido. Kunstfälschertum im Urteil der Zeitgenossen *Schweizerische numismatische Rundschau* (Switzerland), 36 (1954) 31–36.

French abstract in RAA 1954 #1316.
On medallion engravers who imitated antique works.

939

Lindgren, Torgny. När medaljgravören avslöjade sedelförfalskaren. *Nordisk numismatisk Årsskrift* (Sweden), 1950, pp. 91–104, 2 illus.

French abstract in RAA 1952 #2052.

940

Lippens, Jan. Un jeton de l'inauguration de François II. *Cercle d'Etudes numismatiques, Bulletin* (Belgium), 2 (1965) 4–5, 1 illus.

941

Robinson, David M. Unpublished Greek gold jewelry and gems. *American Journal of Archaeology* (USA), 57 no. 1 (January 1953) 5–19, plates 3–25.

See page 13 for Robinson's comments on the Stathatou Aphrodite medallion.

942

Severin, Hans-Georg. Sinistrarum iunctio. *Archäologischer Anzeiger* (Germany), 3 (1982) 595–598, 4 illus., 13 refs.

Forgeries of early Byzantine Christian medallions.

Arms and Armor

See also Exhibitions #1715.

Books

943

Baer, Ilse, et al. *Gefälschte Blankwaffen: galvanoplastische Kopien, Probleme der Authentizität* (Forged cold steel: galvanized copies. Problems of authenticity). Hanover: Verlag Kunst und Antiquitäten, 1980, 83 p., illus. (Reihe Kunst und Falschung 2). Includes bibliographical references.

Reproductions and forgeries of swords.

944

Sanders, Horace. *False Iberian weapons and other forged antiquities from Spain.* N.P. 1913, 10 pp., illus., plates. Caption-Title "From the Proceedings of the Society of Antiquities, February 27, 1913." (Author's presentation copy).

In the collection of the Hispanic Society of America.

Sections of Books

945

Ettmayer, Peter. "Versuch einer metallographischen Authentizitaetsberwertung einer Schallern" (Attempted metallographic authentication of a sallet), in *Wiener Berichte ueber Naturwissenschaft in der Kunst*, vol. 1, edited by Alfred Vendl and Bernhard Pichler, pp. 166–174, 7 illus., 2 refs. Summary in English.

English abstract in AATA vol. 22 (1985) #22-1031.

Periodicals

946

Grancsay, Stephen V. Italian seventeenth century pistols: genuine and false. *Journal of the Walters Art Gallery* (USA), 11 (1948) 62–75.

English abstract in G&U #183.

947

Hayward, John F. A note on a Vienna arms and armor faker. *Waffen-und Kostümkunde* (Germany), 19 no. 1 (1977) 78–81, 3 illus.

The forgeries of goldsmith Salomon Weininger.
English abstract in RILA vol. 4 (1978) #7769.

948

Homma, Kunzan. Common sense useful in the judgment of swords. *Gekkan-Bunkazai* (Tokyo, Japan), no. 3 (1964) 10–15. (in Japanese).

False signatures inscribed on swords; swords fashioned from pieces of different swords, etc.
English abstract in AATA vol. 5 (1964) #4726.

949

Ishikawa, R. and Hiroi, Y. Tsugi Nakago (joined tangs)—Spurious swords and x-ray examination. Museum: A Quarterly Review published by UNESCO (France), no. 179 (1965) 28–34. (In Japanese).

English abstract in AATA vol. 6 (1967) #(6)-H1-24.

950

Knode, Harry C. Collector fakes, *The American Rifleman* (USA), 107 no. 10 (1959) 88–89.

Rare Colt handgun fakes.
English abstract in AATA vol. 3 (1960-1961) #2768.

951

North, Anthony R.E. Two Dutch rapiers. *Connoisseur* (England), 193 no. 776 (October 1976) 113–115. 4 illus.

English abstract in RILA vol. 4 (1978) #1197.

952

Puraye, Jean. Damascus barrels: they faked those, too (part two of Damascus barrel story). *The American Rifleman* (USA), 124 no. 5 (May 1976) 33–35.

English abstract in AATA vol. 13 (1976) #13-1209.

953

Sapunov, B. K istorii sozdanija tak nazyvaemogo noža Ermaka. *Soobščenija Gosudarsvennogo ordena Lenina Ermitaža* (U.S.S.R.), 44 (1979) 34–36, 1 illus. Summary in English.

Two knives, one in the Hermitage Museum, the other in the Historical Museum of Moscow, said to be owned by Ermak Timofeič at the turn of the 15th century are in fact 18th-century forgeries.
French abstract in RAA 1982 #5399.

954

Schedelmann, Hans. Der Waffensammler (The arms collector). *Waffen-und Kostümkde* (Germany), 1963, pp. 99–106, 8 illus.

Faked arms of the 19th century.
French abstract in RAA 1963 #424.

955

Schedelmann, Hans. Der Waffensammler. Gefälschte Prunkwaffen. (The arms collector. Faked dress arms). *Waffen-und Kostumkde* (Germany), 7 no. 2 (1965) 124–132; 8 no. 1 (1966) 53–57, 26 illus.

Faked arms of the 19th and early 20th centuries and items the author identifies as fakes in collections.
English abstract in AATA vol. 6 (1966-1967)#(6)-H4-164.

956

Schedelmann, Hans. Konrad fecit. *Waffen-und Kostümkde* (Germany), no. 1 (1971) 52–61, 26 illus.,

German silver saber forgeries from the early 20th century.

957

Seitz, Heribert. Fakes. Notices on a subject of current interest. *Livrustkammaren, Journal of the Royal Armoury* (Sweden), 12 (1970–1971) 130–160, 11 illus. Summary in Swedish.

Arms and armor forgeries of different centuries.

958

Unsigned article. Disarms forgers. *Photo Methods for Industry* (USA), 14 no. 11 (November 1971) 51.

On authenticating antique arms through the use of industrial x-rays.

959

Unsigned article. This issue's cover subject. *Medical Radiography and Photography* (USA), 47 no. 3 (1971), cover and inside verso, illus.

Photographs and radiographs of forged antique weapons.

960

Vukanovic, T.P. Ubojna kosa iz 15 stoletja (A forgery of war of the 15th century) *Vranjski Glasnik* (Yugoslavia), 7 (1971) 283–286. Summary in German.

961
Wever, Gayle. A Persian puzzle: a bronze sword from Teheran. *Expedition* (USA), 12 no. 1 (Fall 1969) 24–27.

English abstract in AATA vol. 8 (1970–1971) #8-1068.

Brass

See also Technical (Periodicals) #1352, 1353.

Periodicals

962
Craddock, Paul T. The composition of the copper alloys used by the Greek, Etruscan and Roman Civilizations. 3. The origins and early use of brass. *Journal of Archaeological Science* (England), 5 no. 1 (1978) 1–16.

English abstract in AATA vol. 15 (1978) #15-1658.

963
Craddock, Paul T. The first brass: some early claims reconsidered. *Museum of Applied Science Center for Archaeology Journal* (USA), 1 no. 5 (December 1980) 131–133.

Small pins, metal artifacts from early Cypriot tombs, and Luristan cheek pieces are discussed.
English abstract in AATA vol. 18 (1981) #18-661.

964
Lockner, Herman P. Licht für Kirche und Haus. Mitteleuropäische Messingleuchter des 16. Jr. (Light for churches and houses. Middle European brass lamps of the 16th century). Kunst und Antiquitäten (Germany), no. 3 (1977) 30–34, 9 illus.

965
Lockner, Herman P. Oft kopiert und nie erreicht. Nachahmungen, Abformungen, Fälschungen von Beckenschlägerschüssein zwischen 1450 and 1600. *Kunst und Antiquitäten* (Germany), no. 4 (1977) 37–41, 11 illus.

19th century brass imitation wash basins.

966
McLeod, M. A land rich in gold. *Antique Collector* (England), 51 no. 8 (August 1980) 52–54, 10 illus.

Fakes and replicas of West African brass weights for weighing gold dust.
English abstract in ABM vol. 12 (1981) #0409.

967
Power, Robert H. A plate of brass "By Me ... CG Francis Drake." *California History* (USA), 57 no. 2 (1978), pp. 172–185.

Argument for the authenticity of Francis Drake's brass plate.

968

Unsigned article. Tests of Drake's brass plate indicate fake. *Chemical and Engineering News* (USA), 55 no. 32 (8 August 1977) 6–7.

English abstract in AATA vol. 14 (1977) #14-1173.

Bronzes

See also Ceramics (Periodicals) #626, and Technical (Periodicals) #1352, #1353.

Sections of Books

969

Bloch, Peter. "Staufische Bronzen: die Bronzekruzifixe (Hohenstaufen bronzes: the bronze crucifixes), in *Zeit der Staufer: Geschichte, Kunst, Kultur; Band V Supplement: Vortraege und Forschungen.* Edited by Reiner Haussherr and Christian Vaterlein. Stuttgart: Württembergisches Landesmuseum, 1979, 291–330, 48 illus.

970

Faider-Feytmans, Germaine. *Recueil de bronzes de Bavai* (Collection of bronzes from Bavai), Centre National de la Recherche Scientifique, Paris, 1957— 140 p., illus.

Includes a report on 12 doubtful or false bronzes.
English abstract in AATA vol. 2 (1958–1959) #1856.

971

Gettens, Rutherford John. *The Freer Chinese bronzes, Volume II, technical studies.* Smithsonian Institution, Freer Gallery of Art, Oriental Studies, no. 7, Washington, D.C., 1969, 257 p., illus., bibliog (8 pages).

Chapter X is entitled "False patina and repairs."
English abstract and full table of contents in AATA vol. 8 (1970–1971) #8-346.

972

Gettins, Rutherford John; Pope, John Alexander; Cahill, James; and Barnard, Noel. *The Freer Chinese bronzes.* Washington, D.C.: Smithsonian Institution (Publication 4706), 1967, 638 p.

English abstract in AATA vol. 8 (1970–1971) #8-353.

973

Young, William J. "Authentication of works of art," in *Art and technology: a symposium on classified bronzes.* Edited by Suzannah Doehringer, David Gorden Mitten, and Arthur Steinburg. The Massachusetts Institute of Technology, 1970.

English abstract in AATA vol. 8 (1970–1971) #8-1510.

Periodicals

974
Barnard, Noël. "The incidence of forgery amongst archaic Chinese bronzes." *Monumenta Serica* (1968) 91–168.
English abstract in AATA vol. 9 (1972) #9-391.

975
Barnard, Noel. Some remarks on the authenticity of a Western Chou style inscribed bronze. *Monumenta Serica,* 18 (1959) 213–244, 8 plates, 2 illus.
French abstract in RAA 1960 #11019.

976
Chang, Shih-Hsien. An x-ray examination of selected bronzes in the National Palace Museum. *Ku Kung Chi K'an,* 11 no. 3 (1977) 11–18 (English); 41–47 (Chinese).
English abstract in AATA vol. 15 (1978) #15-1653.

977
Chase, W.T. Three bronzes relating to the Princeton P'ou. *Princeton University Art Museum Record* (USA), 27 no. 1 (1968), 11—12.

978
Fleming, Stuart J. Modern scientific techniques for art object authentication. *Electronics and Power,* 20 no. 19 (October 31, 1974) 894–897.
The use of thermoluminescence in authenticating bronzes.
English abstract in AATA vol. 12 (1975) #12-1232.

979
Grummond, Nancy Thomson de. Reflections on the Etruscan mirror. *Archaeology (USA) 34 no. 5 (September/October 1985) 54-58, 8 illus.*
Page 58 has a section on 'forgeries and conservation.' See also #1009.

980
Guglielmi, Stephen. Report on the spurious nature of a Shang Dynasty bronze P'ou. *Princeton University Art Museum Record,* 27 no. 1 (1968) 3–10, illus.

981
Kruger, Gerhard. Über die Entdeckung einer hallischen Werkstatt von Nachbildungen mitteldeutscher Bronzegegenstande. *Wissenschaftliche Zeitschrift der Martin-Luther-Universität, Halle-Wittenberg. Gesellschafts- und sprachwissenschaftliche Reihe* (Germany), 7 (1957–1958) 231–233.
French abstract in RAA 1958 #1794.

982
Lockner, Herman P. Jedes Stück ist ein Individuum. Mitteleuropäische Bronzemörser und ihre Fälscher. *Kunst und Antiquitäten* (Germany), no. 3 (1976), pp. 32–36, 11 illus.

983

Mishara, J. and Meyers, P. Technical examination of a bronze Iranian beaker from Iran. *American Journal of Archaeology* (USA), 78 no. 3 (1974) 252–254.

English abstract in AATA vol. 13 (1976) #13-1206.

984

Otto, Helmut. Die chemische Untersuchung von gefälschten Bronzen aus mitteldeutschen Museen (Chemical examination of false bronzes from central German museums). *Wissenschaftliche Zeitschrift der Martin-Luther-Universitat, Halle-Wittenberg. Gesellschafts-und sprachwissenschaftliche Reihe* (Germany), 7 (1957) 203–229, 18 illus.

English abstract in AATA vol. 2 (1958–1959) #1268.
French abstract in RAA 1958 #1793.

This article also includes a general bibliography on forgeries and falsifications.

985

Potratz, Johannes A.H. Über ein Corpus Aerum Luristanensium. *Iranica antiqua* (Netherlands), 3 (1963) 124–147, 4 illus.

French abstract in RAA 1963 #3111.

986

Rossi, Francesco. Maffeo Olivieri e la bronzistica bresciana del '500 (Maffeo Olivieri and bronze metalwork in Brescia in the 16th century). *Arte lombarda* (Italy), 47–48 (1977) 115–134, 28 illus.

English abstract in RILA vol. 4 (1978) #1536.

987

Rudolph, Richard Casper. Dynastic booty: an altered Chinese bronze. *Harvard Journal of Asiatic Studies* (USA), 11 (1948) 174–180, illus.

An altered inscription on a Chinese bronze bell.
English abstract in G&U #201.

988

Soper, Alexander C. A problematical Chinese bronze vessel: The Ku that was "too good to be true." *Artibus Asiae* (Switzerland), 32 no. 2/3 (1970) 200–211.

English abstract in vol. 8 (1970–1971) #8-1953.

989

Werner, O. Spektralanalytische Untersuchungen antiker und neuzeitlicher indischer Bronzen (Spectro-chemical analysis of ancient and modern Indian bronzes). *Materialprüfung*, 7 no. 12 (1965) 463–470.

English abstract in AATA vol. 7 (1968–1969) #7-1263.

Pewter

See also Exhibitions #1764.

Books

990
Zinn: Kopie, Imitation, Verfälschung (Pewter: copy, imitation, forgery). Hannover: Verlag Kunst und Antiquitäten, 1981, 87 p., illus.

Periodicals

991
Bertram, Fritz. Aktuelle Zinfälschungen auf dem Kunstmarkt (Notice: pewter forgeries on the art market). *Weltkunst* (Germany), 33 no. 5 (1963) 19, 2 illus.

992
Evans, Nancy Goyne. Curators and collectors beware! *Winterthur Newsletter* (USA), 18 no. 5 (May 1972) 4–5.

English abstract in AATA vol. 9 (1972) #9-471.

993
Haedeke, H.U. Wie erkennt man Zinnfälschungen? Eine Antwort, aber keine Patentantwort (How can one recognize pewter forgeries? An answer, but not a patent answer). *Kunst und Antiquitäten* (Germany), no. 2 (1981) 62–67, 10 illus.

994
Hayward, John F. A disputed pewter tankard. *Connoisseur* (England), 136 no. 548 (October 1955) 114–115, 5 illus.

995
Stara, D. Přispevěk k poznání cínových padělků. *Časopis národního Muzea. Historické Muzeum* (Czechoslovakia), 152 no. 1–2 (1983) 57–67, 11 illus. Summary in German.

French abstract in RAA 1985 #10880.

996
Unsigned article. Contre les faus étains (Against forged pewter). *Connaissance des Arts* (France), no. 231 (May 1971) 41.

Silver

See also Exhibitions #1738.

Books

997

Neuwirth, Waltraud. *Wiener Jugendstilsilber: Original, Fälschung oder Pasticcio* (Viennese Jugenstil silver: original, forgery, pastiche). Vienna: Waltrud Neuwirth, 1980, 88 p., 94 plates. In English and German. Available from the Öesterreichisches Museum Fuer Angewandte Kunst, A. 1010 Wien, Stubenring 5.

English abstract in AATA vol. 19 (1982) #19-708 and ABM vol. 14 (1983) #3602.

998

Richter, Ernst Ludwig. *Altes Silber: imitiert, kopiert, gefälscht* (Old silver: imitation, copy, forgery). Munich: Keyser, 1983 (Antiquitäten echt oder gefälscht), 255 p., 240 illus.

999

Unsigned. *Silber: Imitation, Kopie, Fälschung, Verfälschung* (Silver: imitation, copy, forgery, falsification). Munich: Verlag Kunst und Antiquitäten, 1982, (Reihe Kunst und Fälschung 4), 109 pp., 100 illus.

Sections of Books

1000

Boylan, Leona Davis. *Spanish colonial silver*. Santa Fe: Museum of New Mexico Press, 1974, 202 pp., 375 illus., bibliog., index.

English abstract in RILA vol. 2 (1976) #4700.

1001

Emery, John. European spoons before 1700. Edinburgh: J. Donald, 1976, 205 p., 132 illus., diags., bibliog., index.

English abstract in RILA vol. 3 (1977) #4096.

1002

Gans, M.H.: and Wit-Klinkhamer, Th.M. Duyvené de. "Values and forgeries," in their *Dutch silver*, translated by Oliver van Oss. London: Faber and Faber, 1961, pp. 65–74.

1003

Richter, Ernst Ludwig and Kommer, Björn R. "Der spätmittelalterliche Hofbecher und seine nordischen Epigonen; kritische Bemerkungen zu einer Gruppe von Silberbechern mit Lübecker und Bremer Beschauzeichen." (The late medieval *Hofbecher* and its northern imitators; critical notes on a group of silver beakers with inspection marks from Lübeck and Bremen), in *Jahrbuch der Hamburger Kunstsammlungen* (Germany), 24 (1979) 63–76, 17 illus.

English abstract in RILA vol. 7 (1981) #5553.

French abstract in RAA 1982 #5426.

Periodicals

1004

Banister, Judith. Fakes, forgeries and duty-dodgers in English silver. *Antiques* (USA), 88 (September 1965) 330–332.

1005

Banister Judith. Forgers, furbishers and duty-dodgers. *Apollo* (England), 75 (1961) 104–107, 4 illus.

On forged English silver.

1006

Citroen, K.A. Vervalsing en namaak van zilver in Friesland. *Vrije Fries* (Netherlands), 55 (1975), pp. 14–24, 12 illus.

Falsifications of silver, 17th and 18th centuries, in the Netherlands.

1007

Fales, Martha Gandy. Some forged Richardson silver. *Antiques* (USA), 79 no. 5 (May 1961) 466–469, 10 illus.

1008

Fillitz, Hermann. Der Silberschatz der Herzogin Margarete Maultasch in Schloss Ambras. *Pantheon* (Germany), 29 (1971) 320–322, 4 illus.

Two silver goblets and one silver cup forgeries.

French abstract in RAA 1971 #6801.

1009

Fischer-Graf, Ulrike. Der etruskische Silberreliefspiegel in Florenz, eine Fälschung (The Etruscan silver relief mirror in Florence: a forgery). *Antike Kunst* (Switzerland), 25 no. 2 (1982) 117–123, illus.

See also #979.

1010

Grimwade, Arthur. A study of English silver fakes. *Apollo* (England), 116 no. 247 (September 1982) 181–184, 8 illus.

English abstract in ABM vol. 14 (1983) #3600.

1011

Heichelheim, F.M. Modern forgeries in the Mildenhall treasure? *Symboles Osloenses*, 27 (1949) 141–142; 28 (1950) 105–108.

French abstract in RAA 1950–1951 #7183.

1012

Hoving, Thomas. The mystery crèche. *Connoisseur* (England), 212 no. 850 (December 1982) 81, 2 illus.

On silver Gothic creations - with a romantic flavor - from the forger's workshop of L. Marcy in Paris. See also #1023.

1013

Myers, P. Technical studies of Sasanian silver. *Museum of Applied Science Center for Archaeology* (USA), 1 no. 3 (December 1981). 242–245.

English abstract in AATA vol. 19 (1982) #19-704.

1014

Mills, John FitzMaurice. Is it genuine? Silver. *Antique Collector* (England), 50 (December 1979) 79, illus.

1015

Seling, H. Der Silbersammler und seine Welt. (The silver collector and his world.) *Weltkunst* (Germany), 44 no. 12 (1974), pp. 1054–1058, 10 illus.

The collections of the Münchner Residenz.

1016

Van Dievoet, W. Een plaket met valse merken van Gent. *Bulletin des Musées royaux d'Art et d'Histoire* (Belgium), 47 (1975) 211–218, 4 illus. Summary in French.

French abstract in RAA 1977 #13280.

1017

Von Graevenitz, A.; and Gans, L.B. Keine Angst vor Fälschungen holländischen Silbers (No fear about forged Dutch silver). *Weltkunst* (Germany), 45 no. 5 (1975) 344–345, 3 illus.

Forged 17th and 18th century Dutch silver.

1018

Zink, H. Wie die St. Stephanus-Kirche in Hamm-Heessen in den Besitz einer Zweitanfertigung ihres spätgotischen Kelches kam (How the St. Stephanus Church in Hamm-Heessen came to possess a twice fabricated chalice of the late Gothic era). *Westfalen* (Germany), 55 nos. 1–2 (1977) 194–204, 12 illus.

French abstract in RAA 1979 #4670.

Goldsmithing

Sections of Books

1019

Bainbridge, Henry Charles. *Peter Carl Fabergé: goldsmith and jeweller to the Russian Imperial Court*. New York: Spring Books (The Hamlyn Publishing Group, LTD), 1974, pp. 105, 139–140.

1020

Snowman, A. Kenneth. "Wrong attributions, pastiches & forgeries," in his *Carl Fabergé: goldsmith to the Imperial Court of Russia*. New York: Viking Press, 1979, pp. 146–149.

1021

Von Habsburg-Lothringen, G.; and Solodkoff, A. "Fabergé and fake Faberge," in their *Fabergé: court jeweller to the Tsars*. New York: Rizzoli, 1979, pp. 149–150.

Also contains a section on hallmarks and signatures on Fabergé's objects; catalog of Fabergé's easter eggs; bibliography; index.

Periodicals

1022

Albizzati, Carlo. Nuove e vecchie trovate dei fabbricanti d' antichità. *Historia*, 3 (1929) 665 + .

Albizzati claims that the Baurat Schiller Crowns are forgeries.

1023

Blair, Claude and Campbell, Marian. Le mystere de Monsieur Marcy. *Connoissance Arts* (France), 375 (May 1983) 70–73, illus.

See also #1012.

1024

Culican, William. The case for the Baurat Schiller Crowns. *The Journal of the Walters Art Gallery* (USA), vol. 35, pp. 15–35, illus., 104 refs.

1025

Hachmann, Rolf. Die Goldschalen von Leer und Schwäbisch-Gmünd. Zwei Fälschungen aus einer Münchener Goldschmiedewerkstatt (The goldencups from Leer and Schwabia-Gmünd. Two forgeries by a goldsmith state-worker from Munich). *Germania* (Germany), 36 (1958) 436–446, 12 illus.

French abstract in RAA 1958 #1795

1026

Hackenbroch, Yvonne. Reinhold Vasters, goldsmith. *Metropolitan Museum Journal* (USA), 19/20 (1984/1985) 163–268, 205 illus. Exceptionally well researched and written, this booklength article may well become the definitive work on Vasters' life and work. Extensive footnotes with excellent illustrations.

For a review of Hackenbroch's article together with some thoughtful comments on forgeries in general, see Joseph Alsop's 'The faker's art', *New York Review of Books* (USA), 23 October 1986, pp. 25–26, 28–31, 4 illus.

1027

Hartmann, A. Zur Erkennung von Fälschungen antiken Goldschmucks. (How to recognize fake antique gold embellishments). *Archäologischer Anzeiger* (Germany), no. 2 (1975) 300–304, 3 illus.

1028

Hayward, John F. Salomon Weininger, master faker. *Connoisseur* (England), 187 no. 753 (November 1974) 170–179, 15 illus.

English abstract in ABM vol. 6 (1975) #3445.
French abstract in RAA 1975 #3821.

1029

Stevens, Mark. A master forger exposed. *Newsweek* (USA), 103 (January 23, 1984) 59, illus.
On Forger Reinhold Vasters.

1030

Truman, Charles. Reinhold Vasters: the last of the goldsmiths? *Connoisseur* (England), 200 no. 803 (1979) 154–161, 19 illus.

1031

Von Habsburg-Lothringen, G. Fabergé seit 1920 (Fabergé since 1920). *Du* (Switzerland), 37 no. 442 (December 1977) 84–85, 8 illus.

English abstract in ABM vol. 14 (1983) #1509.

1032

Young, Mahonri Sharp. A modern Cellini. *Apollo* (England), 120 (September 1984) 201–202, 5 illus.

On forger Reinhold Vasters.

Minerals, Gems and Jewelry

See also Law (Periodicals) #1654.

Sections of Books

1033
Biesantz, Hagen. *Kretisch-Mykenische Siegelbilder.* Marburg, 1954, pp. 84–122.

On the Thisbe gems.

1034
Emerson, A.R. *Handmade Jewelry.* North Pomfret, Vermont: David & Charles, 1977, 83 p., illus.

Valuable for its examples of Greek and Etruscan granulated jewelry reproductions by Littledale.

1035
Higgins, Reynold. *Greek and Roman jewelry.* 2nd ed. Berkeley and Los Angeles: University of California Press, 1980, 243 p., bibliography and site lists, index, 64 plates.

See pp. 3, 4, 167, 196–197 for forgeries. This is an invaluable reference source for Greek and Roman jewelry. Contains an excellent bibliography.

1036
Nilsson, Martin. P. *The Minoan-Mycenaean religion.* 2nd ed. Traverse City, Michigan: Harry C. Lund, 1950, pp. 40–50, 267.

On the Thisbe gems.

1037
Ogden, Jack. Jewelry of the ancient world. New York: Rizzoli, 1983, 186 p., photos, bibliography, index.

English abstract in AATA vol. 22 (1985) #22-1713.

For a review of Ogden's book, see *Gold Bulletin* (South Africa), 16 no. 4 (October 1983) 110.

Periodicals

1038
Atkinson, R.J.C. The Llanrwst bracelet. *Bulletin of the Board of Celtic Studies* (England), 18 (1958–1960) 206–207.

French abstract in RAA 1960 #1746.

1039

Bailey, Randy. Turquoise: real or fake? An interview with Michael L. Parsons. *American Indian Art Magazine* (USA), 3 no. 1 (Winter 1977) 76–79, 2 color photos.

English abstract in AATA vol. 15 (1978) #15-988.

1040

Bensch, F. Der Wiener Goldschmied Strasser und der Londoner Optiker Dollond. Unechte Brillanten und achromatische Linsen. Josef Strasser und novellistische Bearbeitungen seiner Geschichte (The Viennese goldsmith Strasser and the London optic-maker Dollond. Fake diamonds and achromatic lens. Josef Strasser and the fictional treatment of his life). *Wiener Geschichtsbl.* (Austria), 31 no. 2 (1976) 72–76.

French abstract in RAA 1981 #12438.

1041

Bianchi, Bandinelli R. Pseudo-Alexandre: Pseudo-Pyrgotélès. *Bulletin van de Vereeniging tot de Bevordering der Kennis van de antieke Beschaving* (Netherlands), 24–26 (1949–1951) 76–84, 4 illus.

1042

Carroll, Diana Lee. Drawn wire and the identification of forgeries in ancient jewelry. *American Journal of Archaeology* (USA), 74 no. 4 (1970) 401.

1043

Demortier, G. Analysis of gold jewelry artifacts. Characterization of ancient gold solders by PIXE. *Gold Bulletin* (South Africa), 17 no. 1 (January 1984) 27–38, illus., 21 refs.

English abstract in AATA vol. 21 (1984) #21-2174.

1044

Dunn, Peter J. Copper acetate hydrate with native copper. *The Mineralogical Record* (USA), 12 no. 1 (January–February 1981) 49.

English abstract in AATA vol. 18 (1981) #18-1634.

1045

Dunn, Peter J.; Bentley, Ronald E.; and Wilson, Wendell E. Mineral fakes. *The Mineralogical Record* (USA), 12 no. 4 (July–August 1981) 197–219, 47 color illus., 32 refs.

English abstract in AATA vol. 18 (1981) #18-1552.

1046

Dunn, Peter J.; and Bentley, Ronald E. Mineral fraud. [Guest editorial]. *The Mineralogical Record* (USA), 12 no. 4 (July–August 1981) 194.

English abstract in AATA vol. 18 (1981) #18-1551.

1047

Hoffmann, Herbert. "Greek Gold" reconsidered. *American Journal of Archaeology* (USA), 73 no. 4 (October 1969) 447–451, 2 plates, 18 refs.

A reappraisal of the authenticity of several items exhibited at the "Greek Gold and Jewelry from the age of Alexander the Great" exhibition (22 November 1965–15 June 1966), by the author of the exhibition catalog.

For reviews of the exhibition, see A. Greifenhagen, *Gnomon* (Germany), 40 (1968) 695 + ; and Pierre Amandry, *American Journal of Archaeology* (USA), 74 (1967) 191 + .

1048

Johnson, James R. Stained glass and imitation gems. *Art Bulletin* (USA), 39 (1957) 221–224.

English abstract in AATA vol. 2 (1958–1959) #1858.

1049

Laufer, Berthold. Historical jottings on amber in Asia. *Memoirs of the American Anthropological Association* (USA), 1 no. 3 (February 1907) 211–244.

English abstract in AATA vol. 22 (1985) #22-2186.

1050

Lill, Georg. Die Adlerfibel von 1936 und andere Fälschungen aus einer Münchner Goldschmiedewerkstatt (The eagle clasp from 1936 and another forgery from a Munich goldsmith's workshop). *Germania* (Germany), 28 (1944–1950) 54–62, 2 illus.

French abstract in RAA 1950–1951 #2461.

1051

Reese, K.M. Neutron treatment makes gemstones radioactive. (Newscripts). *Chemical and Engineering News* (USA), 11 October 1982, p. 52.

English abstract in AATA vol. 20 (1983) #20-901.

1052

Von Steinwehr, H.E. Bericht über eine neue Türkisimitation (Report on a new turquoise imitation). *Deutsche Goldschmiede-Zeitung* (Germany), 55 no. 11 (1957) 587.

German abstract in AATA vol. 5 (1964–1965) #5055.

1053

Webster, Robert. Photographic techniques in forensic gemmology. *Forensic Photography* (England), 2 no. 3 (February 1973) 2–8.

English abstract in AATA vol. 10 (1973) #10-541.

Glass

See also Exhibitions #1759.

Books

1054

Glas und Steinzeug: Originale, Kopie oder Fälschung (Glass and stoneware: original, copy or forgery). Hannover: Verlag Kunst und Antiquitäten 1979, (Reihe Kunst und Fälschung 1), 119 p., illus.

1055

Heller, David. *In search of V.O.C. glass.* Cape Town: M. Miller, 1951, 103 p., illus.

Sections of Books

1056

Gros-Galliner Gabriella. "Clear as glass," in her *Glass: a guide for collectors,* New York: Stein and Day, 1970, pp. 145–149.

Pointers on how to spot forgeries.

1057

Unsigned Article. "Reproductions and forgeries," in *The international congress on glass, 9th, Versailles, 1971. Artistic and historical communications.* Paris: l'Institut du Verre, 1972, pp. 113–114.

Periodicals

1058

Bolken, Kandyce Smith. Glass reproductions and fakes. *Depression Glass Daze,* 7 no. 4 (1 June 1977) 30.

1059

Brooks, John. Glass: have you bought the real thing? *The Antique Dealer and Collectors Guide.* January 1980, 71–72, illus.

1060

Elbern, Victor H. A group of pseudo-ancient glass vessels from Italy. *Journal of Glass Studies* (USA), 10 (1968) 171–175, 9 illus.

1061

Goldstein, Sidney M. Forgeries and reproductions of ancient glass in Corning. *Journal of Glass Studies,* (USA), 19 (1977) 40–62, 51 illus.

English abstract in AATA vol. 15 (1978) #15-653.

1062

Lanmon, Dwight P.; Brill, Robert H.; and Reilly, George J. Some blown 'three-mold' suspicions confirmed, *Journal of Glass Studies* (USA), 15 (1973) 143–173, 47 illus., diags., catalog of works.

20th-century forgeries (over 50 pieces) of American blown three-mold glass (The Mutzer group) originally thought to be from the early 19th century. English abstract in RILA vol. 1 (1975) #3181.

1063

Lanmon, Dwight P. Unmasking an American glass fraud. *Antiques* (USA), 123 no. 1 (January 1983) 226–236, 26 illus.

The Mutzer group forgeries.
English abstract in ABM vol. 15 (1984) #5754.

1064

Lappe, Ulrich. Mittelalterliches Glas (Medieval glasses). *Urgeschichte und Heimatforschung* (Germany), 17 (1980) 3–14.

English abstract in AATA vol. 22 (1985) #22-1174.

1065

Mills, John FitzMaurice. Is it genuine? *Antique Collector*, 50 no. 11 (November 1979) 79, illus.

1066

Neuwirth, Waltraud. Anmerkungen zur Kothgasser-Forschung. (Remarks concerning the Kothgasser forgery). *Keramos* (Germany) no. 84 (1979) 69–92, 11 illus.

Neuwirth discusses Kothgasser as a painter on porcelain and glass and discusses imitations and forgeries of Kothgasser glass.
French abstract in RAA 1980 #7169.

1067

Peterson, Arthur G. Glass Reproductions. *Hobbies* (USA), 68 no. 3 (1963) 64–65.

Glass reproductions from the moulds of glass manufacturers who had gone out of business and were sold as originals.
English abstract in AATA vol. 5 (1964–1965) #4727.

1068

Ricke, Helmut. Lampengeblasenes Glas des Historismus: die Hamburger Werkstatt C.H.F. Müeller (Historic lamp-blown glass from the Hamburg workshop of C.H.F. Mueller). *Journal of Glass Studies* (USA), 20 (1978) 45–99, 54 illus. Summary in English.

English abstract in AATA vol. 16 (1979) #16-1595.
French abstract in RAA 1980 #13748.

1069

Unsigned Article. Forgeries and reproductions of ancient painted glass. *Ornamental Glass Bulletin*, 18 (October 1924) 6–7.

1070

Unsigned Article. Making new laboratory items look antique presents problems for Kimble craftsman. *Owens-Illinois Outlook*, no. 201 (April 1977) 2, illus.

Lampworker recreates 18th-century laboratory pieces for Priestly House.

1071

Unsigned Article. Trade problems: let dealers and collectors beware. *Hobbies* (USA), 66 (August 1961) 82, illus.

Two letters to the editor reporting on glass Mother of Pearl reproductions being sold as authentic antique pieces. Reproductions mentioned are: diamond quilted pattern glass lamps; tumblers; cruets, toothpicks; fairy lamps, and miniature lamps.

1072

Werner, A.E.: Bimson, M., and Meeks, N.D. The use of replica techniques and the scanning electron microscope in the study of ancient glass. *Journal of Glass Studies*. (USA), 17 (1975) 158–160.

English abstract in AATA vol. 14 (1977) #14-399.

Ivory and Bone

See also Scrimshaw, Diptych (Periodicals) #1243 and Law (Periodicals) #1671.

Sections of Books

1073

Hoving, Thomas. "Fakes and treasures," in his *King of the confessors.* New York: Simon & Schuster, 1981, pp. 69–88, passim.

The extraordinary story of Thomas Hoving's search, discovery, and purchase of the (authentic) Bury St. Edmons Cross for the Metropolitan Museum of Art, The Cloisters Collection.

Periodicals

1074

Carder, James Nelson. The Louvre *Good Shepherd Christ:* a forgery. *Gesta* (USA), 18 no. 1 (1979) 121–126, 8 illus.

English abstract in RILA vol. 8 (1982) #5231.
French abstracts in RAA 1980 #8580 and RAA 1981 #4811.

1075

Christiansen, T.E. Ivories: authenticity and relationships. *Acta archaeologica*, (Denmark), 46 (1975) 119–133, 10 illus.
French abstract in RAA 1982 #4608.

1076

Dinkel, J. Burrell weeper. *The Scottish Art Review.* (Scotland), 14 no. 4 (1975) 10–12, 5 illus.

French abstract in RAA 1976 #5672.

1077

Elbern, Victor H. A Byzantine ivory relief and its copy. *Journal of the Walters Art Gallery* (USA), 27–28 (1964–1965) 44–47, 2 illus.

1078

Gaborit-Chopin, Danielle. Faux ivoires des collections publiques (Fake ivories in public collections). *Revue de l'Art* (France), no. 21 (1973) 94–101. Summary in English.

French abstract in RAA 1974 #8273.

1079

Leeuwenberg, Jaap. Early nineteenth-century Gothic ivories. *Aachener Kunstblätter* (Germany), 39 (1969) 11–148, 50 illus.

French abstract in RAA 1969 #6098.

1080

Schnitzler, Hermann. Ada Elfenbeine des Barons von Hüpsch. *Festschrift H. von Einem,* 1965, pp. 222–225, 10 illus.

Forgeries of pieces originally thought to be from the time of Charlemagne.

Scrimshaw

Periodicals

1081

Grunfeld, Frederic V. Scamshaw. *Connoisseur* (England), 215 (March 1985) 24–26, illus.

On a flood of fake plastic scrimshaw (weighted with lead inserts) being sold in America, England, and on the Continent.

1082

Prince, D. Scrimshaw: art of the Yankee whaler. *Art and Antiques* (USA), 4 no. 3 (May–June 1981) 108–113, 10 illus.

English abstract in ABM vol. 13 (1982) #2510.

1083

West, Janet. Scrimshaw: recent forgeries in plastic. *Mariner's Mirror* (England), 66 (November 1980) 328–330.

Icons

Books

1084

Teteriatnikov, Vladimir. *Icons and fakes. Notes on the George R. Hann collection.* Translated by Richard David Bosley. New York: Teteriatnikov Art Enterprise Ltd., 1981. Vol. 1, 103 p.; vol. 2, 230 p.; vol. 3, 74 plates, bibliog.

English abstract in AATA vol. 20 (1983) #20-700.

Sections of Books

1085

Heinz, Wolfgang; and Mühleisen, Hans Otto. Ikonen: Aspekte der Kunstfalschung un des Betrugs (Icons: aspects of forgeries and fraud). *Kultur, Kriminalität, Strafrecht: Fetschrift für Thomas Würtenberger zum 70. Geburtstag am 7.10.1977* (Culture, criminality, criminal law: Festschrift for Thomas Würtenberger on the occasion of his 70th birthday). Berlin: Duncker und Humblot, 1977, pp. 219–239.

English abstract in RILA vol. 5 (1979) #4652.

Periodicals

1086

Heinz, Wolfgang; and Mühleisen, Hans Otto. Iconenfalschung: die Beiträge von Kunstwissenschraft und Theologie, von Kriminologie, Kriminalistik und Rechtswissenschaft (The falsification of icons: the contributions of art history and theology, of criminology, the science of criminal behavior and of legal studies). *Münster* (Germany), 30 no. 2 (1977) 93–111, 11 illus. Summary in English.

English abstract in ABM vol. 11 (1980) #1934.

Antiques

See also Exhibitions #1758, #1769.

Books

1087

Cescinsky, Herbert. *The gentle art of faking furniture.* New York: Dover Publications, 1967, 167 pp. 563 photos.

1088

Crawley, W. *Is it genuine?: a guide to the identification of eighteenth-century English furniture.* New York: Hart Publishing Company, Inc., 1972, 188 p., glossary of timbers.

1089

Hammond, Dorothy. *Confusing collectibles.* Leon, Iowa: Mid-America Book Company, 1969, 224 p., 475 color plates, 714 b&w plates.

1090

Lee, Ruth Webb. *Antique fakes and reproductions.* Enlarged and revised. Northborough, Mass: 1950, 317 pp., 167 illus.

1091

Mills, John FitzMaurice. *How to detect fake antiques.* New York: Elliot Publisher: distributed by F. Watts, 1980, 88 p., 53 illus., index.

1092

Mills, John FitzMaurice. *How to detect fake antiques.* London: Arlington Books, 1972, illus., facsims.

1093

Nicolay, Jean. *L'art et la manière des maîtres ébénistes français au xviiie siècle.* Paris, G. Le Prat, 1956–1959. 2 vol. illus., facsims., map.

1094

Nicolay, Jean. *L'art et la manière des maîtres ébénistes français au xviiie siècle. Le truquages, comment reconnaître l'authenticité des meubles anciens.* Paris: G. Le Prat, 1956, 567 p., illus., fold. map.

1095

Peterson, H.L. *How do you know it's old?* New York: Charles Scribner's Sons, 1975, 166 pp., 158 photos, bibliog., index.

On identifying numerous types of American and English antique fakes and forgeries; furniture, glass, pewter, coins, buttons, etc.

English abstract in AATA vol. 14 (1977) #14-56.

1096

Yates, Raymond Francis. *Antique fakes and their detection.* 1st Edition. New York: Harper; London: H. Hamiton, 1950, xi + 229 pp., index, illus. Photographs and drawings by the author.

Sections of Books

1097

Austen, B. *A handbook of styles in English antique furniture.* Slough, England: W. Foulsham, 1974, 186 pp., illus., bibliog.

English abstract in ABM vol. 13 (1982) #1694.

1098

Benjamin, Susan. *English enamel boxes: from the eighteenth to the twentieth centuries.* London: Orbis, 1978, 128 pp., illus., bibliog., index.

Contains a discussion of fakes, forgeries and replicas.
English abstract in RILA vol. 7 (1981) #2048.

1099

Cole, Ann Kilborn. "About reproductions" in her *How to collect the "new" antiques.* New York: David Mckay Company, 1966, pp. 224–229.

1100

Cook, P. *The antique buyer's handbook for Australia.* Terry Hills, Australia: A.H. & A.W. Reed, 1979, 300 pp., 307 illus., bibliog.

Appendix includes a section on how to identify fakes.

1101

Gilbert, Anne. *How to be an antiques collector.* New York: Grosset & Dunlap, 1978, 179 pp., illus.

English abstract in AATA vol. 20 (1983) #20-56.

1102

Gilbert, Anne. *How to be an antiques detective.* New York: Grosset & Dunlap, 1978, pp. 14, 20, 50, 153, 165–166, passim.

1103

Grotz, George. "Prevalent fakes" and "The commonist frauds," in his *Antiques you can decorate with.* Garden City, New York: Doubleday & Company, Inc., 1971 revised edition, pp. 36–45; 46–53; 64–65.

For a review of Grotz' book see "How not to buy an early American drysink" in *Time* (USA), 89 (27 January 1967) 76–77.

1104

Joy, E. *Antique English furniture.* London: Ward Lock, 1972, 192 pp., 136 illus., bibliog.

Includes a section on "Fakes, forgeries and copies."
English abstract in ABM vol. 9 (1978) #5682.

1105

Lorini, M. Campbell, and Williams, Henry Lionel. *How to restore antique furniture.* New York: Pellegrini & Cudahy, 1949. 214 pp., illus.

Includes a section on "Fakes, fakers and reproductions."

1106

Savage, George. *Dictionary of 19th century antiques and other objets d'art.* London: Barrie & Jenkins, 1978, 401 pp., 500 illus.

Appendix contains a section on art forgery in the 19th century. English abstract in ABM vol. 9 (1978) #5356.

1107

Verlet, Pierre. *Le meubles français du xviiie siècle* (French furniture of the 18th century). Paris: Presses Universitaires de France, 1982, 291 p., 171 illus., bibliog., index.

Reprinted from the 1956 edition. A thorough study of French 18th century furniture, including the authentication and detection of forgeries. English abstract in RILA vol. 10 (1984) #1439.

1108

Von Wilckens, Leonie. "Möbel und Spielzeug" (Furniture and toys) in *Das Germanische Nationalmuseum Nürnberg 1852–1977.* Beiträge zur Geschichte; im Auftrag des Museums. Berlin: Deutscher Kunstverlag, 1978, pp. 776–790, 10 illus.

English abstract in RILA vol. 6 (1980) #9166.

Periodicals

1109

Angst, Walter. Collector versus new antiques. *Curator* (USA), 21 no. 4, pp. 265–282, 7 illus.

English abstract in AATA vol. 17 (1980) #17-321.

1110

Allport, Susan. Mr. Severino's cabinet. *Connoisseur* (England), 210 no. 843 (May 1982) 10, 12, 2 b/w photos.

A forged 16th-century cabinet made in the 19th century. English abstract in AATA vol. 20 (1983) #20-1675.

1111

Brown, Raymond Lamont. Detecting the forgeries in English bracket clocks. *Antiques Journal* (USA), 34 no. 8 (August 1979) 16–17, 46–47, 8 illus.

1112

Ennimigazai, M. Antiques, while you wait. *Design* (England), 59 (November 1957) 80–82, illus.

1113

Grice, J.W.H. Faking and selling Chinese antiques. *Country Life* (England), 116 (1954) 350–351, illus.

1114

Gross, Karl-Heinz. Möbelfälschungen des 19. Jahrhunderts (Furniture forgeries of the 19th century). *Forschungen und Berichte* (Staatliche Museen zu Berlin), (Germany), 7 (1965) 105–110, 5 illus.

1115

Himmelheber, G. Die Münchner Christkindwiege (The Munich Christchild cradle). *Zeitschrift für schweizerische Archäologie und Kunstgeschichte* (Switzerland), 41 no. 3 (1984) 143–148, 6 illus. Summaries in German, French, Italian and English.

French abstract in RAA 1985 #1204.

1116

Joy, E. Examining fake and reproduction furniture. *Antique Dealer and Collector's Guide* (England), January 1978, 51–53, 8 illus.

English abstract in ABM vol. 9 (1978) #5670.

1117

Kroll, R.; Steger, E.; and Prescher, H. Ein gravierte Schieferplatte des Meisters W mit der Hausmarke? *Forchungen und Berichte* (Germany), 15 (1973) 57–69, 1 illus.

A plaque with a nativity scene, dated 1467, is the work of Johan Jacob Hock (1750–1829).
French abstract in RAA 1975 #2174.

1118

Loomes, Brian. Fake longcase clocks? *Antique Collector* (England), 53 (October 1982) 104–105, illus.

1119

Marijnissen, Roger H., and Van de Vorde, G. De "Chest of Courtrai." Een vervalsing van het pasticcio-type. (The chest of Courtrai: a pastiche-type forgery). *Meddelingen van de Koninklijke Academie voor Wetenschappen, Letteren en Schone Kunsten van België,"* (Netherlands), 11 no. 3 (1978) 3–24, 9 photos.

A carved wooden chest, the Chest of Courtrai at New College in Oxford, is proven to be a late 19th-century Flemish forgery.
English abstract in RILA vol. 6 (1978) #5392 and AATA vol. 21 (1984) #21-429.

1120

Mehlman, Felice. Close-up on fakes. *Antique Collector* (England), 50 (April 1979) 81, illus.

An illustrated comparison of an original and fake 'Torch Dancer' by F. Preiss. The model is of cold-painted bronze and ivory on a green marble base. Four close-up photos and a brief commentary by Mehlman illustrate the differences between the two.

1121

Oman, Charles. The false plate of medieval England. *Apollo* (England), 55 (1952) 74–75, 3 illus.

A gilded copper plate.

1122

Philip, Peter. How to spot a fake. *The Antique Dealer and Collector's Guide*, March 1975, pp. 68–69.

English abstract in AATA vol. 12 (1975) #12-875.
How to spot fake furniture.

1123

Pratt, Nancy. Beware! Antiques fakery is thriving again. *House Beautiful* (USA), 119 no. 7 (July 1977) 12, illus.

1124

Roth, Cecil. Caveat emptor Judaeus. *Commentary* (USA) 43 no. 3 (March 1967) 84–86.

On the surge of forgeries in Jewish antiques.

1125

Sack, Harold. Authenticity in American furniture. *Art in America* (USA), 48 no. 2 (summer 1960) 72–75, 6 illus.

1126

Unsigned article. Faking it in Moscow. *ARTnews* (USA), 74 (October 1975) 20–22.

On the activities of Naum Nicolayevsky, his antique and Fabergé forgeries, and his arrest by Soviet authorities. Nicolayevsky's story is recounted by Soviet émigré Yuri Brolhin in his *Hustling in Gorky Street*, New York: Dial Press, 1975.

1127

Van Luttervelt, R. Een oude schaal met Marten van Rossem? (A plate decorated with the portrait of Marten van Rossem?) *Berichten van de Rijksdienst voor het oudheidkundig Bodemonderzoek* (The Hague, Netherlands), 10–11 (1960–1961) 539–541, 2 illus.

A plate dated 1530 but believed to be a 19th-century forgery.

1128

Verlet, Pierre, and La Coste-Messelière, M.G. de. Le mobilier des dieux. *L'Oeil* (France), no. 166 (1968) 24–31, 12 illus.

Regarding the authenticity of an ensemble of French chairs.

1129

Wenn, L. Understanding furniture: is it antique or fake? *Antique Collector* (England), 50 no. 1 (January 1979) 68–69, illus.

1130

Winkelmeyer, D. Wege zur Wahrheit. *Weltkunst* (Germany), 52 no. 17 (1982) 2285–2287, 11 illus.

A forged Victorian secretary made of mahogany.

Woodcraft

Periodicals

1131

Roe, F. Gordon. From true to false: a second study in woodcraft. *Connoisseur* (England), 120 (1947) 92.

For Roe's first article on forgeries in woodcraft see RGR #859.

Ethnographic Art

See also Sculpture (Periodicals) #557, Minerals, Gems and Jewelry (Periodicals) #1039, and Law (Periodicals) #1678.

Books

1132

Lund, Marsha Mayer. *Indian jewelry: fact and fantasy.* Boulder, Colorado: Paladin Press, 1976, 159 p., illus.

Contents: Preface; Introduction; Chapter I. The mania; Chapter II. Standards: the past and present; Chapter III. A brief history; Chapter IV. the good guys and the bad guys; Chapter V. Where do you stand?; Chapter VI. Becoming knowledgeable; Chapter VII. Choosing a dealer; Chapter VIII. Tricks of the trade; Chapter IX. Turquoise and the ugly stepsisters; Conclusion; Glossary; Bibliography.

Sections of Books

1133
Bedinger, Margery. "Sterling silver made to order," in her *Indian silver: Navajo and Pueblo jewelers*. Albuquerque, New Mexico: University of New Mexico Press, 1973, pp. 210–213.

1134
Colton, Harold S. "How to identify kachina dolls," in his *Hopi kachina dolls with a key to their identification*. Revised edition. Color photographs by Jack Breed. Albuquerque, New Mexico: The University of New Mexico Press, 1964, pp. 87–141, illus.

1135
Dedera, Don. "Fakes, frauds and foolishness," in his *Navajo rugs: how to find, evaluate, buy and care for them*. Forward by Clay Lockett. Flagstaff, Arizona: Northland Press, 1975, pp. 103–105, passim.

1136
Gathercole, Peter. "Obstacles in the study of Maori carving: the collector, the connoisseur and the faker," in *Art and society: studies in style, culture and aesthetics*. Edited by M. Greenhalgh and V. Megaw. London: Gerlad Duckworth, 1978, XVIII, 350 p., bibliog.

1137
King, Stuart Dale. "True vs. false" and "Thoughts on ethics," in his *Indian silverwork of the southwest, volume two*. Tucson, Arizona: Dale Stuart King, Publisher, 1976, pp. 16–17, 27–32, passim.

An excellent guide to authentic Indian silverwork. Also contains a valuable annotated bibliography.

1138
Rodee, Marian E. "Fiber: the key to identification," in her *Old Navajo rugs: their development from 1900 to 1940*. Albuquerque, New Mexico: University of New Mexico Press, pp. 11–17.

1139
Rooney, Dawn. "Shapes: fakes," in her *Khmer ceramics*. Oxford: Oxford University Press, 1984, pp. 108–109.

1140
Sikorski, Kathryn Ann. *Recent trends in Zuni jewelry*. Master's thesis. University of Arizona, 1958.

Periodicals

1141

Bassani, Ezio. 19th century airport art. *African Arts* (USA), 12 no. 2 (February 1979) 34–35, 90, 7 illus.

A discussion of fake African art sculptures made in the 19th century, and the refusal of a curator/ethnologist to purchase them for what is now the Museo Nazionale Preistorico ed Ethnographico Luigi Pigorini, in Rome.

1142

Berlo, Janet Catherine; and Senuk, Raymond E. Caveat emptor: the misrepresentation of historic Mayan textiles. *Archaeology* (USA), 38 (March/April 1985) 84, illus.

1143

Cornet, Joseph. African art and authenticity. *African Arts* (USA), 9 no. 1 (October 1975) 52–55, 6 illus.

English abstract in ABM vol. 7 (1976) #0229.

1144

Dickey, Herbert Spencer. The head shrinkers of Ecuador. *The Masterkey* (USA), 10 no. 6 (November 1936) 201–203.

English abstract in AATA vol. 18 (1981) #18-1774.

1145

Duthy, Robin. Oceanic fakes and finds. *Connoisseur* (USA), 209 (March 1982) 138–141, illus.

1146

Edge-Partington, James. Maori forgeries. *Man* (England), 9 (1909) 56; 10 (1910) 54–55.

1147

Edge-Partington, James. Note on a forged ethnographical specimen from the New Hebrides. *Man* (England), 5 (1905) 71–72, 1 illus.

On a forged object which appears to be a combination of a pig-killing club and a shell adze.

English abstract in AATA vol. 15 (1978) #15-1292.

1148

Edge-Partington, James. Note on forged ethnographical specimens from the Pacific Islands. *Man* (England), 1 (1901) 68–69.

Forgeries from New Guinea, the New Hebrides and Fiji.

1149

Fakes, fakers, and fakery: authenticity in African art. (Several authors). 9 no. 3 (April 1976) 20–31, 48–74, 92, 25 illus.

Numerous contributions on fakes in African art. This issue of *African Arts* deals almost exclusively with the problem of fakes.

English abstract in ABM vol. 7 (1976) #3738.

1150

Hersey, Irwin. Collecting primitive art in Indonesia. *Arts of Asia* (Hong Kong), 10 no. 5 (September–October. 1980) 156–158, 7 illus.

English abstract in ABM vol. 14 (1983) #1054.

1151

Houlberg, Marilyn Hammersley. Collecting the anthropology of African art. *African Arts* (USA), 9 no. 3 (April 1976) 15–19, 91, 7 illus.

English abstract in ABM vol. 7 (1976) #3739.

1152

Korabiewicz, W. Folklore forgery. *Zeszyty państw. Muz. ethnogr.* (Poland), 1973–1974, pp. 14–15, 111–122, 17 illus. Summary in Polish.

1153

Maurer, Evan. Caveat ethnos: unmasking frauds in ethnographic art. *National Arts Guide* (USA), 3 no. 2 (March–April 1981) 22–25, 5 illus.

This article concentrates on the arts of Africa, Oceania and the Americas.

English abstract in ABM vol. 12 (1981) #5621.

1154

McLeod, M.D. African fakes and their detection. *Antique Collector* (England), 48 no. 6 (June 1977) 97–99, 9 illus.

English abstract in ABM vol. 8 (1977) #5064.

1155

Oldman, William. Polynesian forgeries. *Man* (England) 10 (1910) 188–189, illus.

Forged Polynesian woodcarvings.

1156

Peterson, Frederick A. Faces that are false. *Natural History* (USA), 64 (1955) 176–180.
On numerous types of forgeries—masks, figurines, etc.—from Mexico.
English abstract in AATA vol. 1 (1955–1957) #969.

1157

Turner, G.E.S. Counterfeit "tsantsas" in the Pitt Rivers Museum. *Man* (England), 44 (May–June 1944) 56–58, 2 photos.

English abstract in AATA vol. 15 (1978) #15-1800.

1158

Unsigned article. First word. *African Arts* (USA), 8 no. 4 (Summer 1975) 1, 5–7. Reply by William Fagg. 9 no. 1 (October 1975) 1, 3.

General article on fakes in African art, with a reply by William Fagg.

1159

Van Dusen, Julie. The war on fake carvings. *Macleans* (Canada), 96 no. 20 (16 May 1983) 47–48.

The problem of fake Inuit carvings in Canada.

1160

Watt, Robin. James Edward Little's forged Marquesan stilt steps. *National Museum of New Zealand Records*, 2 no. 7 (1982) 49–63, illus.

Forged Marquesan woodcarvings.

1161

Willett, Frank. True or false? The false dichotomy. *African Arts* (USA), 9 no. 3 (April 1976) 8–14.

1162

Young, D.G. More on authenticity. *African Arts* (USA), 10 no. 1 (October 1976) 97.

Prints

See also Exhibitions #1753, #1766.

Books

1163

Buchanan-Brown, John. *A forged series of woodcuts?* London, 1974, 35 p.

Sections of Books

1164

Batlle, Columba M. "Neue "alte" Holzschnitte in Montserrat (New "old" woodcuts in Montserrat), in *Gutenberg Jahrbuch*, 1962, pp. 411–415, 5 illus.

French abstract in RAA 1963 #1895.

1165

Donson, Theodore B. "Spurious prints: fakes, forgeries, and falsified proofs," in his *Prints and the print market: a handbook for buyers, collectors, and connoisseurs.* New York: Thomas Y. Crowell Company, 1977, pp. 111–147, passim., illus., index.

1166

Hayden, Arthur. *Chats on old prints.* New York: Frederick and Stokes Company, 1906, pp. 48–50, 174, 182, 264–266.

1167

Martindale, Percy H. "Fakes and repairing," in his *Engraving old and modern.* London: Heath Cranton Limited, 1928, pp. 178–188.

1168

Salamon, Ferdinando. "Copies and forgeries," in his *The history of prints and printmaking from Dürer to Picasso: a guide to collecting.* New York: American Heritage Press, 1972, pp. 77–82, passim., bibliog., index.

1169

Trautscholdt, Eduard. "Zu Nachahmungen und Fälschungen. Ein Beitrag aus der Perspektive eines Graphikhändlers (On imitation and forgeries. A contribution from the perspective of a graphics dealer), in *Festschrift H. Ladendorf* (Germany), 1970, pp. 180–183, 11 illus.

French abstract in RAA 1970 #1713.

1170

Turk, Frank. *The prints of Japan.* London: Arco Publications, 1966, pp. 250–252.

1171

Warner, Glen. "Fakes, forgeries and misrepresented prints," in his *Building a print collection: a guide to buying original prints and photographs.* Toronto; New York; Workingham, England: Van Nostrand Reinhold Ltd., 1981, pp. 59–75, passim., illus., index.

English abstract in ABM vol. 14 (1983) #3254.

Periodicals

1172

Austin, G. Alice in Dali-land. *Print Collector's Newsletter* (USA), 3 no. 2 (May–June 1972) 25–26, 2 illus.

1173

Austin, Pat; Harrower, Dee; and Machetanz, Fred. A print by any other name. [Group of articles]. 1. Passing off reproductions as real art. 2. Photographic prints: the investor's point of view. 3. Photomechanical prints: a service to my buyers. *Alaska Journal* (USA), 10 no. 1 (Winter 1980) 73–80.

English abstract in AATA vol. 18 (1981) #18-1150.

1174

Bapi, L. Nel mondo dei falsi. *Quaderni del Conoscitore di Stampe* (Italy), no. 16 (1973) 44–49, 4 illus.

1175

Blunt, Anthony. Jacques Stella, the de Masso family and falsifications of Poussin. *Burlington Magazine* (England), 116 no. 861 (December 1974) 745–751, 8 illus.

English abstract in RILA vol. 1 (1975) #2328.

French abstract in RAA 1975 #6103.

1176

Brown, David; and Landau, David. A counterproof reworked by Perino del Vaga, and other derivations from a Parmigianino Holy Family. *Master Drawings* (USA), 19 no. 1 (Spring 1981) 18–22.

English abstract in AATA vol. 19 (1982) #19-254

1177

Dreyer, P. Tiziansfälschungen des sechszehnten Jahrhunderts. Korrekturen zur Definition der Delineatio bei Tizian und Anmerkungen zur Datierung seiner Holzschnitte (Titian forgeries of the 16th century. Correction of the definition of "delineatio" of Titian and remarks concerning the dating of his wood engravings). *Pantheon* (Germany), 37 no. 4 (1979) 365–375, 18 illus. Summaries in French and English.

French abstract in RAA 1980 #2170.

1178

Dupont, Joan. Decidedly false impression. *Connoisseur* (England), 214 no. 864 (February 1984) 120, 2 illus.

On a disputed lithograph 'after' Cezanne.

1179

Ekkart, R.E.O. Enkele voorbeelden van graveursbedrog. *Vrije Fries* (Netherlands), 55 (1975) 25–31, 6 illus.

1180

Goldman, Judith. The print's progress: problems in a changing medium. *ARTnews* (USA), 75 no. 6 (Summer 1976) 39–46, 8 illus.

English abstract in RILA vol. 3 (1977) #2032.

1181

Hunnisett, B. Studies in the Society's history and archives CXXXVIII: Charles Warren, engraver (1762–1823), and the Society, part I. *Royal Society of Arts Journal* (England), 125 no. 5252 (July 1977) 488–489, 2 illus.

English abstract in ABM vol. 9 (1978) #3809.

1182

Jacques Callot, vero e falso. *Quaderni del Conoscitore di Stampe* (Italy), no. 1 (1970) 56–59, 8 illus.

1183

Karsch, F. Vorsicht—Fälschung (Caution—forgery). *Weltkunst* (Germany), 52 no. 22 (1982) 3284–3285.

On a forged lithograph of Otto Mueller (1874–1930).
French abstract in RAA 1983 #6468.

1184

Kind, J. Mickey Mouse, Dubuffet and faux-graphique. *New Art Examiner* (USA), 7 no. 5 (February 1980) 1, 8, 2 illus.

English abstract in ABM vol. 11 (1980) #7108.

1185

Kuhn, Katherine. The lively art of fakery. *Saturday Review* (USA), 48 (26 June 1965) 46.

General article on fake prints and the need for legislation.

1186

Rodgers, W. Forged prints. *Hobbies* (USA), 79 (July 1974) 140–141.

1187

Sacharow, S. Currier & Ives Prints. *Antique Collector* (England), 53 no. 7 (July 1982) 95, 1 illus.

1188

Salamon, Harry. Dürer vero e falso. Le siliografie. I: I libri. *Quaderni del Conoscitore di Stampe* (Italy), no. 12 (1972) 32–41, illus.

1189

Salamon, Harry. Dürer vero e falso. Le silografie. II. *Quaderni del Conoscitore di Stampe* (Italy), no. 13 (1972) 18–31, 15 illus.

1190

Salamon, Harry. Watermarks: of some use or merely a hazard? *Print Collector* (Italy), Introductory issue, Autumn–Winter 1972, pp. 48–50.

English abstract in AATA vol. 10 (1973) #10-651.

1191

Strieder, Peter. Copies et interprétations du cuivre de Dürer, *Adam et Eve* (Copies and interpretations of Dürer's *Adam and Eve*) *Revue de l'Art* (France), no. 21 (1973) 42–47. Summary in English.

1192

Thomas, D. New prints from old plates. *Antique Collector* (England), 48 no. 11 (November 1977) 100–101, 9 illus.

English abstract in ABM vol. 9 (1978) #3156.

1193

Unsigned article. [Etchings in the Erotic suite from Picasso's 347]. *The Print Collector's Newsletter* (USA) 10 (September 1979), 124, illus.

1194

Unsigned article. Fakes and forgeries: a problem poser forgery. *Print Collector* (Italy), Introductory issue, Autumn—Winter 1972, pp. 72–73, 5 illus.

English abstract in ABM vol. 5 (1974) #1275.

1195

Unsigned article. [Miro print:*A Woman Picking Grapes*]. *The Print Collector's Newsletter* (USA), 10 (September 1979) 125.

1196

Van der Tweel, L.H. An unrecognized woodcut by Werner Van der Valckert or a forgery of the seventeenth century? *Burlington Magazine* (England), 119 no. 893 (1977) 567–568, 2 illus.

French abstract in RAA 1978 #2503.

1197

Zschelletzschky, H.; and Weber, B. Stolpern über ikonologische Fussangeln. Forschungsunfälle im Fachgebiet der Kunstgeschichte (Blunder concerning iconological man-traps. The failure of research in specializations within art history). *Bildende Kunst* (Germany), 27 no. 3 (1979), 117–121, 8 illus.

French abstract in RAA 1979 #8977.

Photography

See also Law (Periodicals) #1697, #1698.

Books

1198

Anscombe, Isabelle. Daylight robbery? Exposing the shady side of the calotype. *Connoisseur* (England), 207 no. 831 (May 1981) 49–51, 6 illus.

English abstract in ABM vol. 12 (1981) #5620.

1199

Busch, R. Collector beware! Which of these ambrotypes are fake? *Popular Photography* (USA), 80 (May 1977) 110–111, 122–123, 132–135, 137, illus.

1200

Duthy, Robin. The world as it was: nineteenth-century photographs—our first pictoral images of real life—will prove to be good investments in time. *Connoisseur* (England), 214 no. 864 (February 1984) 110–111, 113–114.

Duthy briefly mentions the problem of fake calotypes.

1201

Homer, William Innes. On the connoisseurship of photographs. *Print Collector's Newsletter* (USA), 8 no. 5 (November–December 1977) 137–138.

On forging non-silver processes and ways to detect such forgeries. English abstract in AATA vol. 15 (1978) #14-1752.

1202

Horton, Anne. Photography. *American Book Collector* (USA) 2 no. 5 (September–October 1981) 61–62, 1 illus.

Criticism of Isabelle Anscome's article "Daylight robbery?" by the head of the Rare Photography Department at Sotheby Parke Bernet, in New York.

1203

Jay, B. What's in a name? *British Journal of Photography* (England), 129 no. 13 (26 March 1982) 334–335.

On the misattribution of 19th-century photographs, intentional and unintentional. The author concludes that the monetary value of these photographs is in the name of the photographer and not in the aesthetic quality of the images.

1204

Lifson, B. and Solomon-Godeau, A. Photophilia: a conversation about the photography scene. *October* (USA), no. 16 (Spring 1981) 103–118, 4 illus.

English abstract in ABM vol. 13 (1982) #3031.

1205

Osman, Colin. Connoisseur person-ship. *Creative Camera* (England), no. 199 (July 1981) 155.

A letter to the editor regarding Isabelle Anscombe's article "Daylight robbery?"

1206

Poli, Kenneth. Critical focus: collect photographs? Even if you weren't born yesterday you may buy an "old" image that was. *Popular Photography* (USA), 84 no. 3 (March 1979) 6, 222, 2 photos.

1207

Taylor, John Russell. Pictoral photography in the First World War. *History of Photography* (England) 6 no. 2 (April 1982) 119–141, 25 illus.

English abstract in RILA vol. 9 (1983) #2531.

Maps

Books

1208

Skelton, R.A.; Marston, Thomas E.; and Painter, George D. *The Vinland Map and the Tartar Relation*. With a foreword by Alexander O. Vietor. New Haven and London: Yale University Press, 1965, 291 p., illus., index.

Contents: Foreword. By Alexander O. Vietor. List of illustrations and maps; 1. The manuscript: history and description. By Thomas E. Marston. 2. Facsimilies of the Vinland Map and the Tartar Relation. 3. The Tartar Relation. Edited, with Introduction, Translation, and Commentary, by George D. Painter. 4. The Vinland Map. By R.A. Skelton. 5. The Tartar Relation and the Vinland Map: an interpretation. By George Painter. Bibliography (pp.263–269). Indexes, I. General index, II. Proper names in the Latin text of the Tartar Relation, III. Mogol and other non-Latin words in the Tartar Relation (text and commentary).

1209

Washburn, Wilcomb E. (editor). *Proceedings of the Vinland Map Conference*. Chicago, London: The University of Chicago Press, 1971, 185 p.

Contents: Preface by Wilcomb Washburn. Part 1. Provenance and the physical context: Vinland's saga recalled, by Laurence Witten; Is the Vinland Map genuine? By Armando Cortesão; Authenticity and provenance, by John Parker; The case is not settled, by Robert S. Lopez. Part 2. Cartography and the Historical Context: Some reflections on the origin of the Vinland Map, by Thomas E. Goldstein; The Vinland Map and the imperatives of medieval form, by Melvin H. Jackson; Claudius Clavus and the sources of the Vinland Map, by Ib Rønne Kejlbo; The representation of Greenland on the Vinland Map, by Paul Fenimore Cooper, Jr.; The Tartar Relation and the Vinland Map: their significance and character, by Boleslaw B. Szczesniak; The great sea of the Tartars and the adjacent islands, by Vsevolod Slessarev; Linguistic observations on the captions of the Vinland Map, by Konstantin Reichardt; Observations on the relationship between church history and the Vinland Map, by Stephan Kuttner; The companions Bjarni and Leif, by Erik Wahlgren; Bishop Eric and the Vinland Map, by Einar Haugen; A hypothesis for the Vinland Map, by Oystein Ore; Bibliography: 1. Scholarly literature (Arranged by author), pp. 155–172, 2. Popular literature (Arranged chronologically) pp. 173–182; List of participants.

Periodicals

1210

Dahl, Edward H. Facsimile maps and forgeries. *Archivaria* (Canada), no. 10 (Summer 1980) 261–263, 2 photos.

English abstract in AATA vol. 19 (1983) #19-261.

1211

Editorial [Observations with comments on the disclosure of the Vinland map forgery]. *Antiquity* (England), 48 no. 190 (June 1974) 81–82.

1212

Jensen, Oliver. Letter from the editor [The Vinland map forgery]. *American Heritage* (USA), 25 no. 4 (June 1974) 2.

1213

McCrone, Walter C. Authenticity of medieval document tested by small particle analysis. *Analytical Chemistry* (USA), 48 no. 8 (1976) 676A–679A.

Scientific tests conducted by McCrone Associates on the Vinland map. English abstract in AATA vol. 13 (1976) #13-872.

1214

Seifert, Traudl. De Vinlandkaart (The Vinland map). *Spiegel Historiael* (Netherlands), 10 no. 3 (1975) 138–144, illus.

1215

Unsigned article. Ink study suggests Vinland map fraud. *Chemical and Engineering News* (USA), 52 no. 6 (11 February 1974) 21, one halftone plate.

English abstract in AATA vol. 11 (1974) #11-838.

1216

Unsigned article. Microanatomy of a forgery. *Industrial Research* (USA), 16 (March 1974) 19–20.

The Vinland map forgery.

1217

Unsigned article. Tests show 'Vinland map' is forgery. *AB Bookman's Weekly* (USA), 53 (11 February 1974) 542 + .

1218

Unsigned article. Vinland map—a forgery. *Chemistry* (USA), 47 no. 4 (April 1974) 5, illus.

1219

Unsigned article. Yale university library reports that its researchers suggest that the famous Vinland map may be a forgery. *Feliciter* (Canada), 20 (March 1974) 25–26.

1220

Unsigned article. Yale's magnificent forgery. *American Libraries* (USA), 5 no. 4 (April 1974) 175, illus.

The Vinland Map.

Postage Stamps

Books

1221

Atlee, W. Dudley. *The spud papers: an illustrated descriptive catalog of early philatelic forgeries*, by W. Dudley Atlee, Edward L Pemberton, and Robert B. Earée. With an introductory essay and a comprehensive index by Lowell Ragatz. Lucerne: E. Bertrand, 195?, 188 p., illus.

1222

Early forged stamps detector, by Thornton Lewes, Edward Pemberton, and Thomas Dalston. New York, N.Y.: S.J. Durst, c1979, 36, 39 p. Reprint (1st work). Originally published: Edinburgh: printed by Colston, 1863. Reprint (2nd work). Originally published: Gateshead, England: R. Chambers, 1865. Contents: "Forged stamps, how to detect them," by Thornton Lewes and Edward Pemberton. "How to detect forged stamps," by Thomas Dalston.

1223

Fletcher, H.G. Leslie. *Postal forgeries of the world*. Batley: Harry Hayes, 1977, 137 p., illus., facsim. (Harry Hayes philatelic study, no. 26).

1224

Fournier, François. *The Fournier album of philatelic forgeries: a photographic composite for reference purposes*. Edited by Lowell Ragatz. Worthington, Ohio: J. van den Berg, 1970, 175 p., illus.

Contains the author's 1914 price-list of philatelic forgeries, and Album de fac-similés, first published about 1928.

1225

Grasset, Jacques. *Les timbres faux pour tromper la Poste de France*. Brussels, r. de Brabant 91: P. De Méyère, 1976, 134 p., illus., bibliography: p. 133–134.

1226

Hosang, Joachim. *Gezähnte Kriegspropaganda: Handbuch und Katalog der Spionage-und Propagandafälschungen*. Lorch, Württemberg, H.E. Sieger, 1954–1959, v. 4, 1957. 4 vols., illus., stamps.

1227

Karásek, Jan. *Forgeries of Czechoslovak postage stamps, 1918–1939*, by Jan Karasek, Zdenek Kvasnicka, and Bretislav Paulicek. Co-worker: Jan Mrnak. Photographic co-worker: Ferdinand Pertzela.

Translation by the Chicagoland Chapter of the Czechoslovak Philatelic Society, n.p., 1964, 1 vol.

1228

Lowe, Robson. *The Oswald Schröder forgeries.* London: Pall Mall Stamp Co. for Robson Lowe, 1981, 16 p., illus.

1229

Marinho, João Augusto. *Três comunicações: Variações sobre um tema filatelico, O mito dos "tête-bêche" da India Portuguesa e A falsidado do selo nativo de 900 reis.* Luanda: Instituto de Angola, 1972, 41 p., illus.

Summaries in French and English.

1230

Montseny, Monné, Antonio. *Las falsificaciones del sello español.* 1st ed. Barcelona: Ediciones Emeuve, 1968, 207, clxxii p., illus., facsims. (Estudios filatélicos "La Corneta").

1231

Negus, James. *Forgeries of China's "large dragons," 1878.* London: Cinderella Stamp Club, c1978, 14 p., illus. (Cinderella Stamp Club handbook, no. 3).

1232

Smythies, Evelyn Arthur. *B.N.A. fakes and forgeries.* Editor: R.J. Woolley. Thornhill, Ontario: J.F. Webb, 1971, 101 p., illus. (A handbook of the British North America Philatelic Society).

1233

Tyler, Varro E. *Philatelic forgers, their lives and works.* London: Lowe, 1976, iv, 60 p., facsims., ports., index.

1234

Williams, Leon Norman. *Forged stamps of two World Wars: the postal forgeries and propaganda issues for the belligerents, 1914–1918, 1939–1945.* London, 1954, 52 p., illus.

1235

The Yucatan affair: the work of Raoul Ch. de Thuin, philatelic counterfeiter. James M. Chemi, editor-in-chief, James H. Beal and James T. DeVoss, associate editors; detailed and compiled through the assistance of an outstanding specialist editorial staff. Unabridged edition. State College, Pa.: American Philatelic Society, c1974, 523 p., illus. (A.P.S. handbook series).

Periodicals

1236

Frisch, H. Das Isotopenverfahren in der Urkundenprüfung (Isotopes in documentary proof). Landeskriminalamt Berlin. *Archiv für Kriminologie* (Germany) 131 no.s 1–2 (1963) 22–36, 12 illus.

The use of isotopes to detect alterations in stamps.

1237

Herst Jr., Herman. Dealing with counterfeit stamps. *Hobbies* (USA), 86 (May 1981) 116–117.

On the three most infamous stamp forgers: Fournier, Sperati and de Thuin.

1238

Nogéus, Gunilla. Zeiss UV-Sonnar f. 4.3/105mm lens for the Hasselblad 500 C and 500 EL. *Hasselblad* (Published by Evabl Karlsten, Goteberg, Sweden), no. 2 (1970) 19–22.

English abstract in AATA vol. 8 (1970–1971) #8-1609.

On the use of a special lens which, among other uses, could be utilized to detect stamp forgeries.

1239

Rogers, Sherman E. Philatelomania. *Stamps* (USA), 201 (16 October 1982) 133.

Brief article on stamp forger Jean de Sperati.

1240

Tyler, Varro E., and Peck, Garnet E. Characterizations of the genuine stamps, reprints and forgeries of the 1867 and 1868 issues of Roman States by diffuse reflectance spectroscopy. *The American Philatelist* (USA), 92 no. 6 (June 1978) 580–586, 7 illus., 47 figs., 1 table.

English abstract in AATA vol. 15 (1978) #15-1272.

1241

Unsigned article. Charles D. Rehwinkel. *Data* (Italy), vol. 4 no. 11 (Spring 1974) 72, 3 illus. In Italian.

On Charles D. Rehwinkel, stamp forger.
English abstract in ABM vol. 6 (1975) #6373.

1242

Unsigned article. APRL seminar to explore forgeries. *Stamps* (USA), 188 (14 July 1979) 71 + .

Diptych

Periodicals

1243

LaFontaine Dosogne, J. Le *Diptychon Leodiense* du consul Anastase (Constantinople, 517) et le faux des Musées Royaux d'Art et d'Histoire à Bruxelles (The Diptychon Leodiense of Consul Anastase (Constantinople, 517) and the fake in the Brussels Musees Royaux d'Art et d'Histoire (Cinquantenaire)). *Revue Belge d'Archéologie et d'Histoire de l'Art* (Belgium), 49 no. 2 (1980–1981) 5–19, 10 illus.

English abstract in AATA vol. 21 (1984) #21-2336.

1244

Lauant, A. Identification d'un mystérieux insigne de pèlerinage échoué à Hautrage (Identification of a mysterious insignia of a stranded pilgrimage at Hautrage). *Mémoires et Publications de la Société des Sciences, des Arts et des Lettres du Hainaut* (Belgium), 90 (1979) 9–19, 2 plates.

Tapestry

Periodicals

1245

Wie alt und wie echt? Ueber die Alters-und Echtheitsbestimmung von Teppichen. Ein interessantes Kapitel aus dem neuen Ullstein-Teppichbuch von Reinhard Hubel (How old and how genuine? On determining the age and authenticity of tapestry. An interesting chapter on the new Ullstein-Tapestry of Reinhard Hubel). *Artis* (Germany), no. 9 (1966) 31–34, 3 illus.

Mosaic

Periodicals

1246

Börker, C. Zum Blumenkorb-Mosaik im Vatikan (Concerning the flower-basket mosaic in the Vatican). *Archäeologischer Anzeiger* (Germany), no. 3 (1978) 442–448, 2 illus.

French abstract in RAA 1980 #9351.

Miniatures

Periodicals

1247

Amar, S.S. Divagazioni su un falso. *Studi piemontesi* (Italy), 4 no. 1 (1975) 123–124, 1 plate.

French abstract in RAA 1975 #12837.

1248

Selinova, T. Iskusnaja poddelka (A clever imitation). *Hudožnik* (USSR), 15 no. 3 (1973) 45–46, 2 illus.

A forged miniature portrait of A. Pouchkine, signed A. Linev, 1834. The miniature is in the Historic Museum, Moscow.

French abstract in RAA 1974 #6912.

1249

Vikan, Gary. A group of forged Byzantine miniatures. *Aachener Kunstblätter* (Germany), 48 (1978–1979) 53–70, 37 illus.

Byzantine manuscripts and single leaves with 20th-century forged miniatures from Greek icon painter Demetrios Pelekasis.

English abstracts in RILA vol. 10 (1984) #783 and AATA vol. 22 (1985) #22-1798.

French abstract in RAA 1982 #4447.

1250

Wieck, R.S. A late medieval miniature in the Houghton Library. *Harvard Library Bulletin* (USA), 29 no. 2 (1981) 212–214, 1 illus.

French abstract in RAA 1982 #1247.

Netsuke

Sections of Books

1251

Bushell, Raymond. *Collector's netsuke.* New York & Tokyo: Walker/Weatherhill, 1971, 1st edition, pp. 16–17, 21–24, 44–47, 115, 119, illus., bibliog., index.

1252

O'Brien, Mary Louise. *Netsuke: a guide for collectors.* Rutland, Vermont & Tokyo, Japan: Charles E. Tuttle Company, 1965, pp. 120, 148, 152–153, 164.

Cameos

1253

Rosenberg, Pierre. On the origins of a cameo at Versailles. *Burlington Magazine* (England), 119 no. 893 (August 1977) 570–573, illus.

1254

Rosenberg, Pierre. On the origins of a cameo at Versailles, part II: a fake. *Burlington Magazine* (England), 123 no. 945 (December 1981) 747–748.

English abstract in RILA vol. 9 (1983) #5922.
French abstract in RAA 1982 #5441.

Book Bindings and Bookplates

Books

1255

Helwig, Hellmuth. Einbandfälschungen (Binding forgeries). Stuttgart: Hettler, 1968, 98 p., illus.

Sections of Books

1256

Nixon, H.M. Binding forgeries. *International Kongress Bibliophilen*, 6th, (Vienna 1969), Austria, 1971, pp. 69–83.

Summaries in French and German.

Periodicals

1257

Lee, B. North. Authenticity of bookplates. *Book Collector* (England), 30 (Spring 1981) 62–73.

1258

Lee, B. North. A problem for the bookplate collector. *Private Library* (England), 6 no. 3 (Autumn 1973) 123–132, 5 illus.

English abstract in ABM vol. 7 (1976) #1307.

1259

Pollard, Graham. Changes in style of bookbinding, 1550–1830. *The Library* (England), 11 no. 2 (1956) 71–94.

English abstract in AATA vol. 4 (1962–1963) 3679.

1260

Swarzenski, H. The niello cover of the Gospelbook of the Sainte-Chapelle and the limits of stylistic criticism and interpretation of literary sources. *Gesta* (USA), 20 no. 1 (1981) 207–212, 4 illus. (Essays in honor of Harry Bober).

French abstract in RAA 1981 #11638.

1261

Unterkircher, Franz. F. Steenbock: Der kirchliche Prachteinband im frühen Mittelalter. Von den Anfängen bis zum Beginn der Gotik (F. Steenbock: ornamented church volumes in the early middle ages. From the beginning to the start of the gothic period). *Österreichische Zeitschrift für Kunst und Denkmalpflege* (Austria), 21 (1967) 61–62.

Music and Musical Instruments

See also Literary—Manuscripts, Letters, and Documents (Periodicals) for the forged letters of Chopin, Verdi and Berlioz; Sale Stamps and Certificates of Authenticity (Periodicals) #1289, #1291, and Law (Periodicals) #1659.

Books

1262

Ripin, Edwin M. *The instrument catalogs of Leopoldo Franciolini.* Hackensack, New Jersey: N.J. Boonin, Inc., 1974, 210 p., illus. On the musical instrument forger Leopoldo Franciolini. Besides reproducing Franciolini's instrument catalogs, contents of Ripin's book includes: Photographs of instruments listed in catalog #6; Other photographs; Drawings; Notes on the photographs and drawings; Instrument labels from Franciolini's shop; Note on the indexes; Index of names; Index of instruments; Appendix I: Franciolini's trial; Appendix IIL: A selling trip made by Franciolini's son.

Periodicals

1263

Blankenhorn, V.S. Traditional and bogus elements in 'MacCrimmon's Lament.' *Scottish Studies* 22 (1978) 45–67, illus.

1264

Block, Steven D. George Rochberg: progressive or master forger? *Perspectives of New Music* (USA), 21 nos. 1–2 (1982–1983) 407–409.

1265

Cudworth, Charles L. Notes on the instrumental works attributed to Pergolesi. *Music and Letters* (England), 30 no. 4 (Oct. 1949) 321–328.

1266

Cudworth, Charles L. Ye olde spuriousity shoppe; or, put it in the Anhang. *Notes* (USA), 12 no. 1 (Dec. 1954) 25–40; 12 no. 4 (Sept. 1955) 533–553.

A two part article on spurious musical works. Cudworth divides spuriousities into three groups, each of which is subdivided: Group 1. spuriousities traceable to composers; Group 2. spuriousities traceable to publishers; Group 3. spuriousities traceable to editors and musicologists. The second article consists of a listing of composers and spuriousities. The articles are confined to classical music from around 1600 to 1900.

1267

Degrada, F. Alcuni falsi autografi Pergolesiani: *Rivista italiana di Musicologia* (Italy), 1 no. 1 (1966) 32–48, illus.

1268

Germann, Sheridan. 'Mrs Crawley's Couchet' reconsidered. *Early Music* (England) 7 no. 4 (October 1979) 473–481.

1269

Howell, Standley. Beethoven's Maelzel canon—another Schindler forgery? *The Musical Times* (England), 122 no. 1642 (December 1979), 987–990.

1270

Jahr, Dan. Instrument forgers—yesterday and today. *Folk Harp Journal* (USA), no. 44 (March 1984) 45, 47.

1271

Lewin, Robert. The art of deception. *The Strad* (England), 8 (June 1969) 57, 59, 61, 63.

On violin forgeries.

1272

Lewin, Robert. Problems of authenticity. *The Strad* (England), 91 no. 1092 (April 1981) 887–888.

On violin forgeries.

1273

Lewin, Robert. Tricks of the trade. *The Strad* (England), 80 (April 1970) 555 + .

On violin forgeries.

1274

Newman, William S. Ravenscroft and Corelli. *Music and Letters* (England), 38 no. 4 (October 1957) 369–370.

1275

Newman, William S. Yet another Beethoven forgery by Schindler? *Journal of Musicology* (USA), 3 no. 4 (Fall 1984) 397–422.

1276

Piper, Towry. The gentle art of fiddle-faking. *The Strad* (England), 84 (February 1974) 629, 631, 633.

1277

Ripin, Edwin M. A suspicious spinet. *Metropolitan Museum of Art Bulletin* (USA), 30 (1971–1972) 196–202, 8 illus.

1278

Sheppard, Leslie. The "Balfour" Strad. *The Strad* (England), 91 no. 1089 (January 1981) 644–647, illus.

1279

Sturt-Penrose, Barrie. Salerooms. *Art and Artists* (England), 4 no. 6 (September 1969) 8, 1 illus.

On fake Stradivari violins.

1280

Walker, Frank. Two centuries of Pergolesi forgeries and misattributions. *Music and Letters* (England), 30 no. 4 (October 1949) 297–320.

Scientific Instruments

Sections of Books

1281

Mills, John FitzMaurice. "Forgery and fakes," in his *Encyclopedia of antique scientific instruments*. New York: Facts on File Publications, 1983, pp. 245–248.

Periodicals

1282

Gingerich, Owen; King, David; and Saliba, George. The 'Abd al-A'imma astrolabe forgeries. *Journal for the History of Astronomy* (England), 3 (1972) 188–198.

1283

Gingerich, Owen. Astronomical scrapbook: fake astrolabes. *Sky and Telescope* (USA), 63 no. 5 (May 1982) 465–468, 6 illus.

1284

Horský, Zdeněk. Falsa mezi historickými vědeckými přistroji (Forgeries among ancient scientific instruments). *Muzejní a vlastivědní Práce* (Czechoslovakia), 6 (1968) 78–84, 4 illus.

Postcards

Periodicals

1285

Ripley, John W. The art of postcard fakery. *Kansas Historical Quarterly* (USA), 38 no. 2 (1972) 129–131, illus.

On fake color postcards of the early 20th century, created by German lithographers touring the United States.
English abstract in ABM vol. 8 (1977) #6464.

Papier Mâché

Periodicals

1286

Booth-Jones, T. Papier mâché. *Antique Collector* (England), 53 no. 2 (February 1982) 52–55, 19 illus.
English abstract in ABM vol. 14 (1983) #7087.

Sale Stamps and Certificates of Authenticity

See also Law (Periodicals) #1677.

Periodicals

1287
Duthy, Robin. Fiddling on a grand scale. *Connoisseur* (England), 212 no. 848 (October 1982), 124, 126, 128, 130, illus.

The prices for fine violins have risen between 500 and 1,000 percent since 1970. The demand for fine violins outstrips the supply. In Japan forgers have taken advantage of the situation by forging violin certificates (e.g. "the Kanada scandal"). An example of a forged William E. Hill & Sons certificate is given. The Japanese forgers were betrayed by their faulty American spelling and pidgin English.

1288
Johnson, Lee. Pierre Andrieu, un "polisson"? (Pierre Andrieu, a "rascal"?). *Revue de l'Art* (France), no. 21 (1973) 66–69. Summary in English.

On the illegitimate use of the Delacroix sale stamp by Pierre Andrieu and reattribution of several works from Delacroix to Andrieu.

1289
Lewin, Robert. Artful dodger. *The Strad* (England), 95 no. 1135 (December 1984) 608–609, illus.

Lewin discusses the history of forged violin certificates, the current problem, and offers tips on how to detect forgeries.

1290
Pauwels, H. Enquête betreffende adviesverleningen en echtheidsverklaringen door Musea en Museumpersoneel ten behoeve van particulieren. *Museumleven* (Belgium), 1 (1974) 5–12. Summary in English.

(Investigation concerning the appraisals and certificate of authenticity delivered to private persons by the museums and by their personnel.)

1291
Unsigned article. Forged certificates. *The Strad* (England), 93 no. 1107 (July 1982) 178, 1 illus.

The problem of forged certificates of musical instruments in Japan.

1292
Wintersgill, Donald. Faked credentials for 'antiques' cause a stir. *ARTnews* (USA), 72 no. 6 (Summer 1973) 91.

Media

1293

Niggemeyer, Hanneliese. Tontrager als Historische Quellen. Moglichkeiten ihrer manipulation, Verfälschung und Fälschung und deren Erkennbarkeit (Tapes and sound records as historical sources: the possibilities of manipulation, adulteration, and forgery and their perception). Archivar (Germany), 28 no. 3 (1975) 291–302.

Computer Art

Periodicals

1294

Biship, Bobbie. Art forgery and the computer. *School Arts* (USA), 85 no. 7 (March 1986) 22–24, illus.

Intended for the elementary school art teacher, this article promotes artistic creativity in students using microcomputers by encouraging them to copy or "forge" the works of popular artists, such as Mondrian, whose works can be simulated by computer technology.

Technical

Books

1295

Fleming, Stuart J. *Authenticity in art: the scientific detection of forgery.* Foreword by S.A. Goudsmit, London, Bristol: Institute of Physics, 1975; New York: Crane, Russack, 1976, XII + 164 p., illus. (color), bibliog., index.

English abstract in ABM vol. 8 (1977) #1434 and RILA vol. 2 (1976) #3844.

Sections of Books

1296

Barker, Harold. "Scientific criteria in the authentication of antiquities," in *Application of science in examination of works of art,* edited by William J. Young. Proceedings of the Seminar, June 15–19, 1970. Museum of Fine Arts, Boston, 1973, pp. 187–192.

English abstract in AATA vol. 11 (1974) #11-412.

1297

Barnard, Noel. "The special character of metallurgy in ancient China," in *Application of science in examination of works of art*, Proceedings of the Seminar, September 7–16, 1965, Museum of Fine Arts, Boston, Massachusetts, 1967, pp. 184–204. Maps and illustrations.

English abstract in AATA vol. 15 (1978) #15-1637.

1298

Buehler, M. "Méthodes de détection de faux," in *International Council of Museums. Quatrième conference générale de l'ICOM* (Bâle, Berne, Zurich, Schaffhouse, Neuchâtel, Geneve, 2–9 juillet, 1956). Paris, 1958, pp. 136–137.

1299

Daniels, Vincent D. "A photographic method for detecting the oxidation of materials", in *ICOM Committee for Conservation, 7th Triennial Meeting*. Copenhagen, 10–14 September 1984, Preprints. Working Group: New Applications of Methods of Examination, vol. I, pp. 84.1.51–84.1.53. 3 b&w photos, 6 refs.

English abstract in AATA vol. 21 (1984) #21-1231.

1300

Fleming, Stuart J. "A evaluation of physico-chemical approaches to authentication," in *Authentication in the visual arts: a multi-disciplinary symposium*. Amsterdam, 12th March 1977, pp. 103–139, 16 illus., diags.

English abstract in RILA vol. 8 (1982) #5041.

1301

Keisch, Bernard. "Nuclear applications at the National Gallery of Art Research Project: seven years of progress," in *Applicazione dei metodi nucleari nel campo delle opere d'arte*. Congresso internazionale, Roma-Venezia, 24–29 Maggio 1973 (Applications of nuclear methods in the field of works of art. International congress, Rome-Venice, 24–29, May 1973). Accadamia Nazionale Dei Lincei, Rome, 1976, pp. 359–379, 14 illus, 11 refs.

English abstract in AATA vol. 14 (1977) #14-691.

1302

Perlman, Isadore; Asaro, Frank; and Michel, Helen V. "Nuclear applications in art and technology," in *Annual Review of Nuclear Science* (U.S.A.), 22 (1972) 383–426.

English abstract in AATA vol. 10 (1973) #10-43.

1303

Riederer, Josef. "Die naturwissenschaftliche Echtheitspruefung von Kunstwerken" (The scientific examination of the authenticity of works of art), in *Jahrbuch Preuss. Kulturbesitz* (Germany), 16 (1981) 73–82, 4 photos.

English abstract in AATA vol. 18 (1981) #18-878.

1304
Vana, Norbert. "Der derzeitige Stand der Thermolumineszenz-Datierung" (The present state of thermoluminescent dating), in *Wiener Berichte ueber Naturwissenschaft in der Kunst*, vol. 1, edited by Alfred Vendl and Bernhard Pichler, pp. 49–57, 2 illus., 23 refs. Summary in English.

English abstract in AATA vol. 22 (1985) #22-57.

1305
Young, William J. "Examination of works of art embracing the various fields of science," in *Application of science in examination of works of art*. Proceedings of the Seminar, September 15–18, 1958, Museum of Fine Arts, Boston, Massachusetts, 1959, pp. 17–30.

English abstract in AATA vol. 15 (1978) #15-1053.

Periodicals

1306
Bleck, Rolf-Dieter. Archäologische Chemie—Chemie im Dienste der Urgeschichtsforschung (Archaeological chemistry in the service of prehistory). *Alt-Thüringen* (Germany), 8 (1966) 7–19.

English abstract in AATA vol. 8 (1970–1971) #8-1689.

1307
Borrelli Vlad, Licia. Sul carattere du autenticità di alcuni graffiti. *Bollettino dell' Istituto Centrale del Restauro* (Italy), 13 (1953) 47–59.

English abstract in AATA vol. 1 (1955–1957) #958.

1308
Brandone, A.; Oddone, M.; Riganti, V.; and Saletti, C. Use of instrumental techniques for studying archaeological relics. *Rassegna Chimica* (Italy), 34 no. 1 (1982) 3–9. [In Italian].

English abstract in AATA vol. 20 (1983) #20-173.

1309
Daniels, Vincent D. The Russell Effect—a review of its possible uses in conservation and the scientific examination of materials. *Studies in Conservation* (England), 29 no. 2 (1984) 57–62.

English abstract in AATA vol. 21 (1984) #21-1232.

1310
Dornberg, John. Artists who fake fine art have met their match—in the laboratory. *Smithsonian* (USA), 16 no. 7 (October 1985) 60–69, illus.

On Josef Riederer and his work at the Rathgen Research Laboratory, at Berlin's State Museums of Prussian Cultural Property.

1311

Fleming, Stuart J. Art forgery: III, beyond the eye. *National Antiques Review,* 8 no. 2 (August 1976) 26–28, 6 illus.

English abstract in AATA vol. 15 (1978) #15-144.

1312

Fleming, Stuart J. Faking the past: science attacks the forger. *Museum of Applied Science Center for Archaeology Journal* (U.S.A.), 1 no. 1 (December 1979) 24–26.

1313

Fleming, Stuart J. Freewheeling in fakes. *Archaeology* (U.S.A.), 35 no. 2 (March–April 1982) 74–75.

English abstract in AATA vol. 19 (1982) #19-553.

1314

Fleming, Stuart J. Science detects the forgeries. *New Scientist* (England), 68 no. 978 (1975) 567–569.

1315

Frankel, Richard. Detection of art forgeries by x-ray fluorescence spectroscopy. *Isotopes and Radiation Technology* (U.S.A.), 8 no. 1 (1970) 65–68.

English abstract in AATA vol. 8 (1970–1971) #8-1627.

1316

Frisch, Bruce. How science uncovers art fakes. *Science Digest* (U.S.A.), 62 no. 2 (August 1967) 6–11, illus.

1317

Gairola, T.R. Fakes in bronzes and paintings. *Roopa-Lekhá* (India), 27 no. 2 (1956) 37–41.

English abstract in AATA vol. 5 (1964–1965) #4475.

1318

Gillespie, R.; Gowlett, J.A.J.; Hall, E.T.; and Hedges, R.E.M. Radiocarbon measurement by accelerator mass spectrometry: an early selection of dates. *Archaeometry* (England), 26 no. 1 (February 1984) 15–20, appendix, 12 refs.

English abstract in AATA vol. 21 (1984) #21-1245.

1319

Grenberg, Y.I. Scientific technical examination of works of art. *Soobscenija WCNILKR* (U.S.S.R.), no. 21 (1968) 3–26. [In Russian. Summary in English].

English abstract in AATA vol. 8 (1970–1971) #8-59.

1320

Hanson, Victor F. Quantitative elemental analysis of art objects by energy-dispersive, x-ray fluorescence spectroscopy. *Applied Spectroscopy* (U.S.A.), 27 no. 5 (September 1973) 309–333.

English abstract in AATA vol. 11 (1974) #11-14.

1321

Harbottle, G. Activation analysis in archaeology. *Radiochemistry* (England), 3 (1976) 33-72.

English abstract in AATA vol. 14 (1977) #14-689.

1322

Harper, Mr. After hours: bitter pill. *Harper's Magazine* (U.S.A.), 210 (May 1955), 80–82.

On Dr. Paul Coremans, his work at the Laboratoire Centrale des Musées Belgique, and the lawsuit filed against him by the Dutch collector, Mr. van Beuningen, for his publication of a Vermeer (*Last Supper*) as a forgery.

1323

Herz, Norman, and Wenner, David B. Tracing the origins of marble. *Archaeology* (U.S.A.), 34 no. 5 (September–October 1981) 14–21.

English abstract in AATA vol. 18 (1981) #18-1566.

1324

Johnson, Ben, B., and Cairns, Thomas. Report for analytical chemists. Art conservation: culture under analysis. Part II. *Analytical Chemistry* (U.S.A.), 44 no. 2 (1972) 30A–38A.

Contains a brief section on authentication methods.
English abstract in AATA vol. 9 (1972) #9-492.

1325

Keisch, Bernard, and Miller, H.H. Recent art forgeries: detection by carbon-14 measurements. *Nature* (England), 240 no. 5382 (22 December 1972) 491–492.

English abstract in AATA vol. 10 (1973) #10-561.

1326

Komarik, Dénes. A müemlékek tudományos kutatása és a Velencei Karta (The scientific examination of monuments and the Charter of Venice). *Müemlékvédelem* (Hungary), 28 no. 4 (1984) 275–278.

English abstract in AATA vol. 22 (1985) #22-1485.

1327

Kowalski, H. Nuclear radiation exposes art forgers and coin counterfeiters. *Euro Spectra-Scientific and Technical Review of the European Communities* (Belgium), 2 no. 2 (June 1972) 47–55.

English abstract in AATA vol. 9 (1972) #9-458.

1328

Lyon, Marjorie. Pairing physics and archaeology into new insights on ancient materials. *Technology Review* (U.S.A.), 83 no. 6 (May–June 1981) A4–A5, 1 photo.

English abstract in AATA vol. 18 (1981) #18-1415.

1329

Oddy, W.A. Is it fake? Spectroscopy in the authentication of metallic antiquities. *European Spectroscopy News* (England), no. 34 (1981) 31–34.

English abstract in AATA vol. 18 (1981) #18-710.

1330

Partington, J.R. History of alchemy and early chemistry. *Nature* (England), 159 (1947) 81–85.

English abstract in G&U #30.

1331

Riederer, Josef. Die chemische Analyse in der kulturgeschichtlichen Forschung (Chemical analysis for historical research). *Fresenius Zeitschrift fuer Analytische Chemie* (USA), 1984, pp. 300–303.

English abstract in AATA vol. 22 (1985) #22-90.

1332

Riederer, Josef. Die Echtheitspruefung von Kunstwerken am Rathgen-Forschungslabor (Authenticity testing at the Rathgen Research Laboratory). *Kunst und Faelschung* (Germany), no. 1 (1979) 24–32, 5 photos.

English abstract in AATA vol. 16 (1979) #16-1062.

1333

Riederer, Josef. Die Echtheitsprüfung von Kunstwerken mit naturwissenschaftlichen Methoden (Authenticity testing by scientific methods). *Der Sachverständige* no. 7–8 (1984) 166–168, 5 photos.

English abstract in AATA vol. 22 (1985) #22–1382.

1334

Riederer, Josef. Die Erkennung von Faelschungen kunst und kulturgeschichtlicher Objekte aus Kupfer, Bronze und Messing durch naturwissenschaftliche Untersuchungen (The detection of forgeries of art objects of copper, bronze and brass by scientific analysis). *Berlinger Beitraege zur Archaeometrie* (Germany), 2 (1977) 85–95.

English abstract in AATA vol. 15 (1978) #15-1718.
French abstract in RAA 1980 #7356.

1335

Riederer, Josef. Die Erkennung von Fälschungen mit naturwissenschaftlichen Methoden (The identification of forgeries with scientific techniques). *Katalog Fälschung und Forschung* (Germany), 1976, pp. 187–199.

English abstract in AATA vol. 14 (1977) #14-57.

1336

Riederer, Josef. Fälschungen von Marmor-Idolen und Gafässen der Kykladenkultur (Forgeries of marble idols and vessels of the cycladic culture). *Kunst der Kykladen* (Germany), 94 (1976) 94–96.

English abstract in AATA vol. 13 (1976) #13-1149.

1337

Riederer, Josef. Die Untersuchung Von Kunstwerken mit Mineralogischen Methoden (The examination of art objects by mineralogical methods). *Atti Della XLIX Riunione Della S.I.P.S.* (Italy), September 1967, pp. 1133–1140.

English abstract in AATA vol. 8 (1970–1971) #8-29.

1338

Riederer, Josef. Die Untersuchung von Sinter und Patina zur Echtheitspruefung antiker Bodenfunde (The examination of sinter and patina to check the authenticity of antiquities). *Archäeologisher Anzeiger* (Germany), no. 2 (1975) 295–299.

English abstract in AATA vol. 12 (1975) #12-1181.

1339

Riederer, Josef. Die Tricks der Faelscher (The tricks of forgers). *Bild der Wissenschaft* (Germany), 15 no. 11 (1978) 70–81, 14 photos.

English abstract in AATA vol. 17 (1980) #17-896.

1340

Riederer, Josef. Naturwissenschaft entlarvt Fälschungen (Science detects forgeries). *Weltkunst* (Germany), 47 no. 3 (1977) 124–125.

English abstract in AATA vol. 14 (1977) #14-700.

1341

Rosen, David. Photomicrographs as aids in the study of decorative arts. *Walters Art Gallery Journal* (USA), 15–16, Special Technical Issue (1952–1953) 80–96, illus.

1342

Rowlett, Ralph M.; Manderville, Margaret D.; and Zeller, Edward J. The interpretation and dating of humanly worked siliceous materials by thermoluminescent analysis. *Proceedings of the Prehistoric Society* (England), 40 (1974) 37–44.

English abstract in AATA vol. 12 (1975) #12-1186.

1343

Schur, Susan E. Laboratory profile: the Boston Museum of Fine Arts Research Laboratory. *Technology and Conservation of Art, Architecture, and Antiquities* (USA), 77 no. 2 (Summer 1977) 14–37.

English abstract in AATA vol. 14 (1977) #14-752.

1344

Ślesiński, Marek K. Metody fałszowania przedmiotow z metali (Techniques of forging metal objects). *Ochrona Zabytków* (Poland), 35 no. 3–4 (1982) 187–192. Summary in English.

An excerpt from the author's thesis entitled *Techniques of forging: the works of art made of metal and methods of their identification.*

English abstract in AATA vol. 22 (1985) #22-1106.

1345

Strauss, Irmgard. Uebersicht ueber synthetisch organische Kuenstlerpigmente und Moeglichkeiten ihrer Identifizierung (A survey of synthetic organic artists' pigments and their possible identification). *Maltechnik-Restauro* (Germany), Jahrgang 90 no. 4 (1984) 29–44, 9 tables.

English abstract in AATA vol. 22 (1985) #22-650.

1346

Stross, Fred H. Authentication of antique stone objects by physical and chemical methods. *Analytical Chemistry* (USA), 32 (1960) 17A–36A.

English abstract in AATA vol. 3 (1960–1961) #3089.

1347

Unsigned Article. Art frauds beware. *Popular Mechanics* (USA), 158 no. 5 (Nov. 1982) 149, illus.

Brief article on the use of the cyclotron at the University of California, Davis (Crocker Nuclear Laboratory) in authenticating antiquities and art objects, and detecting forgeries.

1348

Unsigned Article. Atoms for detection. *Time* (USA), 91 (5 April 1968) 87.

Thermoluminescence testing and "atomic fingerprinting" of paintings by old masters.

1349

Unsigned Article. Fakes from Father Christmas. *Economist* (England), 269 (23 December 1978) 83–85, illus.

Survey article on the latest scientific methods used to detect forgeries.

1350

Unsigned Article. New technique exposes fake lacquer. *New Scientist* (England), 98 no. 1354 (21 April 1983) 149.

English abstract in AATA vol. 20 (1983) #20-2244.

1351

Unsigned Article. The lady is a phony. *Technology Review* (USA), April 1960, pp. 25–28, 52.

General article on methods of identifying forgeries at the Research Laboratory of the Boston Museum of Fine Arts.

1352

Werner, O. Analysen mittelalterlicher Bronzen und Messinge (Analysis of medieval bronzes and brasses). *Berliner Beitraege zur Archaeometrie* (Germany), 7 (1982) 24–93.

English abstract in AATA vol. 20 (1983) #20-1098.

1353

Werner, O. Zusammensetzung neuzeitlicher Nachguesse und Faelschungen mittelalterlicher Messinge und Bronzen (Composition of modern copies or forgeries of brasses and bronzes from the middle ages). *Berliner Beitraege zur Archaeometrie* (Germany), no. 5 (1980) 11–35, 2 illus., 21 refs.

English abstract in AATA vol. 19 (1982) #19-740.
French abstract in RAA 1982 #10969.

1354

Woods, William W. The quantitative analysis of soil phosphate. *American Antiquity* (USA), 42 no. 2 (April 1977) 248–252.

English abstract in AATA vol. 14 (1977) #14-818.

1355

Zimmerman, David W. Thermoluminescence: a dating and authenticating method for art objects. *Technology and Conservation* (USA), 3 no. 1 (1978) 32–37.

English abstract in AATA vol. 15 (1978) #15-1054.

Architecture

Periodicals

1356

Bresc-Bautier, Geneviève. Un 'faux' du XIXe siècle: le plan du Saint-Sépulcre de l'abbatiale de Saint-Denis (A 'fake' of the 19th century: the plan of the Church of the Holy Sepulchre from the abbey of Saint-Denis). *Bullentin monumental* (France), 140 no. 3 (1982) 197–201, 3 illus., plans, elevations.

English abstract in RILA vol. 11 (1985) #452.

Patents

1357

Davies, R.A. Method of producing a simulated oil painting. British patent #1,517,515, 2 p.

English abstract in AATA vol. 17 (1980) #17-529.

1358

International Art Registry (U.K.) Ltd. (Inventors: Chapman, Michael J.; and Gerrard, Martin J.). Improvements in or relating to the authentication of works of art. British patent #1,357,734, 3 p., 2 p. illus. English abstract in AATA vol. 12 (1975) #12-1001.

Literary

See also Law (Periodicals) #1702.

(A) *Literature*

Books

1359

Brox, Norbert. *Falsche Verfasserangaben: zur Erklärung der frühchristlichen Pseudepigraphie* (Forged authorship: clarifying the early Christian pseudoepigraphica). Stuttgart: KBW Verlag, c1975, 132 p., bibliography (pp. 131–132). (Stuttgarter Bibelstudien; 79).

1360

Chambers, Sir Edmund Kerchever. *The history and motives of literary forgeries: being the Chancellor's English essay for 1891.* Norwood, PA: Norwood Editions, 1977, 37 p. Reprint of 1891 edition. Includes bibliographical references.

1361

Ehrsam, Theodore George. *Major George Gordon Byron and his Shelley, Byron, and Keats forgeries.* Dissertation Abstracts International, SO14, sec. 6 (New York University), Ph.D., 1948, 193 p. University Microfilms order number ADG73-17845.

1362

Ehrsam, Theodore George. *Major Byron: The incredible career of a literary forger.* New York: Charles S. Boesen; London: John Murray, 1951, 217 p., illus.

1363

Farrer, James Anson. *Literary forgeries.* With an introduction by Andrew Lang. London, New York: Longmans, Green, 1907. Reprinted. Detroit: Gale Research Co., 1969, xxvi, 282 p.

1364

Ganzel, Dewey. *Fortune and men's eyes: the career of John Payne Collier.* Oxford: Oxford University Press, 1982, x, 454 p.

For a review of Ganzel's book, see Arthur Freeman's *"A new victim for the old corrector," Times Literary Supplement,* (England), 22 April 1983, pp. 391–393, illus.

1365

Goodspeed, Edgar Johnson. *Modern apocrypha.* Boston: Beacon Press, 1956, 124 p., illus.

On forged modern Christian writings.

1366

Grebanier, Bernard. *The great Shakespeare forgery: a new look at the career of William Henry Ireland.* Norwood, PA: Telegraph Books, 1983, 308 p. Reprint of 1966 edition.

1367

Hamilton, Charles. *Scribblers & scoundrels.* Introduction by Diane Hamilton. New York: P.S. Eriksson, 1968, viii, 282 p., illus.

1368

Ingleby, Clement Mansfield. *A complete view of the Shakespeare controversy concerning the genuineness of manuscript matter affecting the works and biography of Shakespeare.* London: Nattali and Bond, 1861, xvi, 350 p. xviii facsims. "The bibliography of the Shakespeare controversy": pp. 339–348.

1369

Irving, Clifford. *The hoax.* Sagaponack, N.Y.: Permanent Press, 1981, vi, 378 p. Originally published as: *Clifford Irving: what really happened.* 1972.

1370

Kaiser, Bruno. *Der gefälschte Don Quijote: literarische Missetaten aus drei Jahrhunderten* (The forged Don Quijote: literary criminals from three hundred years). Berlin, Rütten & Loening, 1957, 129 p., illus.

1371

Lehmann, Paul Joachim Georg. *Pseudo-antike Literatur des Mittelalters* (Pseudo-ancient literature of the middle ages). (Unveränderter reprografischer Nachdruck der Ausg. Leipzig und Berlin 1927). Darmstadt: Wissenschaftliche Buchgesellschaft, 1964, 108 p., 6 p. of illus. (For members only).

1372

Mair, John. *The fourth forger: William Ireland and the Shakespeare papers.* New York: Macmillan, 1939, 244 p., index.

1373

Meder, M.D. *Bibliography of material on literary forgeries and hoaxes available in Carnegie Library of Pittsburgh.* Thesis (M.L.S.) Carnegie Institute of Technology, 1949, 64 p.

1374

Meyerstein, Edward Harry William. *A life of Thomas Chatterton.* New York: Russell & Russell, c1972, 584 p., illus. Reprint of 1930 Ed.

1375

Morahan, Richard E. *I. Samuel Johnson and William Lauder's Milton forgeries. II. Poetry in space: Disjunction in language and state action in Johnson's Sejanus. III. Jane Austen's endings.* Dissertation Abstracts International, Pt. A, 0419–4209; Pt. B, 0419–4217; Pt. C, 0307–6075, Ann Arbor, MI, 32:3318A–19A (Rutgers), 1971, 123 p.

1376

Morrissette, Bruce Archer. *La bataille Rimbaud: l'affaire de La chasse spirituelle. Avec inédits, illus., et une anthologie de pastiches rimbaldiens.* [Traduction française de Jean Barré] Paris: A.G. Nizet, 1959, 402 p., illus., facsims.

1377

Morrissette, Bruce Archer. *The great Rimbaud forgery: The affaire of La chasse spirituelle, with unpublished documents and an anthology of Rimbaldian pastiches.* Saint Louis, Committee on Publications, Washington University, 1956, iii, 333 p., illus., facsims. (Washington University Studies).

1378

Quercu, Matthias. *Falsch aus der Feder geflossen: Lug, Trug und Versteckspiel in der Weltliteratur.* (Forgery from the fresh ink of a pen: falsehood, deceit, and ambush in world literature). Munich: Ehrenwirth Verlag, 1964, 282 p., illus., facsims., ports. (Das Moderne Sachbuch, Bd. 26).

1379

Rhodes, Henry Taylor Fowkes. *The craft of forgery.* London: John Murray, 1934, 307 p., plates, facsims., bibliography (pp. 293–294).

1380

Roushead, William. *The riddle of the Ruthvens and other studies.* Revised edition. Edinburgh, London: The Moray Press, 1936.

On forger A.H. "Antique" Smith, Scottish literature and Scottish history forgeries.

1381

Smith, Robert Metcalf, et al. *The Shelley legend.* New York: Charles Scribner's Sons, 1945, 343 p., index.

For a highly critical examination of this book, see *An examination of the Shelley legend* by White, Jones and Cameron, #1387.

1382

Speyer, Wolfgang. *Die literarische Fälschung im heidnischen und christlichen Altertum: ein Versuch ihrer Deutung* (The literary forgery in pagan and Christian ancient times: an inquiry concerning their meaning). Munich: Beck, 1971, XXIV, 343 p. (Handbuch der Altertumswissenschaft, 1. Abt., 2. T.)

1383

Stamp, A.E. *The disputed Revels accounts.* London, 1930.

On John Payne Collier.

1384

Tannenbaum, Samuel Aaron. *Shakespere forgeries in the Revels accounts.* Norwood, PA: Norwood Editions, c.1978, xii, 109 p., facsims. Includes bibliographical references and index. Reprint of the 1928 ed. Published by Columbia University Press, New York.

On John Payne Collier.

1385

Tatlock, John and Perry, S. *Legendary history of Britain.* Staten Island, NY: Gordian, 1975. Reprint of 1950 edition.

1386

Thomas, Ralph. *Handbook of ficticious names: being a guide to authors chiefly in the lighter literature of the XIXth century, who have written under assumed names, and to literary forgers, imposters, plagiarists, and imitators,* by Olphar Hamst, Esq. (Ralph Thomas), London: J.R. Smith, 1868. Detroit: Gale Research Co., 1969, xiv, 235 p.

1387

White, Newman I., Jones, Frederick L. and Cameron, Kenneth N. *An examination of the Shelley legend.* Philadelphia: University of Pennsylvania Press, 1951, 114 p.

See also #1381.

1388

Whitehead, John. *This solemn mockery: the art of literary forgery.* London: Arlington Books, 1973, 177 p., 8 pages of plates, ports., bibliography (pp. 172–177).

Sections of Books

1389

Barker, Nicolas. "Le Contrefaçon littéraire au XIXe siècle et la bibliographie matérielle," in *La Bibliographie matérielle,* edited by Roger Laufer. Paris: CNRS, 1983, pp. 43–52.

1390

Brook, G.L. *Books and Book Collecting.* Lexington, MA: Lexington Bks, 1980, 176 p.

Includes a section on forgers.

1391

Chambers, Sir Edmund Kerchever. *William Shakespeare.* Oxford, 1930, pp. 384–393.

1392

Devoe, Alan. "Psalmanazar the fabulous forger," in *Carrousel for bibliophiles*, edited by William Targ. New York: Philip C. Duschnes, 1947, pp. 79–81.

1393

Donno, Elizabeth Story. "Forgery, literary," in the *Encyclopedia Americana, International Edition*. Danbury, Connecticut: Grolier Incorporated, 1985, vol. 11, pp. 597–598, bibliog.

1394

Friedman, Joan M. "Fakes, forgeries, facsimiles, and other oddities," in *Book collecting: a modern guide*, edited by Jean Peters. New York: R.R. Bowker, 1977, pp. 116–135.

1395

Halliday, F.E. "Shakespeare incorporated," in his *The cult of Shakespeare*. New York: Thomas Yoseloff, 1957, pp. 135–146.

1396

Starretts, Vincent. "The fine art of forgery," in *Carrousel for bibliophiles*, edited by William Targ. New York: Philip C. Duschnes, 1947, pp. 313–329.

1397

Storm, C. and Peckham, H.H. *Invitation to book collecting: its pleasures and practices*. New York: R.R. Bowker, 1947, pp. 232–247.

Contains a section on fakes, forgeries, facsimiles and thefts.

1398

Tannenbaum, Samuel Aaron. *Shakespearian scraps and other Elizabethan fragments*. New York: Columbia University, 1933, 217 p., facsims. Bibliographical references included in "Notes" pp. 191–210.

On John Payne Collier.

1399

Thomas, Alan G. "First editions, fakes and forgeries," in his *Great books and book collectors*. New York: G.P. Putnam's Sons, 1975, pp. 234–251, illus.

1400

Thompson, Lawrence S. "Forgeries, frauds, etc.," in *The encyclopedia of library and information science*. New York: Marcel Dekker, Inc., 1973, vol. 9, pp. 12–17, bibliog.

A historical overview of literary forgery from antiquity to the 20th century. There is also a brief bibliography on p. 17.

1401

Wilson, Robert A. "Fakes, forgeries and facsimiles" (chapter thirteen), in his *Modern book collecting: a guide for the beginner who is buying first editions for the first time*. New York: Alfred A. Knopf, 1980, pp. 191–200.

Periodicals

1402

Abbott, Craig S. The case of Scharmel Iris. *Papers of the Bibliographical Society of America* (USA), 77 no. 1 (1983) 15–34. Includes bibliography.

1403

Anderson, Richard Lloyd. The fraudulent Archko volume. *Brigham Young University Studies* (USA), 15 no. 1 (1974) 43–64.

1404

Arafat, W. An aspect of the forger's art in early Islamic poetry. *School of Oriental and African Studies Bulletin* (England), 28 (1965) 477–482.

1405

Barker-Benfield, Bruce C. A Shelley fake. *Bodleian Library Record* (England), 11 (May 1983) 99–104.

1406

Baron, Hans. The anti-Florentine discourses of the Doge Tommaso Mocenigo (1414–1423): their date and partial forgery. *Speculum* (USA), 27 no. 3 (July 1952) 323–342.

1407

Becker, Helen. To coin a phrase . . . *Carnegie Magazine* (USA), 27 (February 1953) 65–66.

On the long history of literary forgery: ancient Greek classics; early Christian gospels; the view that Lord Bacon wrote Shakespeare's works; the case of George Psalmanazar; etc.

1408

Bolz, Norbert. Are Robert Greene's "Autobiographies" fakes? The forgery of the "Repentance of Robert Greene." *The Shakespeare Newsletter* (USA), 29 (1979), 43.

1409

Brownlee, Marina Scordilis. The Trojan palimpsest and Lemarte's metacritical forgery. *MLN* (USA), 100 no. 2 (March 1985) 397–405.

1410

Dawson, Giles E. John Payne Collier's great forgery. *Studies in Bibliography: Papers of the Bibliographical Society of the University of Virginia* (USA), 24 (1971) 1–26.

1411

Dickinson, A.D. Frauds, forgeries, fakes and facsimiles. *Library Journal* (USA), 60 (15 February 1935) 135–141.

1412

Folkenflik, Robert. MacPherson, Chatterton, Blake and the great age of literary forgery. *The Centennial Review* (USA), 18 (1974), 378–391.

1413

Fraenkel, Eduard. The Culex. *Journal of Roman Studies*, 42 parts I & II (1952) 1–9.

On a forged work of Virgil.

1414

Fruman, Norman. Originality, plagiarism, forgery and romanticism. *Centrum: Working Papers of the Minnesota Center for Advanced Studies in Language, Style, and Literary Theory* (USA), 4 (1976), 44–49.

1415

Ganzel, Dewey. The "Collier Forgeries" and the Ireland controversy. *The Shakespeare Newsletter* (USA), 34 (Spring 1984) 6.

1416

Goodacre, S.H. Enquiry into the nature of a certain Lewis Carroll pamphlet. *Book Collector* (England), 27 (Autumn 1978) 325–342, illus.

1417

Haraszti, Z. Ireland's Shakespeare forgeries. *More Books* (USA), 9 (November 1934) 333–350.

1418

Haywood, Ian. Chatterton plans for the publication of the forgery. *Review of English Studies* (England), 36 no. 141 (February 1985) 58–68.

1419

Haywood, Ian. The making of history: historiography and literary forgery in the eighteenth century. *Literature and History: a New Journal for the Humanities* (England), 9 no. 2 (Autumn 1983), 139–151.

1420

Hazen, Allen T. Literary forgeries and the library. *Columbia Library Columns* (USA), 22 (November 1972) 6–13.

1421

Holstein, Mark. Five foot shelf of literary forgeries. *Colophon* (USA), 2 no. 4 (1937) 550–567.

1422

Hopkins, F.M. Forgeries in the New York Public Library. *Publishers Weekly* (USA), 138 (16 November 1940) 1926.

1423

Houtchens, Lawrence H. *The Spirit of the Times* and a "New work by Boz." *PMLA* (USA), 67 no. 2 (March 1952) 94–100.

1424

Hughes, Merritt Y. New evidence on the charge that Milton forged the Pamela prayer in the Eikon basilike. *The Review of English Studies* (England), 3 no. 10 (April 1952) 130–140.

1425

Ingalls, Daniel H.H. The Krsnacarita of Samudragupta: a modern forgery. *American Oriental Society Journal* (USA), 85 (January 1965) 60–65.

1426

Jones, W.R. Palladism and the papacy: an episode of French anti-clericalism in the nineteenth century. *Journal of Christian Studies* (USA), 12 (Autumn 1970) 453–473.

1427

Jorgensen, Peter A. Hafgeir's saga flateyings: an eighteenth-century forgery. *Journal of English and Germanic Philology* (USA), 76 (1977) 155–164.

1428

Jorgensen, Peter A. Thjostolf's saga hamramma: the case for forgery. *Gripla,* 3 (1979) 96–103.

1429

Kaplan, J.H. Thomas Middleton's epitaph on the death of Richard Burbage, and John Payne Collier. *The Papers of the Bibliographical Society of America* (USA), 80(1986) 225–232.

1430

Kemp, J. Valuable collection of literary forgeries. *Texas Libraries* (USA), 29 (Winter 1967) 249–252.

1431

Knight, G.W. Colman and Don Leon. *Twentieth Century* (England), 159 (June 1956) 562–573.

Forgeries of Byron.

1432

Knight, G.W. Who wrote Don Leon? *Twentieth Century* (England), 156 (July 1954) 67–79.

1433

Kondratiev, Alexi. New myths for old: the legacy of Iolo Morgannwg and Hersard de la Villemarque. *Mythlore* (USA), 10 no. 1, (Spring 1983) 31–47; 10 no. 2 (Summer 1983) 43–46.

1434

Lange, Thomas V. Two forged plates in *America*, copy B. *Blake* (USA), 16 no. 4 (Spring 1983) 212–218.

1435

Lin, Ching-Chang. The problem of current forged books. *Journal of Educational Media and Library Science* (Taiwan), 22 no. 2 (Winter 1985) 186–198, 8 refs.

Many works from Mainland China have been pirated by printers in Taiwan. This article examines the problem and proposes a solution.

1436

Lynch, Katherine L. Homer's Iliad and Pope's vile forgery. *Comparative Literature* (USA), 34 no. 1 (Winter 1982) 1–15.

1437

McDonald, G.D. Forgeries in the Library. *Bulletin of the New York Public Library* (USA), 41 (August 1937) 623–628.

1438

McDonald, G.D. Shelf of forgeries. *Bulletin of the New York Public Library* (USA), 37 (March 1933) 200–204.

1439

Marcuse, Michael J. The gentleman's magazine and the Lauder/Milton controversy. *Bulletin of Research in the Humanities* (USA) 81 no. 2 (1978) 179–209.

1440

Marcuse, Michael J. The Lauder controversy and the Jacobite cause. *Studies in Burke and his Time* (USA), 18 no. 1 (1977) 27–47.

1441

Marder, Louis. Chettle's forgery of the *Groatsworth of wit* and the "Shakescene" Passage. *The Shakespeare Newsletter* (USA), 20 (1970) 42.

1442

Metzger, B.M. Literary forgeries of canonical pseudepigrapha. *Journal of Biblical Literature* (USA), 91 (March 1972) 3–24.

1443

Momigliano, A. Unsolved problem of historical forgery: the *Scriptores Historiae Augustae*. *Journal of the Warburg and Courtauld Institutes* (England), 17 (January 1954) 22–46.

1444

Norman, Philip. The marvellous boy: Thomas Chatterton, the teenage poet who "Discovered" the works of a medieval priest. *The Sunday Times Magazine* (England), 8 March 1970, pp. 22–23, 25–26, 28 [Photographs by Robert Freson].

1445

Paley, Morton D. John Camden Hotten, A.C. Swinburne, and the Blake facsimiles of 1868. *Bulletin of the New York Public Library* (USA), 79 no. 3 (Spring 1976) 259–296, illus.

1446

Pellan, Francoise. Virginia Woolf's posthumous poem. *Modern Fiction Studies* (USA), 29 (Winter 1983) 695–700.

1447

Piggott, S. William Stukeley: new facts and an old forgery. *Antiquity* (England), 60 (July 1986) 115–122.

1448

Rambaud-Buhot, J. La critique des faux dans l'ancien droit canonique (Critique on forgeries of ancient canon law). *Bibl. Ec. Chartes* (France), 126 no. 1 (1968) 5–62.

1449

Ringler, William. Another Collier forgery. *Times Literary Supplement* (England) 29 October 1938, pp. 693–694.

1450

Rodger, William. The Ireland forgeries: a magnificent hoax. *Hobbies* (USA) 85 no. 7 (September 1980) 100–101, 104–105.

1451

Salomon, Richard G. Poggio Bracciolini and Johanes Hus: a hoax hard to kill. *Journal of the Warburg and Courtauld Institutes* (England), 19 nos. 1&2 (January–June 1956), 174–177.

1452

Schimmel, S.B. Living with forgers. [1st Robert F. Metzdorf Memorial Lecture]. *University of Rochester Library Bulletin*, (USA), 32 (Winter 1979) 41–60.

1453

Schoenbaum, S. The crimes and repentance of John Payne Collier. *Times Literary Supplement* (England), 26 June 1969, p. 709, illus.

1454

Schottenloher, K. Der schwankdichter Michael Lindener als schriftenfälscher (Popular poet Michael Lindener as literary forger). *Zentralblatt fuer Bibliothekswesen* (Germany), 56 (July 1939) 335–347.

Includes a bibliography of Lindener's writings, including his forgeries.

1455

Schumacher, John N. The authenticity of the writings attributed to Father Jose Burgos. *Philippine Studies* (Philippines), 18 no. 1 (1970) 3–51.

1456
Spencer, Hazelton. The forger at work: a new case against Collier. *Philological Quarterly* (USA), 6 (1927) 32–38.

1457
Starr, Phyllis. Forgers in the public library. *Vogue* (USA), 138 (1 August 1961) 126–127, 129–130.
Starr discusses several of the more prominent literary forgers whose works can be found in the rare book room at the New York Public Library.

1458
Thomas, John P. A disputed novel of Basil II. *Greek, Roman and Byzantine Studies* (USA) 24 (Autumn 1983) 273–283.

1459
Thompson, S.O. Vrain-Denis Lucas, 'prince of forgers.' *AB Bookman's Weekly* (USA), 70 (13 September 1982) 1627 +.

1460
Timpanaro, S. Di alcuni falsificazioni di scritti Leopardiani. (On several falsifications of writings of Leopardi). *G. stor. Lett. ital.* (Italy), 143 no. 441 (1966) 88–119.

1461
Tolstoy, Nikolai. The diary of nobody at all: Penguin, the BBC and a spurious documentary. *Encounter* (England), 58 no. 5, (May 1982), 35–39.

1462
Tout, T.F. Medieval forgers and forgeries. *John Rylands Library Bulletin* (England), 5 (1919) 208–234.

1463
Trevor-Roper, Hugh. The Ossian forgeries: wrong but romantic. *The Spectator* (England), 16 March 1985, pp. 14–15.

1464
Viscomi, Joseph. Facsimile or forgery? an examination of *America*, plates 4 and 9, copy B. *Blake* (USA) 16 no. 4 (Spring 1983), 219–223, illus.

1465
Walters, Raymond Jr. The James Gallatin diary: a fraud? *American Historical Review* (USA), 62 no. 4 (July 1957) 878–885.

1466
Wells, Anna Mary. ED forgeries. *Dickinson Studies* (USA), 35 (1979) 12–16.

1467
Wilson, J. Dover and Hunt, R.W. The authenticity of Simon Forman's 'Booke of Plaies.' *Review of English Studies* (England), 23 (1947) 193–200.

1468
Wormser, R.S. Spectra and other hoaxes. *Columbia Library Columns* (USA), 22 (November 1972) 14–21.

1469
Zall, P.M. The cool world of Samuel Taylor Coleridge: George Steevens, antic antiquarian. *The Wordsworth Circle* (USA), 13 no. 4 (1982) 211–213.

1470
Zug, Charles G., III. Sir Walter Scott and the Ballad forgery. *Studies in Scottish Literature* (USA), 8 (1970) 52–64.

Literary

(B) Manuscripts, Letters and Documents
Books

1471
Allegro, John Marco. *The Shapira affair.* New York: Doubleday, 1965, 139 p., illus., maps.

1472
Fuhrmann, Horst. *Einflus und Verbreitung der pseudoisidorischen Fälschungen: von ihrem Auftauchen bis in d. neuere Zeit* (Influx and spread of the pseudo-isidoris. Forgery from its sudden appearance to recent times). Stuttgart: Hiersemann, 1972–1974, 3 vols., 1127 p., ficisms. (Schriften der Monumenta Germaniae Historica, Deutsches Institut für Erforschung des Mittelalters; Bd.24). Vol. 3 has individual title: *Texte, Untersuchungen,* Übersichten.

1473
Gualazzini, Ugo. Falsificazioni di fonti dell'età paleochristiana e altomedievale nella storiografica cremonese. Cremona, 1975, 132 p., facsims., indexes. (Annali della Biblioteca statale e libreria civica di Cremona; 23).

1474
Hamilton, Charles. *Great forgers and famous fakes: the manuscript forgers of America and how they duped the experts.* 1st Edition. New York: Crown Publishers, c1980, viii + 278 p., illus., index.

1475
Hector, Leonard Charles. *Paleography and forgery.* London: St. Anthony's Press, 1959, 18 p., plates, facsims. (St. Anthony's Hall publications, no. 15).

1476

Ravier, André. *Saint François de Sales et ses faussaires.* Avec le concours de Albert Mirot. Annecy, Académie salésienne, 1971 (reprinted 1973), 217 p., illus. (Mémoires et documents, t. 83). (Collection Bibliothèque salésienne, no. 2). Bibliography: pp. 211–212.

Sections of Books

1477

Andrews, John F. "Taylor-made Shakespeare? Or is "Shall I die" the long-lost text of Bottom's Dream?", in the *Dictionary of literary biography yearbook: 1985.* Edited by Jean W. Ross. Detroit, Michigan: Gale Research Company, 1986, pp. 40–48, bibliog. (p. 48).

An excellent summary of the controversy surrounding the poem "Shall I die?", discovered at the Bodleian Library and attributed to Shakespeare by Shakespeare scholar Gary Taylor. The article also includes a copy of the poem, "comments from other scholars and poets," and a bibliography. The bibliography is especially valuable for its newspaper and book review citations.

1478

Jänichen, Hans. Zur Herkunft der Reichenauer Fälscher des 12ten Jahrhunderts (The descent of the Reichenauer forgery of the 12th century). In *Die Abtei Reichenau: neure Beitrhase zur Geschichte und der Insel-Pfarreien Reichenau.* Edited by Helmut Maurer. Sismarinsen: Thorbecke, 1974, pp. 277–287.

1479

Kosean-Mokrau, Alfred. "Die gefälschten memoiren des pandurenobristen Franz von der Trenck." (The falsified memoirs of the Panduren Colonel Franz von der Trenck). *Jahrbuch des Inst. für Deutsche Geschichte* (Israel), 4 (1975) 13–51.

1480

Lutz, Cora Elizabeth. "A forged manuscript in Boustrophedon," in his "The oldest library motto, and other library essays." Hamden, CT: Archon Books, 1979, pp. 65–72.

1481

Spawforth, A.J.S. "Fourmontiana. IG v^1. 515: another forgery 'from Amyklai'," in *The Annual of the British School at Athens,* (England), 71 (1976) 139–145, illus.

Periodicals

1482

Alsop, J.D. The Shakespearian forgeries of 1796: an insertion in a Tudor manuscript. *Notes & Queries* (England), 28 (August 1981) 315.

1483

Backhouse, Janet. The "Spanish Forger." *British Museum Quarterly*, (England), 33 (Autumn 1968) 65–71, illus.

1484

Belknap, George N. Oregon Twenty Acts: a tale of bibliographic detection. *Pacific Northwest Quarterly* (USA), 67 no. 2 (1976), 63–68, 2 photos.

Forgery of the Oregon Territorial Laws.

1485

Bevan, J. and Shapiro, I.A. [Discussion]. Donne and the Walton forgeries—a correspondence. *The Library* (England) 4 no. 3 (1982) 329–339.

1486

Black, Lydia. "The Daily Journal of Reverend Father Juvenal": a cautionary tale. *Ethnohistory* (USA), 28 no. 1 (1981) 33–58.

1487

Brooke, Christopher Nugent Lawrence. Approaches to medieval forgery. *Journal of the Society of Archivists* (England), 3 no. 8 (October 1968) 377–386, 2 plates.

1488

Burgess, Anthony. Is it really Shakespeare? *The New York Times Book Review* (USA), 22 December 1985, p. 3.

1489

Caraci, Giuseppe. Le lettere del Vespucci non poterono, dunque, essere contraffatte? (Is it impossible that Vespucci's letters were forgeries?). *Nuova Rivista Storica* (Italy), 42 no. 3 (1958) 393–444.

1490

Cashin, Edward J., Jr. George Walton and the forged letter. *Georgia Historical Quarterly* (USA), 62 no. 2 (1978) 133–145.

1491

Cheney, C.R. Magna Carta Beati Thome: another Canterbury forgery. *Bulletin of the Institute of Historical Research*, 36 (May 1963) 1–26.

1492

Denton, J.H. The forged Bull of St. Botolph's Colchester. *Bulletin of the John Rylands University Library of Manchester*, (England), 55 no. 2 (Spring 1973) 324–345.

1493

Deutsch, Otto Erich. Spurious Mozart letters. *The Music Review* (England) 25 (May 1964) 120–123.

1494

Fehrenbacher, Don E. Lincoln's lost love letters. *American Heritage* (USA), 32 no. 2 (1981) 70–80.

1495

Friedrich, Otto and Holmes, Steven. "Shall I die? Shall I fly. . . .": a U.S. scholar claims discovery of a poem by Shakespeare. *Time* (USA), 9 December 1985, p. 76, illus.

1496

Galbraith, V.H. *The Modus tenendi Parliamentum. Journal of the Warburg & Courtauld Institutes* (England) 16 nos. 1–2 (1954) 81–99.

A 14th-century Latin document.

1497

Goshen-Gottstein, Moshe H. The Shapira forgery and the Qumran scrolls. *Journal of Jewish Studies* (England) 7 (1956) 187–193, 1 plate.

1498

Harasowski, Adam. Fact or forgery? *Music and Musicians* (England), 21 no. 7 (March 1973) 28–33.

On the authenticity of the Chopin-Potocka letters. The article contains fragments of the letters, published for the first time.

1499

Higgins, Thomas. Delphine Potocka and Frederic Chopin. *Journal of the American Liszt Society* (USA), Part I. 8 (1980) 64–74; Part II. 9 (June 1981) 73–87.

1500

Hopkinson, Cecil. [Letter to the Editor]. Berlioz discoveries. *Fontes Artis Musicae* (Germany), 16 nos. 1–2 (January–June 1969), 28–29.

1501

Huart, Suzanne d'. Vraies du fausses? Le lettres de Marie-Antoinette (True or false? The letters of Marie-Antoinette). *Histoire* (France), no. 51 (1982) 91–93.

1502

Jack, R.I. Forgery of medieval documents. *Australian Library Journal* (Australia), 14 (March 1965) 12–19.

1503

Johansson, J.V. De Rudbeckianska förfalskningarna i *Codex Argenteus.* (The Rudbekian forgeries in the *Codex Argenteus.*) *Nordisk Tidskrift för Bok- och Biblioteksväsen* (Sweden) 42 no. 1 (1955), 12–27. Summary in English.

1504

Johnsen, Thomas C. Historical concensus and Christian science: the career of a manuscript controversy. *New England Quarterly* (USA), 53 no. 1 (March 1980) 3–22.

1505

Kent, F.W. Letters genuine and spurious of Giovanni Rucellai. *Journal of the Warburg and Courtauld Institutes* (England), 37 (1974) 342–349.

1506

Klein, John W. Verdian forgeries—a summing-up. *The Music Review* (England) 20 nos. 3&4 (August–November 1959) 244–252.

1507

Lacy, Norris J. The Kansas manuscript of L'istoire de Jehan Coquault. *Manuscripta* (USA), 25 no. 3 (1981) 172–176.

1508

Lancaster, Paul. Faking it. *American Heritage* (USA), 33 no. 6, (October/ November 1982) 50–57, illus.

On faking newspaper stories in early American newspapers.

1509

Lapp, John C. On some manuscripts of La Fontaine in America. *Modern Language Notes* (USA), 75 (June 1960) 490–497.

1510

Lizardi, Ramos, Cesar. Another Maya falsification. *American Antiquity* (USA), 25 (1959) 120–121.

The thirty-third forged Maya manuscript to be identified.

English abstract in AATA vol. 3 (1960-1961) #3087.

1511

Lutz, Cora Elizabeth. Forged manuscript in Boustrophedon. *Yale University Library Gazette* (USA), 53 (July 1978) 38–44.

1512

McKay, D.A. The historian and the forger. *Amateur Historian* (England), 3 no. 3 (1957) 105–107.

1513

Macdonald, Hugh; Cairns, David; and Tyson, Alan. [Letter to the Editor]. Berlioz forgeries. *The Musical Times* (England), 110 no. 1511 (January 1969) 32.

1514

Mackenzie, D.N. Pseudoprotokurtica. *Bulletin of the School of Oriental and African Studies* (England), 26 (1963) 1970–1973.

1515

Phillips, H. The Book of the duchess, lines 31-96: are they a forgery? *English Studies* (Netherlands), 67 (April 1986) 113-125.

1516

Quesnell, Quentin. Mar Saba Clementine: a question of evidence. *Catholic Biblical Quarterly* (USA) 37 (Jan. 1975) 48–67; Reply to Morton Smith. 38 (April 1976) 200–203.

1517

Rabinowicz, O.K. Shapira scroll: a nineteenth-century forgery. *Jewish Quarterly Review* (USA), 56 (July 1965) 1–21.

1518

Rapport, Leonard. Forging the past. *OAH Newsletter* (USA) 11 no. 3, (1983) 11–15.

On the forging of historical documents.

1519

Reily, Duncan. Reunion shenanigan: Bishop William Capers' "Letter" of 1854. *Methodist History* (USA), 15 (January 1977) 131–139.

1520

Rodger, William. The king of forgers. *Hobbies* (USA) 83 no. 6, (August 1978) 138–139, 147, 156, 161.

On the life and activities of Simonidies, mss forger.

1521

Shapiro, I.A. Donne and the Walton forgeries. *The Library* (England), 6th ser. 3 (September 1981) 232; Discussion. 4 (September 1982) 329–339.

1522

Sjögren, P. Erland Hjärne om Adolf Ludvig Stierneld som historieförfalskare (Erland Hjärne on Adolf Ludvig Stierneld as a forger of historical documents). *Nordisk Tidskrift för Bok-och Biblioteksväsen* (Sweden), 67 no. 1 (1980) 11–15.

1523

Southern, R.W. The Canterbury forgeries. *English Historical Review* (England), 73 (1958) 193–226.

1524

Taylor, Gary. Who's sorry now? *The New York Times Book Review* (USA) 22 December 1986, p. 3.

A brief reply to Anthony Burgess' article entitled, "Is it really Shakespeare?"

1525

Thompson, J. Eric, S. The Grolier Codex. *The Book Collector*, (England), 25 no. 1 (Spring 1976) 64–75.

1526

Unsigned article. Lincoln forgeries. *USA Today* (USA), 109 no. 2425, (October 1980) 15–16.

The forged Lincoln love letters.

1527

Unsigned article. Mayan muddle. *ARTnews* (USA), 75 (Nov. 1976) 20, 22.

The Grolier Codex.

1528

Unsigned article. Warning of fraud. *Library Journal* (USA), 64 (1 September 1939) 656.

The sale of stolen Stephen Collins Foster facsimiles as first editions and forged Foster letters and manuscripts on the market.

1529

Vesela-Prenosilova, Zdenka. A propos d'une falsification des documents Ottomans en 1804 (Concerning a falsification of Ottoman documents in 1804). *Prilozi za Orijentalnu Filologiju* (Yugoslavia), 22–23 (1972–1973) 149–162.

1530

Walker, Frank. Verdi [Letter to the editor]. Response to John W. Klein's article. *Music Review* (England), 21 no. 1, (February 1960), 83–84; 21 no. 2 (May 1960) 175; Response from John W. Klein, 21 no. 2 (May 1960) 175–176; 21 no. 3 (August 1960) 264.

1531

Walker, Frank. Verdian forgeries: letters hostile to Catalani. *Music Review* (England) 20 no. 1 (February 1959) 28–37.

1532

Walker, Frank. Verdian forgeries: letters of Giuseppina Verdi to her confessor. *Music Review* (England) 19 no. 4 (November 1958), 273–282.

1533

Winter, Paul. Letter from Pontius Pilate. *Novum Testamentum*, (Netherlands), 7 no. 1 (1964) 37–43.

1534

Winter, Paul. Une lettre de Ponce-Pilate. *Foi et Vie* (France), 62 no. 2 (1963) 1C1–108.

1535

Winter, Paul. News from Pilate in Liverpool. *Encounter* (England), 21 (August 1963) 68–70.

Literary

(C) Thomas James Wise

Books

1536

Atkin, E.J. *Examination of Thomas J. Wise and his literary forgeries.* Thesis (M.A. in L.S.), Kent State University, 1959, 55 p.

1537

Barker, Nicolas and Collins, John. *A sequel to an enquiry: the forgeries of Forman and Wise re-examined.* Berkeley: Scholar Press, 1984, 368 p., illus.

For an extended review, see Donald Gallup's, "The Carter and Pollard Enquiry fifty years after," *Papers of the Bibliographical Society of America* (USA), 78 no. 4, (1984) 447–460.

1538

Carter, John and Pollard, Graham. *An enquiry into the nature of certain nineteenth century pamphlets.* Edited by Nicolas Barker and John Collins. Berkeley: Scholar Press, 1984, 464 p., illus. Reprint of 1934 edition.

1539

Carter, John and Pollard, Graham. *Enquiry into the nature of certain nineteenth century pamphlets.* (English Literature Series no. 33). New York: Haskell, 1971. Reprint of 1934 edition.

1540

Carter, John and Pollard, Graham. *The firm of Charles Ottley, Landon & Co.: footnote to an enquiry.* London: Rupert Hart-Davis; New York: Charles Scribner's Sons, 1948, 95 p.

1541

Carter, John and Pollard, Graham. *The forgeries of Tennyson's plays.* Oxford: B.H. Blackwell LTD. Distributors, 1967, 21 p. (Working papers for a second edition of "An enquiry into the nature of certain nineteenth century pamphlets," no. 2).

1542

Carter, John and Pollard, Graham. *Gorfin's stock.* Oxford: Distributed for the authors by B.H. Blackwell, LTD., 1970, 36 p. (Working papers for a second edition of "An enquiry into the nature of certain nineteenth century pamphlets," no. 4). Limited edition of 400 copies.

1543

Carter, John and Pollard, Graham. *The Mystery of "The Death of Balder."* Oxford: distributed for the authors by Blackwell, 1969, 21 p., 4 facsims. (Working papers for a second edition of "An enquiry into the nature of certain nineteenth century pamphlets," no. 3).

1544

Carter, John and Pollard, Graham. *Precis of Paden: or, the sources for the new Timon.* Oxford: distributed for the authors by Blackwell, LTD., c 1967, 24 p., facsims., table. (Working papers for a second edition of "An enquiry into the nature of certain nineteenth century pamphlets," no. 1).

1545

Foxon, D.F. *Thomas J. Wise and the pre-restoration drama.* London: The Bibliographical Society, 1959, viii, 42 p., 4 plates.

Publication of the research carried out by D.F. Foxon into the theft of leaves from quartos in the British Museum by Thomas J. Wise.

For a book review by Graham Pollard, see *The Book Collector*, (England) 8 no. 3 (Autumn 1959) 319–320, 323.

1546

Partington, Wilfred George. *Forging ahead: the true story of the upward progress of Thomas James Wise, prince of book collectors, bibliographer extraordinary, and otherwise.* New York: Cooper Square Publishers, 1973, xv, 315 p., illus. Reprint of 1939 ed. "The bibliography of the bibliographer; a record of his compilations, privately printed publications, edited works, forgeries, piracies, etc.": pp. 283–304.

For review by John Carter, see "Lowdown on Wise," *Publishers Weekly* (USA) 136 (25 November 1939) 1974–1975.

A revised edition was published in London, in 1947, under title: *Thomas J. Wise in the original cloth.*

1547

Partington, Wilfred George. *Thomas J. Wise in the original cloth: the life and record of the forger of the nineteenth-century pamphlets.* With an appendix by George Bernard Shaw. Folkestone, England: Dawsons of Pall Mall, 1974, 372 p., illus.

Reprint of the 1947 edition published by R. Hale, London, which was an enlarged edition with alterations of the author's "Forging ahead," published in New York, 1939. "The bibliography of the bibliographer": pp. 323–346.

1548

Pedley, Katharine Greenleaf. *Moriarty in the stacks: the nefarious adventures of Thomas J. Wise.* Berkeley: Peacock Press, 1966, 27 pages, frontispiece.

1549

Ratchford, Fannie E. *A review of reviews: Part I. An enquiry; part II. Wise's letters.* Austin: The University of Texas, 1946, 71 p., illus., facsims.

1550

Ratchford, Fannie E. (Editor). *Letters of Thomas J. Wise to John Henry Wrenn: a further enquiry into the guilt of certain nineteenth century forgers.* New York: Alfred A. Knopf, 1944, 591 p., index xvi p.

1551

Todd, William Burton. *Suppressed commentaries on the Wiseian forgeries.* Austin: Humanities Research Center, University of Texas at Austin, 1969, 50 p., facsim. (Bibliographical monograph no.1).

1552

Todd, William Burton (Editor). *Thomas J. Wise: centenary studies.* Essays by John Carter, Graham Pollard, and William B. Todd. Austin: University of Texas Press, 1959, 128 p., port., facsim. [Also pre-published as a supplement to *The Texas Quarterly*, vol. 2 no. 4, winter, 1959.]

For a review, see Roland Baughman's article in *The Book Collector* (England), 9 no. 2 (Summer 1960) 232, 235–236.

1553

Thompson, R.F. *Evaluation of Thomas J. Wise.* Thesis (M.S.L.S.), Drexel Institute of Technology, 1951, 52 p.

Periodicals

1554

Alden, John. [Bibliographical Notes and Queries]. Query 104 (Winter 1958). T.J. Wise and *Tales of the wild and wonderful. The Book Collector* (England), 8 no. 3 (Autumn 1959) 300–303. Additional letter from Joseph Rubenstein, pp. 303–306.

1555

Angeli, H.R. *Cor cordium* and Thomas J. Wise. *New Colophon* (USA), 2 (September 1949) 237–244.

1556

Baughman, Roland. Some Victorian forged rarities. *Huntington Library Bulletin* (USA), no. 9 (April 1936) 91–117.

1557

Baughman, Roland. Peccancies of T.J. Wise, et al.; some aftermaths of the exposure. *Columbia Library Columns* (USA), 3 (May 1954) 12–28.

1558

Bissell, E.E. [Bibliographical Notes and Queries]. Note 115. Goose, Wise and Swinburne. *The Book Collector* (England), 8 no. 3, (Autumn 1959) 297–299.

1559

Carter, John. Puzzle of Thomas J. Wise. *Publishers Weekly* (USA), 131 (29 May 1937) 2213–2214.

1560

Carter, John. [Bibliographical Notes and Queries]. Query no. 36. Thomas J. Wise's *Verses*, 1882 & 1883. *The Book Collector* (England), 2 no. 2 (Summer 1953) 158–159.

1561

Carter, John. [Bibliographical Notes and Queries]. Note 110. Thomas J. Wise and 'Richard Gullible'. *The Book Collector* (England), 8 no. 2 (Summer 1959) 182–183.

1562

Carter, John. How we got Wise. *Sunday Times Magazine* (England), 8 March 1970, pp. 38–39, 41, 43–44, illus.

1563

Carter, John. Wise after the event. *Bookseller* (England), 5 September 1964, pp. 1296–1297.

1564

Collingwood, F. Case of Thomas Wise (1859–1937). *Library World* (England), 61 (August 1959) 33–36.

1565

Commentary. [Thomas J. Wise forgeries sold at auction by Yale University]. *The Book Collector* (England), 10 no. 4 (Winter 1961), 390–392.

1566

Commentary. [On Fannie Ratchford's efforts to link Sir Edmund Gosse to the Thomas Wise forgeries as a fellow-conspirator]. *The Book Collector* (England), 7 no. 3 (Autumn 1958) 237–238.

1567

Commentary. [Fannie E. Ratchford's research at the British Museum]. *The Book Collector* (England), 6 no. 4 (Winter 1957) 340–341.

By collating Ashley Library copies, purchased by the British Museum, with copies from the Wrenn library, Austin, Texas, Ratchford determined that T.J. Wise had 'improved' the copies he had sold to the Wrenn with pieces he had taken from quartos in the British Museum.

1568

Cox, J.T. New date for a Wiseian forgery: Tennyson's trial issue of Becket (1879). *Papers of the Bibliographical Society of America* (USA), 68 (July 1974) 335–336.

1569

Dearden, James S. Wise and Ruskin, *The Book Collector* (England), 18 (Spring 1969) 45–56.

1570
Dearden, James S. Wise and Ruskin. Forgeries. *The Book Collector* (England), 18 (Summer 1969) 170–188, illus.

1571
Dearden, James S. Wise and Ruskin. Wise's editions of letters from John Ruskin. *The Book Collector* (England), 18 (Autumn 1969), 318–339.

1572
Fletcher, E.G. Proof that Forman knew. *Library Chronicle*, (USA), 2 (Fall 1946) 136–155.

1573
Foxon, D.F. and Todd, William Burton. Thomas J. Wise and the pre-restoration drama: a supplement. *The Library* (England), 16 (December 1961) 287–293.

1574
Freeman, Arthur. The workshop of Thomas J. Wise. *Times Literary Supplement* (England), 17 September 1982, p. 990.

1575
Gearty, Thomas J., Jr. Thomas J. Wise: a brief survey of his literary forgeries. *The Courier* (USA) 11 no. 1 (1973) 51–64.

1576
Gross, M.J.H. Some sources of John Whitehead's *This Solemn Mockery*. *Papers of the Bibliographical Society of America* (USA), 72 (January 1978) 113–129.

1577
Hilliard, Celia. The Thomas Wise forgeries: the case of the Wrenn Library. *Chicago History* (USA), 9 no. 4 (1980–1981) 212–218.

1578
Hopkins, F.M. Victorian forged pamphlets. *Publishers Weekly* (USA), 130 (18 July 1936) 200–203.

1579
Kendall, L.H. Not-so-gentle art of puffing: William G. Kingsland and Thomas J. Wise. *Papers of the Bibliographical Society of America* (USA), 62 (January 1968) 25–37.

1580
McDonald, Dwight. Annals of crime: the first editions of Thomas J. Wise. *New Yorker* (USA), 38 no. 38 (10 November 1962) 168 +.

1581

Muir, P.H. Elkin Mathews VIII: sherry and shibboleths. *The Book Collector* (England), 3 no. 1 (Spring 1954) 11–27.

Lengthy article centering primarily on Thomas J. Wise, and John Carter and Graham Pollard who published the *Enquiry* which exposed Wise.

1582

The new *Enquiry*: a preview. *The Book Collector* (England), 31 no. 4 (Winter 1982), 463–480, illus.; A Preview: Part Two, 32 no. 1 (Spring 1983), 67–77; A Preview: Part Three, 32 no. 2, (Summer 1983), 189–200.

Excerpts from *A sequel to an enquiry*, companion volume to John Carter and Graham Pollard's *An enquiry into the nature of certain nineteenth century pamphlets*, revised edition.

1583

Pariser, Maurice. A T.J. Wise collection. *Private Library*, (England), 2 no. 6 (October 1959) 86–89.

1584

Park, Julian. [Bibliographical Notes and Queries]. Query 104. *Tales of the wild and the wonderful*. 1825. *The Book Collector* (England), 7 no. 4 (Winter 1958) 417.

A note inquiring into the authorship of *Tales of the Wild and the Wonderful*. Park notes that T.J. Wise attributed the work to George Borrow. For a reply, see letters from John Alden and Joseph Rubenstein.

1585

Todd, William Burton. Some Wiseian ascriptions in the Wrenn catalogue. *The Library* (England), 23 (June 1968) 95–107.

1586

Todd, William Burton. T.J. Wise's later benefactions to the Wrenn Library. *Papers of the Bibliographical Society of America* (USA), 67 (July 1973) 341–344.

1587

Trevanian, Michael. Thomas J. Wise's descriptive formula. *The Book Collector* (England), 13 (Autumn 1964) 355–356.

1588

Unsigned article. Additional items in Guildhall Library associated with Thomas J. Wise. *Guildhall Miscellany* (England), 2 (September 1965) 305–306.

1589

Wells, T. Looking Back at Thomas J. Wise. *Rub-Off* (USA), 17 (November 1966) 1–6.

Literary

(D) Detection

Books

1590
Conway, James V.P. *Evidential documents.* Springfield, IL: Charles C. Thomas, 1959, 267 p. (2nd printing 1972).

English abstract in AATA vol. 17 (1980) #17-1079.

1591
Harrison, Wilson R. *Forgery detection: a practical guide.* New York: Praeger, 1964, 232 p., illus.

1592
Harrison, Wilson R. *Suspect documents: their scientific examination.* Chicago: Nelson Hall, 1981, 594 p.

Sections of Books

1593
Hamilton, Charles. "Thirteen rules for spotting fakes," in his *Great forgers and famous fakes: the manuscript forgers of America and how they duped the experts.* New York: Crown Publishers, Inc., pp. 261–268.

Periodicals

1594
Bendikson, L.; and Haselden, R.B. Detection of manuscript forgeries. *Library Journal* (USA), 59 (15 May 1934) 442.

1595
Bendikson, L. Facsimile reprints of rare books. *Library Journal* (USA), 63 (15 February 1938) 140–143.

1596
Bliss, A.S. Cyclotron analysis and a fake gospel lectionary of 1328. *Scriptorium* (Belgium), 38 no. 2 (1984) 322–325, 1 plate.

French abstract in RAA 1985 #9918.

1597
Brown, T.J. The detection of fake literary MSS. *The Book Collector* (England), 2 no. 1 (Spring 1953) 6–23, plates.

Contents: I. Introduction; II. Points of examination, 1. Pedigree, 2. Contents, 3. Physical appearance, a. Materials, b. The handwriting; III. Notes on the plates.

1598

Hazen, Allen T. Watermarks and forgeries; the role of watermarks in the examination and condemnation of certain eighteenth century productions. *Print* (USA), 2 (Summer 1941) 21–31.

1599

Krueger, William C. Paper and forensic science. *Journal of the Technical Association of the Pulp and Paper Industry* (USA), 67 no. 6 (June 1984) 42–45, 2 photos.

English abstract in AATA vol. 21 (1984) #21-1596.

1600

Lacy, G.J. Questioned documents. *American Archivist* (USA), 9 (October 1946) 267–275.

1601

Mackenzie, Norman H. Forensic document techniques applied to literary manuscripts. *Bodleian Library Record* (England), 9 (June 1976) 234–240.

1602

Price, Cheryl A. Document examination in American archives. *Special Libraries* (USA), 68 no. 9 (September 1977) 299–304.

Price recommends an increasingly scientific approach to document authentication, and outlines ways the archivist can detect forged documents.

1603

Rapport, L. Fakes and facsimiles: problems of identification. *American Archivist* (USA), 42 no. 1 (January 1979) 13–58, illus. Comment by J. Lancaster [Letter], 42 (July 1979) 276.

1604

Schofield, M. Evidence in or on paper. *Papermaker* (England), 130 no. 1 (July 1955) 30; *Bull. Inst. Pap, Chem.*, 26 (1955–1956) 21.

English abstract in AATA vol. 3 (1960–1961) #3088.

1605

Shell, E.R. Pursuit of fakery. *Technology Illustrated* (USA), 3 no. 9 (September 1983) 22–27, 10 illus.

English abstract in AATA vol. 22 (1985) #22-1792.

1606

Strini, A. Il rimpiccolimento dei fogli. *Accademie e Biblioteche d'Italia* (Italy), 12 (April 1938) 167–170.

1607

Werthmann, B.; Schiller, W.; and Griebenow, W. Naturwissenschaftliche Aspekte der Echtheitspruefung der sogenannten "Hitler-Tagebuecher" (Scientific aspects of authenticity testing of the so-called "Hitler diaries"). *Maltechnik-Restauro* (Germany), Jg. 90 no. 4 (1984) 65–72, 16 refs.

English abstract in AATA vol. 22 (1985) #22-528.

Law

Books

1608

Chatelain, Jean. *Forgery in the art world*. Brussels: Commission of the European Communities, 1979, 190p., bibliog., 7 appendices.

English abstracts in ABM vol. 13 (1982) #5489 and AATA vol. 21 (1984) #21-51.

1609

Drachsler, Leo and Torczyner, Harry (Eds.) *Forgery in art and the law: a symposium held under the auspices of the Federal Bar Association of New York, New Jersey and Connecticut*. New York: Federal Legal Publishers, 1956, 61p.

English abstract in AATA vol. 3 (1960–1961) #3090.

1610

Van De Waal, H., et al. *Aspects of art forgery: a symposium organized by the Institute of Criminal Law and Criminology of the University of Leiden*. The Hague: Martinus Nijhoff, 1962, 53 p.

Contents: Foreword, by J.M. Van Bemmelen; "Forgery as a stylistic problem," by Dr. H. Van De Waal; "Criminological and criminal-law problems of the forging of painting," by Dr. Thomas Würtenberger; "Criminalistic aspects of art forgery," by Dr. W. Froentjes.

1611

Würtenberger, Thomas. *Der Kampf gegen das Kunstfälschertum in der deutschen und schweizerischen Strafrechtspflege* (The battle against the art forgeries in the German and Swiss criminal courts). Weisbaden: F. Steiner, 1951, xi + 179p, 17 illus.

1612

Würtenberger, Thomas. *Das Kunstfälschertum: Entstehung und Bekämpfung eines Verbrechens vom Anfang des 15. bis zum Ende des 18. Jahrhunderts* (Art forgery: uprise and battle against criminals from the beginning of the 15th century to the end of the 18th century). [2., im Text unveränderte, durch einen Anhang vermehrte Auflage]. Weimar: H. Böhlaus Nachfolger, 1940. [Leipzig, Zentralantiquariat der Deutschen Demokratischen Republik, 1970], xiii + 264p.

Sections of Books

1613

Arnau, Frank (Pseud.) "Some cases in brief," in his *Three thousand years of deception in art and antiques.* Translated from the German by J. Maxwell Brownjohn. London: Jonathan Cape, 1961, pp. 295–328.

Arnau reports on the court cases of Otto Wacker, Han van Meegeren, and Lothar Malskat. For the contents of Arnau's entire book, see #78.

1614

Bochicchio, Sergio; and Mastelloni, Adriano. *Guida giuridica Bolaffi dell'arte: corredata da richiami giurisprudenziali e bibliografici nelle singole voci, da un appendice legislativa e da una bibliografia di interesse generale.* Torino: G. Bolaffi, 1973, 297 p., bibliography (pp. 291–294), index.

1615

Brandow, Wendy Waldron. "Art fraud and forgery," in her *Selected bibliography on law and fine art.* Chicago: The John Marshall Law School Library, 1984, pp. 55-57.

1616

Crawford, Tad. *Legal guide for the visual artist.* New York: Hawthorn Books, Inc., 1977, pp. 195–198.

1617

Duboff, Leonard D. "Authentication" (Chapter XI), in his *The deskbook of art law,* 1st Ed. Washington, D.C.: Federal Publications, Inc., 1977, pp. 384–475, passim. Supplemented by *The deskbook of art law supplement 1984.* Washington, D.C.: Federal Publications, Inc., 1984, pp. XI-1–XI-8.

Contents of Chapter XI: A. Incentives for forgery; B. Defining the problems; C. Experts & establishing authenticity; D. Methods of authentication; E. attempted legal solutions; F. Art & the Uniform Commercial Code; G. UCC-express warranties; H. UCC-implied warranties; I. Remedies for breach of warranty; J. Fine print legislation; K. Other suggested solutions.

1618

Duboff, Leonard D. "Authentication," in his *Art law in a nutshell* (Nutshell Series), St. Paul, Minnesota: West Publishing Co., 1984, pp. 66–100, passim.

1619

Duboff, Leonard D. "The authentication of art" (Part Three), in *Art law: domestic and international.* South Hackensack, N.J.: Fred B. Rothman & Co., 1975, pp. 475-559, passim.

English abstracts in RILA vol. 2 (1976) #3702 and ABM vol. 8 (1977) #0553.

1620

DuBoff, Leonard D. and Frantz, Julie S. "What is real: authenticity or aesthetics in art," in *Law and the visual arts*, Leonard D. DuBoff and Mary Ann DuBoff. Portland, 1974, 303 + .

1621

Duffy, Robert E. "Theft and art fakes, scientific verification and fine art prints," in his *Art law: representing artists, dealers, and collectors*. New York: Practicing Law Institute, 1977, pp. 4–12, 57–74.

Includes a section on the California and Illinois Print Acts, New York state statute and legislation regarding prints.

1622

Feldman, Franklin and Weil, Stephen. *Art works: law, policy, practice.* New York: Practicing Law Institute, c1974, passim.

Coverage in the areas of frauds and forgeries include: legislation, prevention, the Uniform Commercial Code, liability, remedies against frauds and forgeries, and court cases.

1623

Goodrich, Lloyd. "Lawsuits," in his *Art fakes in America.* New York: The Viking Press, pp. 133–155.

For contents of Goodrich's entire book see #90.

1624

Hodes, Scott. *The law of art and antiques: a primer for artists and collectors.* New York: Oceana Publications, Inc., 1966, pp. 54–55, 107.

1625

Hodes, Scott, "Art forgery—protection for artists and collectors," in his *Legal rights in the art and collectors' world* (Legal almanac series no. 56). Dobbs Ferry, New York: Oceana Publications, Inc., 1982, pp. 27–34.

1626

Hollander, Barnett. "Fakes, forgeries and frauds," in his *The international law of art for lawyers, collectors and artists.* London: Bowes & Bowes, 1959, pp. 175–196, passim.

English abstract in AATA vol. 3 (1960–1961) #2808.

1627

Lerner, Ralph E. (Chairman) *Representing artists, collectors, and dealers.* New York: Practicing Law Institute, 1981, pp. 715–727.

Reproduced are: "Questions regarding authentication formulated by the Art Committee of the Bar of the City of New York"; "Part A: Certificate of Authenticity, Ownership and Value—International Art Registry Limited"; "Part B: Model certificate of authenticity"; "What is an original print? (Principles recommended by the Print Council of America)"; "Sale of fine prints (The Illinois statute)."

1628

Malaro, Marie E. *A legal primer on managing museum collections.* Washington, D.C.: Smithsonian Institution Press, 1985, pp. 61–63.

1629

Merryman, John Henry, and Elsen, Albert E. *Law, ethics and the visual arts: cases and materials.* 2 vols., Looseleaf. New York: Matthew Bender, 1979, vol. II, Chapter VI, pp. 6-1–6-182.

This is an invaluable source for the professional who must deal with the legal points surrounding fakes and forgeries, or any area of the visual arts. Comments from the authors are coupled with excerpts from books, articles from journals, Uniform Commercial Code excerpts, case law, etc. Relevant areas covered in Chapter VI are: A. The acquisition of art; The art market; B. The acquisition of art at auction; C. Consumer protection and the fine arts: (1) Prints, (2) Sculptural reproduction, (3) Fakes and forgeries, (4) Experts and expertise, (5) The disposition of counterfeit art, (6) Theft and art-napping.

1630

Olin, Charles. "The problem of authentication of oil paintings," in Leonard D. DuBoff, and Mary Ann DuBoff, *Law and the Visual Arts*, Portland: 1974, p. 333 + .

1631

Ripin, Edwin. "Franciolini's trial" (Appendix I), in his *The instrument catalogs of Leopoldo Franciolini*. Hackensack, N.J.: Joseph Boonin, Inc., 1974, pp. 181–199. In Italian and English.

The *Sentenza* from musical instrument forger Leopoldo Franciolini's trial in Italy, 1910–1911. For the full contents of Ripin's book see #1262.

1632

Wear, Bruce. "Appendix C: trial- A case on Remington bronzes," in his *The second bronze world of Frederic Remington*. Ranch Publishing Company, 1976.

For the full contents of Wear's book see #488.

Periodicals

1633

Akston, J.J. Art, fraud and equity. *Arts* (USA) 40 (1966) 12; Discussion. 40 (March 1966) 11; 40 (April 1966) 8; 40 (June 1966) 8; 40 (September 1966) 6, 10.

1634

Anderson, Lanie. (Comment) Consumer protection legislation in the sale of original prints: a proposal for Michigan. *University of Detroit Journal of Urban Law* (USA), 57 no. 1 (Fall 1979) 55–93.

Contents: I. Introduction; II. What is an original print?; III. The forgery problem and the buyer's remedies under the Uniform Commercial Code; IV. Existing art print legislation; V. Model art print legislation.

1635

Bauman, Lawrence Scott. Legal control of the fabrication and marketing of fake paintings. *Stanford Law Review* (USA), 24 (May 1972) 930–946.

1636

Baynes-Cope, David. Museum frauds and forgeries, intentional and unintentional. *Medico-Legal Journal* (England), 43 Part I (1975) 25–34.

1637

Berkowitz, Rhoda. Law and the visual arts: an annotated bibliography. *Law Library Journal* (USA), 70 (February 1977) 5–13.

Contains a short section on consumer protection, of value chiefly for its scope. This is a good introduction to the legal literature covering the entire field of the visual arts.

1638

Brooks, Valerie F. Forgeries charged in Louisiana. *ARTnews* (USA), 84 no. 9 (November 1985) 22.

Art dealer David Lucier, of Mount Clemens, Michigan, is sued for $260,000 by the Louisiana Auction Exchange, in Baton Rouge. Jacob Wientraub, a New York dealer, is also a plaintiff in the case. The LAE claims that eleven artworks consigned to them by Lucier are forgeries and that he never delivered papers to them documenting their authenticity and provenances.

1639

Brooks, Valerie F. A horse of a different color. *ARTnews* (USA), 84 no. 5 (May 1985) 19, 1 illus.

"A painting once thought to be an original George Stubbs, but whose authorship is now in doubt, is the center of a dispute between Sotheby's in New York, which auctioned the work last year, and the picture's consignor, who blames the auctioneers for his being unable to collect the sale proceeds or to reclaim the painting." (From the article).

1640

Cahn, Joshua Binion. What is an original print? *New York State Bar Journal* (USA), 37 no. 6 (December 1965) 546–553.

1641

Chamberlain, Betty. Appraising art acquisitions. *American Artist* (USA), 45 (May 1981) 14, 86, 87.

Chamberlain discusses Art Appraisal and Information, Inc., in Montclair, New Jersey; especially its role in the authentication of art works.

1642

Chamberlain, Betty. Fraudulence curtailed. *American Artist* (USA), 46 no. 476 (March 1982) 10, 71–72.

On the New York state law regulating the sales of prints and photographs in editions.

1643

Chamberlain, Betty. Gold brick control. *American Artist* (USA), 45 no. 464 (March 1981) 10–11.

A discussion of fakes and frauds in prints and sculpture, and the need for effective legislation.

1644

Cillario, A. Ho comprato un quadro. È falso. Che cosa faccio? (I have bought a picture. It's a fake. What do I do?) *Bolaffiarte* (Italy) 6 no. 48 (March–April 1975) 64.

English abstract in ABM vol. 6 (1975) #4819.

1645

Colin, Ralph F. The Art Dealers Association of America, Inc. *Museum News* (USA), 41 no. 10 (1963) 25–26.

English abstract in AATA vol. 4 (1962–1963) #3895.

1646

Colin, Ralph F. Legal problems involved in art forgery. *Lex et Scientia*, 73 (April/June 1968) 73, 84–85.

1647

The Committee on Art, the Association of the Bar of the City of New York. (Franklin Feldman, Chairman). Disposition of fake art. *The Record of the New York City Bar Association* (USA), 26 no. 7 (Oct. 1971) 591–600.

Contents: Introduction; "Continuing confiscation" of fake art; Re-entry of fake art into commerce, (1) Reliance on existing law, (2) Making the object to denote its fake status (3) Establishing a central registry of fake art, (4) Establishing an "Archive of Fake Art," (5) Allowing the artist or his estate to destroy or reclaim a fake object, (6) Issuance of an appropriate court order or directive to the fake object's present owner; Conclusion.

1648

The Committee on Art, the Association of the Bar of the City of New York. (Harris B. Steinberg, Chairman). Legal problems of art authentication. *The Record of the New York City Bar Association* (USA), 21 no. 2 (February 1966) 96–102.

Contents: Introduction; Paintings and drawings; Prints; Sculpture; Antiquities; Conclusion.

1649

Deighten, E. Art and the law. *Art and Artists* (England), 4 (September 1969) 6.

1650

Duboff, Leonard D. Controlling the artful con: authentication and regulation. *Hastings Law Journal* (USA), 27 no. 5 (May 1976) 973–1021.

"The author discusses forgeries of art works, examines methods of detection, and analyzes existing legislation designed to protect art purchasers. He offers proposals which would further protect art customers and reduce the incidence of art fraud." (Abstract of article).

1651

Duffy, Robert E. Jr. Disclosure requirements in connection with the sale of fine art prints. *California State Bar Journal* (USA), 48 no. 5 (September/ October 1973) 528–534, 605, illus.

1652

Easby, Dudley T. Jr. and Colin, Ralph F. The legal aspects of forgery and the protection of the expert. *Metropolitan Museum of Art Bulletin* (USA), 26 (1967–1968) 257–261.

1653

Elsen, Albert and Merryman, John Henry. Art replicas: a question of ethics. *ARTnews* (USA) 78 no. 2 (February 1979) 61.

1654

Feldhaus, F.M. Imitation emerald problems in the 16th century. *The Gemologist.* (England), 23(1954) 174.

On court cases in Nuremberg from 1480–1588.

1655

Feldman, Franklin. New protection for the art collector—warranties. Opinions and disclaimers. *The Record of the Association of the Bar of the City of New York* (USA), 23 (1968) 661–668.

1656

Froentjes, W. The van Meegeren case. The scientific investigation. *International Criminal Police Review* (France), 3 (December 1948) 7–15, illus.

English abstract in G + U #181.

1657

Gibson, Michael. For the love of Mondrian. *ARTnews* (USA), 84 no. 8 (October 1985) 121–122, 1 illus.

In September 1984, a French court ruled that 3 Mondrians purchased by the Musée National d'Art Moderne at the Pompidou Center are forgeries. Payment had not yet been made on the paintings; the court ordered Simone Verde, the seller of the paintings, to pay the museum one franc in symbolic damages, 10,000 francs (about $1,000) to Harry Holtzman, Mondrian's heir, and 20,000 francs to a collector, Baron Hans Heinrich Thyssen-Bornemisza, who purchased a forged Mondrian from Verde in 1976.

1658

Grant, Julius. Forensic scientist—still at large! *Medico-Legal Journal* (England), 50 Part 2 (Summer 1982) 61–74.

1659

Harvey, Brian. Violin frauds, fakes and misdescriptions: the law. *The Strad* (England), Part 1, 93 no. 1106 (June 1982) 93–94, illus.; Part 2, 93 no. 1107 (July 1982) 173–175; Part 3, 93 no. 1108 (August 1982) 261–262.

"Parts 1 and 2 looked at the law one hundred years ago and the law today, examining the differences. Part 3, the last in the series, discusses the problem of authentication." (Abstract to the articles).

1660

Hess, Thomas B. The modest faker: a cautionary history of the recently arrested Paris ring of art forgers, followed by some modest suggestions for improving the trade. *ARTnews* (USA), 61 no. 3 (May 1962) 42.

English abstract in AATA vol. 4 (1962–1963) #3675.

1661

Hirt, R. Straftaten im Zusammenhang mit dem Kunst und Antiquitätenhandel. Teil 1 und 2 (Offenses connected with the fine art and antique trade. Parts 1 and 2). *Kriminalistik* (Switzerland), 1 (1983) 47–52; 2 (1983) 114–118.

1662

Hochfield, Sylvia. Problems in the reproduction of sculpture: flagrant abuses, pernicious practices and counterfeit sculpture are widespread. *ARTnews* (USA), 73 (November 1974) 20–29, 10 illus.; Discussion. 74 (January 1975) 22; 74 (December 1975) 24 +.

English abstracts in ABM vol. 9 (1978) #3409 and RILA vol. 1 (1975) #474.

1663

Hochfield, Sylvia. Quando lo scultore si rivolta nella tomba: lo scandalo delle fusioni (When the sculptor turns in his grave: the casting scandal). *Bolaffiarte* (Italy) 7 no. 65 (December 1976–January 1977) 26–37, 6 illus.

On the abuses in sculptural reproduction after an artist's death. This article also includes the entire text of the "Declaration on the norms for the reproduction of sculpture and on the preventative measures in opposing bronze castings contrary to ethics," drafted by Albert Elsen. English abstract in ABM vol. 8 (1977) #5067.

1664

Hodes, Scott. Art legislation for Illinois a reality. *Illinois Bar Journal* (USA), 60 (1972) 370–374.

1665

Hodes, Scott. 'Fake' art and the law. *Federal Bar Association Journal* (USA), 27 (1967) 73–78.

1666

Hodes, Scott. Wanted: art legislation in Illinois. *Illinois Bar Journal* (USA), 57 (1968) 218–222.

1667

Houseman, Lee Ann. Current practices and problems in combating illegality in the art market. *Seton Hall Law Review* (USA), 12 no. 3 (Summer 1982) 506–567.

Contents: Forgery; A. Methods of art forgery, B. Methods of detecting art forgery; Fraud; Art theft; Stolen antiquities; Marine antiquities; Non-legal solutions; Legal solutions; Conclusion.

1668

Hoving, Thomas. Let the seller beware. *Connoisseur* (England), 214 no. 874 (December 1984) 25, 1 illus.

Hoving recalls how, during the early 1960s, "The law of the art business was 'Caveat Emptor'—let the buyer beware." He notes how this situation has changed. Museums now demand that their money be returned when they discover they have purchased a fake, and are willing to go to court to seek redress. The seller should guarantee that an artwork can be returned and the sale price refunded if it is proven that the artwork was "incorrectly described" as to provenance, date or maker.

1669

Isnard, Guy. L'expertise scientifique des oeuvres d'art. (Scientific expertise of works of art). *Revue Internationale de police criminelle* (France), no. 68 (1953) 138–150, illus.

1670

Isnard, Guy. La répression des fraudes artistiques en France. *Gazette des Beaux-Arts* (France), 48 (1956) 177–182, 6 illus. Summary in English.

Description of an organization in France, created by the author to eliminate art frauds.

1671

Jordon, H.; Simon, A.; Pforte, K.; and Kaiser, R. Counterfeit ivory miniatures— contribution to problems of antique forgery. *Kriminalistik und Forensische Wissenschaften* (Germany) 1977 no. 30 (1977) 67–80.

1672

Ketchum, Linda E. Forgery producer infiltrates market with fakes. *Western Association for Art Conservation Newsletter* (USA), 5 no. 3 (September 1983) 3–5.

On the activities of Forgery of the Month, Inc., in Chicago. The company sells fake lithographs and drawings attributed to masters.

English abstract in AATA vol. 21 (1984) # 21–359.

1673

Kiejman, Mme Georges. Le faux en art et sa répression par le droit français (Fakes in art and its repression by French law). *Revue de l'Art* (France), no. 21 (1973) 125–128. Summary in English.

1674

Kincaid, Robert M., Jr. [Comment]. The Uniform Commercial Code warranty provisions and the theory of strict liability in tort as solutions to art counterfeiting in paintings: a critical analysis. *St. Louis University Law Journal* (USA), 20 no. 3, (1976) 531–558.

1675

Lane, Alvin S. The case of the careless collector. *Art in America* (USA), 53 no. 5 (October–November 1965) 90–95, illus.

"The purpose of this article is to touch on some of the abuses and questionable practices that currently exist in the field of contemporary art and to recommend solutions. Reference will be made to the roles of the collector, dealer, auction gallery, foundry, artist, museum and customs office" (From the article).

1676

Lane, Alvin S. Lawyer finds public needs protection. *Trial* (USA), 2 no. 6 (October–November 1966) 36–37.

The author purchased a forged Jean Harp sculpture which was accompanied by a forged certificate of authentication. He recounts the story and how his money was eventually returned. He suggests that a national registry of art be created, and offers other proposals that would protect collectors.

1677

Martin, Daniel L. Art warranties and certificates of authentication, or the case of the sterile bull. *New York State Bar Journal* (USA), 48 No. 3 (April 1976) 193–195.

An examination of the New York state law relating "to certificates of authentication and warranties as to works of art."

1678

McKay, Shona. Con game that fakes real art. *MacLeans* (Canada), 92 (8 October 79) 10–11, illus.

This article touches on the prevalence of forgeries on the market, fakes in the Royal Ontario Museum's African Art Collection, and the Routhier case in Canada, involving forged paintings purchased by the National Gallery in Ottawa.

1679

Merryman, John Henry, and Duffy, Robert E. Art and the law. *Art Journal* (USA), 34 no. 4 (Summer 1975) 332–336.

English abstract in ABM vol. 6 (1975) #3976.

1680

The new Visual Arts Multiples Law: its impact on artists, dealers and collectors. *Print Review* (USA), 16 (1983) 65–78.

An edited transcript of a discussion held on 9 March 1982, concerning the new Visual Arts Multiples Law. It was held at the Association of the Bar of the City of New York. Panel members were: Renato Beghe, Moderator; Gustav Harrow; Sylvan Cole, Jr.; Norman J. Itzkoff; Franklin Feldman; Daniel L. Kurtz; with commentary by Bill Barnet.

1681

Nicol, Andrew. Fakes and facsimiles: legal aspects. *Museums Journal* (England), 83 (March 1984) 207–210.

1682

Penelope, M. Speculazione e inganno (Speculation and fraud). *Arte a Stampa* (Italy), no. 7 (May–June 1979) 16–17, 1 illus.

On the surge of fake prints in Italy and the relation between this proliferation and legislation passed by the Italian Parliament in 1976.
English abstract in ABM vol. 16 (1985) #5630.

1683

Pollock, Phillip. Art print legislation in California: a critical review. *Stanford Law Review* (USA), 25 (April 1973) 586–604.

1684

Ragghianti, Carlo Ludovico. Il caso de Chirico (The de Chirico case). *Critica d'arte* (Italy), 44 no. 163–165 (January–June 1979) 3–54, 199 illus.

English abstracts in RILA vol. 7 (1981) #7018 and ABM vol. 11 (1980) #5007.
French abstract in RAA 1980 #6949.

1685

Rasky, F. Interpol mountie who sleuths down fake, forged and stolen art. *Arts Magazine* (USA), 56 (November–January 1981–82) 73–76.

1686

Ruggles, Mervyn. An art fraud case—a conservator's evidence given in court. *American Institute for Conservation Journal, Preprints* (USA), Toronto, May 30–June 1 (1979), 116–121, photos, 9 refs.

English abstract in AATA vol. 16 (1979) #16-1519.

1687

Saunders, Laura. Get it in writing. *Forbes* (USA), 137 no. 5, (10 March 86) 96.

An art collector sold two of his paintings at a substantial loss after he discovered they were fakes, and deducted the remaining portion of the purchase price from his taxes as a theft loss. The IRS disallowed the deduction for the Poussin and let stand the deduction for the William Merritt Chase. The Poussin was not signed; the Chase bore his "signature."

1688

Schulder, Diane. Art proceeds act: a study of the *Droit de Suite* and a proposed enactment for the United States. *Northwestern University Law Review* (USA), 61 no. 1 (March–April 1966) 19–45.

1689

Shientag, Florence. Some legal aspects of art and fake art. *Women Lawyers' Journal* (USA), 54 no. 1 (1968) 23–27.

1690

Skolnik, Peter Barry. Art forgery: the art market and legal considerations. *Nova Law Journal* (USA), 7 (Winter 1983) 315–352.

Contents: Introduction; I. Art forgery—a philosophical enigma; II. Art forgery—A reflection of the history and development of the art market, A. Early history, B. The modern market; III. Art forgery—legal considerations, A. Factors perpetuating art forgery, B. Other problems to be considered, C. The Uniform Commercial Code—the problem continues, D. New York legislation leads the way; Conclusion.

1691

Stein, Claire. Demand, documentation and definition. *National Sculpture Review* (USA), 24 no. 4 (Winter 1975–1976) 7, 27.

Abuses in the reproduction and sale of sculpture. The need to establish ethical guidelines requiring careful documentation of sculptural works and the establishment of precise definitions for documentation purposes. The role of the College Art Association in establishing ethical guidelines is discussed.

1692

Stolow, Nathan. This art was a crime. *Canadian Art* (Canada), 21 no. 6 (November/December 1964) 354–357, illus.

Summary of the scientific and technical evidence used in the Canadian art fraud case (forged paintings).

English abstract in AATA vol. 5 (1964–1965) #5054.

1693

Tedeschi, G. Art forgeries and their prevention. *Israel Law Review* (Israel), 4 no. 3 (July 1969) 364–370.

1694

Trustman, Deborah. Abuses in the reproduction of sculpture. *ARTnews* (USA), 80 no. 6 (June 1981) 84–92, 6 illus.

"Despite efforts by the College Art Association and others to raise public consciousness about methods—ethical and unethical—of sculptural reproduction, 'pernicious practices and counterfeit sculpture' are still widespread." (Abstract to the article).

1695

Unsigned article. The artists speak: how to protect the public. *Time* (USA), 87 (7 January 66) 59.

On interviews with artists held by New York Attorney General Louis Lefkowitz regarding art forgeries and fakes.

1696

Unsigned article. Checklist of legal and other aspects of art forgery, or the gentle art of faking. *Record of the Association of the Bar of the City of New York* (USA), 29 no. 516 (May–June 1974) 512–517.

1697

Unsigned article. [Comment]. *British Journal of Photography* (England), 127 no. 6281 (12 December 1980) 1229–1230.

Jury trial of two men in England (the Ovenden hoax) for selling fake Victorian photographs.

1698

Unsigned article. [Comment]. *British Journal of Photography* (England), 126 no. 6211 (10 August 1979) 753–754.

An Oldham man is convicted and sentenced to 12 months in prison for selling forged Daguerreotypes to the North Western Museum of Science and Industry, in Manchester.

1699

Unsigned article. Crying 'fake' in a crowded gallery. *ARTnews* (USA), 80 no. 2 (February 1981) 22.

Lawsuit by Diane Gilson against Anne Gould Hauberg for claiming Matisse drawings were fakes at the opening of Gilson's Matisse exhibition.

1700

Unsigned article. Dealing from Park Avenue. *Time* (USA), 89 no. 21, (26 May 1967) 75.

David Stein is indicted on charges of counterfeiting and grand larceny.

1701

Unsigned article. Fake's progress. *Newsweek* (USA), 66 (29 November 1965) 90.

Hearing held by New York State Attorney General Louis J. Lefkowitz on art forgeries.

1702

Unsigned articles. Forged literary works. *AB Bookman's Weekly* (USA), 62 (December 18–25, 1978) 3815.

Robert Frost expert, Thomas E.F. McNamara of Ashland, New Hampshire, is sentenced to one year in federal prison on six counts of mail fraud. McNamara was convicted for selling forged works of American poets.

1703

Unsigned article. Forged Vlamincks and Utrillos. *Apollo* (England), 57 no. 336 (February 1953) 62.

1704

Unsigned article. Master forger. *Time* (USA), 65 (7 February 1955) 64, 67.

The trial of Lothar Malskat and Dietrich Fey for forging Saint Mary's gothic murals in Lubeck, Germany.

1705

Unsigned article. A Paris judge uncovers an art fraud. *Geo* (USA), 6 (August 1984) 100, illus.

Three Piet Mondrian paintings sold to the Pompidou Center by Simone Verde are declared forgeries by a Paris judge.

1706

Unsigned article. Personal business: con men frame naive collectors ... *Business Week* (USA) 20 May 1967, pp. 165–166.

Brief article on the need to get a written guarantee of authenticity when purchasing art.

1707

Unsigned article. Personal business: some perils that face the art buyer. *Business Week* (USA), 2 November 1968, pp. 137–138.

On the need to authenticate paintings and prints at the time of purchase.

1708

Unsigned article [note]. Protecting the public interest in art. *Yale Law Journal* (USA), 91 no. 1 (November 1981) 121–143.

1709

Unsigned article [note]. Uniform Commercial Code warranty solutions to art fraud and forgery. *William & Mary Law Review* (USA), 14 (1972) 409–429.

1710

VerMeulen, M. The case of the curious Cassatt ... or elementary my dear Watson. *New Art Examiner* (USA), 4 no. 8 (May 1977), 1, 8, 1 illus.

English abstract in ABM vol. 10 (1979) #1090.

1711

Walker, Richard W. New York cracks down on Dali forgeries *ARTnews* (USA), 85 no. 5 (May 1986) 28.

Seven people indicted on 27 counts for the sale of forged Dali lithographs.

1712
Wallach, Amei. The trouble with prints: abuses in today's market. *ARTnews* (USA), 80 no. 5 (May 1981) 60–69, 11 illus.
English abstract in RILA vol. 8 (1982) #3785. French abstract in RAA 1981 #12980.

1713
Würtenberger, Thomas. Criminal damages to art—a criminological study. *De Paul Law Review* (USA), 14 no. 1 (Autumn 1964) 83–92.

Chronological List of Some Exhibitions and Exhibition Catalogs of Fakes and Forgeries

1714
Whitechapel Art Gallery, London, Spring Exhibition, 1908.
The exhibition was of copies of pictures only.

1715
Exhibition of Reproductions and Forgeries, Armor Department, Metropolitan Museum of Art, Continuing Exhibition in the Main Gallery, 1914–.

1716
Copenhagen, Danske Kunstindustrimuseum, 1915.
Copenhagen: Danske Kunstindustrimuseum. *Fortrolig Fortegnelse over en raekke Forfalskninger. Forsög til en Bibliografi over Forfalskninger af Kunsthaandvaerk.* 2 vols. [Illustrated Catalogue of an Exhibition of Forgeries, and Bibliography]. 1915.

1717
Fakes and Reproductions, Pennsylvania Museum, Philadelphia, PA, 1916.
Exhibition of fakes and reproductions. Preface by Edwin Atlee Barber. Philadelphia, PA, 1916, 64 p., illus.
The exhibition was limited to the industrial arts.

1718
20 Fake Aubrey Beardsley's Exhibited in New York, 1919.

1719
Austellung gefälschte Kunstwerk, Kunsthistorische Museum, Vienna, September–October 1923.

1720

London, Burlington Fine Arts Club, 1924.

Catalogue of a Collection of Counterfeits, Imitations and Copies of Works of Art. London: Privately printed for the Burlington Fine Arts Club by Frederick Hall, Oxford University Press, 1924, 28 p., bibliography (p. 28).

1721

Sculpture by Aleco Dossena, National Art Galleries, Inc., New York, March 9, 1933.

1722

Facsimiles & Forgeries, William L. Clements Library of American History, Michigan University, Ann Arbor, Michigan, 1934.

Michigan University. William L. Clements Library of American History. *Facsimiles & forgeries: a guide to a timely exhibition in the William L. Clements Library.* Ann Arbor, 1934, 14 p., front. (Its Bulletin no. 21). 1000 copies printed.

1723

Copies des Maitre, Kunst Museum Basel, September–November 1937.

1724

Kunsthistoriches Museum, Vienna, 1937.

1725

A Jekyll-and-Hyde Exhibition, Colby College Library, Waterville, Maine, May 1938. (A two week exhibition on Thomas J. Wise forgeries, commencing on the 13th of May 1938, the 1st anniversary of his death).

A Jekyll-and-Hyde Exhibition. Colby College Library, N. Orwin Rush, Librarian. Waterville, Maine, May 13, 1938. Maine: Colby College Library, 9 p., 1 illus.

1726

Art: Genuine or Counterfeit? Fogg Art Museum, Cambridge, Massachusetts, 1940.

Art: Genuine or Counterfeit. A loan Exhibition arranged by Professor Paul Sachs' Museum Class. Cambridge, MA: The Fogg Museum of Art, Harvard University, 1940, 16 p. & 1 p. bibliog.

1727

University of Texas, 1–30 October 1942.

Texas. University. *An exhibition of manuscripts and printed books at the University of Texas, October 1–30, 1942: Alfred, Lord Tennyson, 1809–1892.* Austin, 1942, 20 p. Signed: Fannie E. Ratchford. The Wise forgeries, pp. 16–20.

1728

Certain Nineteenth Century Forgeries, University of Texas, Austin, 1946.

Texas. University. Library. *Certain nineteenth century forgeries. An exhibition of books and letters at the University of Texas, June 1–September 30, 1946.* Described by Fannie E. Ratchford, Austin, 1946, 57 p.

A descriptive catalog of certain forgeries sold by Thomas J. Wise to John Henry Wrenn but now a part of the Rare Book Collection of the University of Texas Library.

1729

Facsimiles & Forgeries, William L. Clements Library of American History, Michigan University, Ann Arbor, Michigan, 1950.

Michigan University. William L. Clements Library of American History. *Facsimiles & forgeries: a guide to a timely exhibition in the William L. Clements Library.* Ann Arbor, 1950, 26 p. (Its Bulletin 59, revised and enlarged from Bulletin 21). Introduction by Howard Mumford Jones.

1730

Forgeries, Facsimiles and Questioned Documents, The National Society of Autograph Collectors, Exhibited in the Library of Congress, 1950.

1731

Fakes and Forgeries in Museums, Ashmolean Museum, Oxford, England, 1952.

1732

Vals of Echt? (True or False?) Stedlijk Museum, Amsterdam, 1952.

Van Dantzig, Maurits Michel; Kersten, W.W.; Jaffe, H.L.C.; Sandberg, W.; and Friedlander, Max. *Vals of Echt?* Introduction by Max Friedlander. Amsterdam, Netherlands: Stedlijk Museum, 28 p., 3 b&w illus. Summary in English and French.

1733

True or False? Corning Museum of Glass, Corning, New York, 1953–1954. (The "Vals of Echt?" exhibition from Amsterdam).

Van Dantzig, Maurits Michel; and Buechner, Thomas S., et al. *True or false?* Catalog of an exhibition organized and circulated in Europe by the Stedelijk Museum in Amsterdam, Netherlands. Circulated in the USA by the Corning Museum of Glass, Corning Glass Center, Corning, N.Y., 1953–1954. Amsterdam, Keesing's Systems, 1953, 51 p., 46 illus.

1734

Take Care, Brooklyn Museum, 1954. Organized by Mr. and Mrs. Sheldon Keck.

Emphasis of the exhibition was on the conservation of paintings, authentication, and detection of fakes.

1735

Le faux dans l'art et dans l'histoire, Paris, Grand palais, 1954.

1736

Exhibition of Thomas J. Wise Books, University of Texas, Austin, The Wrenn Library, 1959.

Todd, Dr. William B. *Various extraordinary books procured by Thomas J. Wise and displayed on All Fools Day in observance of the centenary of his birth.* Austin, Texas: The Humanities Research Center, The University of Texas, 1959, 18 p.
300 copies printed.

1737

Forgeries and Deceptive Copies, The British Museum, London, 1961.

British Museum. *An exhibition of forgeries and deceptive copies held in the department of prints and drawings.* London: British Museum, 1961, 30 p., index. (Includes floor plan of the exhibition).

1738

Silver Stummers, London, Black Starr & Gorham, 1961.

An exhibition of forged silver-plated English pieces, together with authentic pieces, on display at Black Starr & Gorham's 150th Birthday anniversary exhibition.

1739

Crime and the Literati: Fraud and Forgery in Literature, Peabody Institute Library, Baltimore, Maryland 15 May–15 June 1962.

Peabody Institute, Baltimore. Library. *Crime and the literati: fraud and forgery in literature. Exhibition at the Peabody Institute Library, Baltimore, May & June 1962.* Baltimore: the library, 1962, 35 p., index, bibliography (pp. 29–33).

1740

Wise After the Event, Manchester Central Library, September, 1964.

Haslam, George Eric, (Ed). *Wise after the event: a catalogue of books, pamphlets, manuscripts and letters relating to Thomas J. Wise displayed in an exhibition in Manchester Central Library, September, 1964.* Manchester: Manchester Libraries Committee, 1964, xii, 86 p., facsims.
500 copies printed.

1741

Art: Authentic and Fake, Graham Gallery, New York, May 1967.

1742

Fakes and Frauds, Madison Art Center, Madison, Wisconsin, November–December, 1967.

1743

Fakes, Frauds and Forgeries, Portland Art Museum, Portland, Oregon, February, 1969.

1744

David Stein Forgeries, The Wright-Hepburn Gallery, London, 1969.

Paintings exhibited under his own name.

1745

David Stein Forgeries, The Wright-Hepburn-Webster Gallery, New York, 1970.

Paintings exhibited under his own name.

1746

Know What You See, The Renaissance Society of the University of Chicago, Chicago, October–November, 1970.

1747

Elmyr de Hory Forgeries, The Wright Hepburn Gallery, London, May, 1971.

1748

Rodin Drawings, True and False, National Gallery of Art, Washington, D.C., November 20, 1971–January 23, 1972; The Solomon R. Guggenheim Museum, New York, March 9–May 14, 1972.

Varnedoe, J. Kirk T.; and Elsen, Albert. *The drawings of Rodin.* With additional contributions by Victoria Thorson and Elizabeth Chase Geissbuhler. New York: Praeger Publishers, 1971, 191 p., 152 illus., bibliog. See especially "True and false," pp. 157–185 by J. Kirk T. Varnedoe.

1749

Documents Famous and Infamous, New York Public Library, 1972–1973.

Szladits, Lola L. *Documents: famous & infamous; selected from the Henry W. and Albert A. Berg Collection of English and American literature.* New York: New York Public Library, 1972, 34 p., illus.

1750

Problems of Authenticity in Nineteenth and Twentieth Century Art, The Art Museum, Princeton University, June 1–30, 1973.

1751

Fakes and Forgeries, Minneapolis, Minneapolis Institute of Arts, 12 July 1973–29 September 1973.

Minneapolis Institute of Arts. *Fakes and forgeries: [Catalog of an exhibition] the Minneapolis Institute of Arts, July 11–September 29, 1973.* Introduction by Samuel Sachs, II. Essay by Kathryn C. Johnson. Minneapolis: The Institute, 1973, 272 p., 292 illus. Bibliography: pp 264–270.

1752

Copias, Replicas, Pastiches, Louvre, Paris, 1974.

1753

Dürer Through Other Eyes: His Graphic Art Mirrored in Copies and Forgeries of Three Centuries. Williamstown, Massachusetts, Sterling and Francine Clark Art Institute, 1975.

Adams, Judith; Cogswell, Elizabeth; Cohn, Anna; Fisher, Jay; and Held, Julius. *Dürer through other eyes: his graphic art mirrored in copies and forgeries of three centuries* (Includes an essay on techniques of copying and extensive bibliographical notes). Williamstown, Massachusetts: Sterling and Francine Clark Art Institute, 1975, 99 p., 71 b&w illus., 7 p. bibliography, footnotes.

1754

Falshung und Forschung (Forgery and Research). Essen, Museum Folkwang, October 1976–January 1977; Berlin, Stattliche Museen Preussischer Kulturbesitz, Skulpturenabteilung, January–March 1977.

Fälschung und Forschung: Ausstellung Museum Folkwang Essen, Oktober 1976–Januar 1977: Skulpturengalerie, Staatliche Museen Preussischer Kulturbesitz Berlin, Januar-März 1977. Katalogbearb., Heinz Althöfer, et al. Essen: Museum Folkwang; Berlin: Skulpturengalerie, 1976, 208 p., 109 illus., bibliog., 219 works shown.

For a brief description of the exhibition with the titles and authors of seven essays in the catalog, see RILA vol. 3 (1977) #3731.

1755

Forgery—Literary and Historical, Manuscript and Printed. New York, The Grolier Club, Autumn Exhibition, 1977.

1756

The Eye of the Beholder: Fakes, Replicas and Alterations in American Art, New Haven, Connecticut, Yale University Art Gallery, 14 May–10 July 1977.

Yale University, Art Gallery. *The eye of the beholder: fakes, replicas and alterations in American art, Exhibition 14 May–10 July 1977.* Edited by Gerald W.R. Ward. New Haven, Connecticut: Yale University, Art Gallery, 1977, 95 p., 110 illus., bibliog., 130 works shown.

Contents: Preface by Alan Shestack; List of lenders; Foreword by Charles F. Montgomery; Introduction: fakes, replicas and alterations in American art; Misattributions; Alterations and adaptions; Restorations; Fakes; Revivals; Reproductions; Questionables; Note on the application of science to the examination of works of art.

1757

Wiener Porzellan—echt oder gefälscht, Österreichisches Museum für Angewandte Kunste, Vienna, Austria, 19 Nov. 1976–31 March 1977.

Neuwirth, Waltraud. *Der Bindenschild als Porzellanmarke: original, imitation fälschung, verfälschung* (The Bindenschild as porcelain mark: original,
imitation, forgery). 16 p., 71 b&w photos, bibliog. [Booklet published in
conjunction with the exhibition].

Neuwirth, Waltraud. *Wiener Porzellan: Original, Kopie, Verfälschung,
Fälschung* (Viennese porcelain: original, copy, falsification, forgery). Vienna:
Dr. Waltraud Neuwirth, 1979, 612 p. Also in English and French. 600 illus.,
bibliog. Based on the exhibition 'Wiener Porzellan—echt oder gefälscht?'

1758

Genuine Antiques and their Counterfeits, Southport-Westport Antiques Show,
Fairfield County Hunt Club, Long Lots Road, Westport, Connecticut, 22
April 1977–24 April 1977.

1759

Deceptions in Glass, Toledo Museum of Art, 1977.

Deceptions in Glass. Toledo, Ohio: Toledo Museum of Art, 1977, 4 p., 13
b&w illus.

1760

The Spanish Forger, New York, Pierpont Morgan Library, 19 May–19 July
1978.

Voelkle, William, and Assisted by Roger S. Wieck. *The Spanish Forger.
Exhibition 19 May–29 July 1978.* New York: Pierpont Morgan Library, 76 p.,
130 plates, 316 b&w illus., 6 color illus., 1 p. bibliog., footnotes including
chronology.

The exhibition catalog is the first attempt to publish a catalog of all the
known paintings of the Spanish Forger. English abstract in RILA vol. 5 (1979)
#3622.

1761

Exhibition of Fakes, Forgeries, Hoaxes, and Deceptions, Founders Memorial
Library, Northern Illinois University, Dekalb, Illinois, 1980.

Literary forgeries: T.J. Wise, John Payne Collier, William Henry Ireland,
Chatterton, Ossian, Psalmanazar, etc. The Exhibition covered a period of
400 years.

1762

Original-Kopie-Replik-Paraphrase (Original-copy-replica-paraphrase). Vienna,
Austria, Akademie der Bildenden Kunste, 1980.

Hutter, Heribert; Klauner, Friederike; Kortan, Helmut; Schutz, Karl; Berger, G.; and Polleross, F. *Original-Kopie-Replik-Paraphrase* (Original-copy-
replica-paraphrase). Vienna, Austria: Bildhefte der Akademie der bildenden
Kuenste in Wien 12/13, Vienna, 1980, 60 p., 45 b&w illus., 9 color illus.,
footnotes including chronology.

English abstract in AATA vol. 18 (1981) #18–451.

1763

Seeing is Not Believing, National Gallery of Scotland, The Mound, Edinburgh, 1 July–20 September 1981.

National Gallery of Scotland. *Seeing is not believing. Exhibition 1 July–20 September 1981.* Edinburgh: National Gallery of Scotland, 8 p., 28 illus., 39 works shown.
English abstract in RILA vol. 9 (1983) #1286.

1764

Zinn (Pewter). Dusseldorf, Kunstmuseum, 27 September 1981–31 January 1982.

Schepers, Bearbeitet von Wolfgang. *Zinn.* Dusseldorf: Kunstmuseum, 87 p., illus., 115 works shown, bibliog.
English abstract in RILA vol. 10 (1984) #414.

1765

Cast and Recast: the Sculpture of Frederic Remington. Smithsonian Institution, National Museum of American Art, Washington, D.C., 18 Sept. 1981–3 Jan. 1982.

Shapiro, Michael Edward. *Cast and recast: the sculpture of Frederic Remington.* Smithsonian Institution, National Museum of American Art, Washington, D.C., 127 p., diagrams, 98 illus., bibliog.

1766

The Discerning Eye: A Study in Print Connoisseurship. Philadelphia, Pennsylvania, Associated American Artists, 1982.

1767

Bartolomeo Cavaceppi, Clarenden Gallery, London, 23 November-22 December 1983.

An exhibition of the works of Bartolomeo Cavaceppi—restorer, copyist, forger—and of his employees and contemporaries.

1768

Echt Vals? (Real Fakes?), Allard Pierson Museum, Amsterdam, 1983.

1769

Fakes and Forgeries, Marriages and Deceptions No. 2, 14th Annual Hunt Valley Antiques Show, 24 February-26 February 1984.

At Marriot's Hunt Valley Inn, (North of Baltimore) Maryland.

1770

Seeing is Deceiving: Forgery and Imitation in Pictures. Manchester, England: Whitworth Art Gallery, 17 March-7 May 1984. Organized by the Postgraduate Course in Art Gallery and Museums Studies at the University of Manchester.

Seeing is deceiving: forgery and imitation in pictures. Manchester, England: Whitworth Art Gallery, 1984, 20 p., 18 illus., bibliog.
English abstract in ABM vol. 16 (1985) # 5634.

1771
From our attic, The Buffalo Bill Historical Center, Billings, Montana, 1985.

1772
Forgeries by Thomas J. Wise and H. Buxton Forman, William Andrews Clark Memorial Library, University of California, Los Angeles, Los Angeles, California, October 1985-December 1985.

1773
Investigations/The F.B.I. Collects, Washington, D.C. The Mcintosh/Drysdale Gallery, May 15-June 18, 1986. Arranged through the cooperation of the Federal Bureau of Investigation.

1774
Don't Trust the Label, Nottingham University Art Gallery; York City Art Gallery; Exeter Royal Albert Memorial Museum, 1986.

Exhibition Reviews

(Numbers in parentheses at the end of each entry indicate which exhibition is reviewed.)

1775
Grancsay, Steven V. An exhibition of forgeries. *Metropolitan Museum of Art Bulletin* (USA), 27 (February 1932) 46–48, 1 illus.

1776
Barber, Edwin Attlee. Special exhibition of fakes and reproductions. *Bulletin of the Pennsylvania Museum* (USA), 14 no. 54, (April 1916) 20–23. (#1715).

1777
Meulenkamp, W.G.J.M. Aubrey Beardsley, John Lane en Leonard Smithers: enn tekenaar en zijn uitgevers (Aubrey Beardsley, John Lane and Leonard Smithers: a draughtsman and his publishers). *Antiek* (Netherlands) 17 no. 3 (Oct. 1982) 139–151, 14 illus. Summary in English. (#1718).

This article contains a discussion of the exhibition of Beardsley forgeries in New York in 1919.

English abstract in ABM vol. 14 (1983) #0724.

1778
Unsigned Article. Genuine and counterfeit. *Magazine of Art* 33 (1940) 374–376, illus. (#1726)

1779
Plenderleith, H.J. Fakes and forgeries in museums. *Museums Journal* (England), 52 (1952) 143–148. (#1731).

1780

Blom, J. Falsch oder echt? Zur Ausstellung im Stedelijk-Museum, Amsterdam. (Forged or genuine? The exhibition in the Stedelisk-Museum in Amsterdam) *Weltkunst* (Germany), 22 no. 20 (1952) 2, 4 illus. (#1732)

1781

Unsigned Article. Falsch oder Echt? Kunstfälschungen aus drei Jahrhunderten. *Werke, Bauen & Wohnen* (Germany), 4 (February 1953), supp., 15–16. (#1732).

1782

Chanin, A.L. Counterfeits and conservation. *Art Digest* 28 no. 9 (1 February 1954), 10, 25, illus. (#1733).

1783

Larsen, Erik. Views and news of art in America. *Apollo* (England), 59 no. 352 (June 1954), 180. (#1733)

1784

Frankfurter, Alfred. The gentle art of faking. *ARTnews* (USA), 52 no. 10 (February 1954) 16–19, 66–67, 10 illus. (#1733).

1785

Charles, J. Le plus grands faux du monde se sont donné rendez-vous au Grand palais. *France Illustration* (France), no. 424 (July 1955) 66–68, illus. (#1735).

1786

Isnard, Guy. Les faux dans l'art et dans l'histoire. *Jardin des Arts* (France), no. 9 (1955), 539–543, 12 illus. (#1735).

1787

Mathey, Francois. Vrai ou faux. *Médecine de France* (France), no. 62 (1955) 17–32, 22 illus. (#1735)

1788

Unsigned Article. [*Le Faux dans l'art et dans l'historie* Exhibition at the Grand Palais, Paris] *New Yorker* (USA), 31 no. 20, (2 July 1955) 65–66. (#1735).

1789

Unsigned Article. Big Paris show displays forgeries of art to warn against fakery. *Life* (USA), 39 (26 September 1955) 141–144 +, illus. (#1735).

1790

Wiske, Eva. Das Falsche in der Kunst. *Maltechnik* (Germany), 61, (1955) 109–115, 13 illus. (#1735).

1791

Commentary [Exhibition of Thomas J. Wise Forgeries at the University of Texas, at Austin]. *The Book Collector* (England), 8 no. 3 (Autumn 1959) 239–240. (#1736).

1792

Cole, Sonia. Forgeries and the British Museum. *Antiquity* (England), 35 no. 138 (June 1961) 103–106, plates. (#1737).

1793

Commentary [Forgeries and deceptive copies at the British Museum]. *The Book Collector* (England), 10 no. 2 (Summer 1961) 140, 143. (#1737).

1794

Croft-Murray, Edward. An exhibition of forgeries and deceptive copies held in the Department of Prints and Drawings from 9 February 1961. *British Museum Quarterly* (England), 24 (1961) 29–30 (#1737).

1795

Haskell, Francis. When scholars are deceived: forgeries in art and antiques. *The Listener* (England), 65 (16 February 1961) 303, illus. (#1737).

1796

Savage, George. Collector versus forger. *Studio* (England), 161 no. 817 (May 1961) 195–197, illus. (#1737).

1797

Unsigned Article. Confessions of a museum. *Time* (USA), 77 (17 February 1961) 81. (#1737).

1798

Unsigned Article. British Museum shows "deceptions." *ARTnews* (USA), 60 no. 1 (March 1961) 68. (1737).

1799

Unsigned Article. Gentle art of duping the expert: a London exhibition of forgeries and deceptions. *Illustrated London News* (England), 238 (4 February 1961) 174–175, photos. (#1737).

1800

Hughes, Graham. Silver stumers. *Antiques* (USA), 79 no. 4 (April 1961) 376–379, 10 illus. (#1738).

1801

Unsigned Article. True or false? *Newsweek* (USA), 69 (15 May 1967) 106, illus. (#1741).

1802

Unsigned Article. Fact or fake. *Art and Artists* (England), 4 no. 2, (May 1969), 64, illus. (#1744).

1803

Unsigned Article. Forging a career. *Newsweek* (USA), 12 October 1970, p. 105. (#1745).

1804

Pomerantz, Louis. Know what you see. *Museum News* (USA), 50 no. 4 (December 1971) 16–23, 23 illus. (#1746).

1805

Spencer, Charles. Master faker. *Art and Artists* (England), 6 no. 2 (May 1971) 78, 1 illus. (#1747).

1806

Raynor, Vivian. Rodin drawings at the Guggenheim. *Art in America* (USA), 60 (May 1972) 35 +. (#1748).

1807

Varnedoe, J. Kirk T. Rodin drawings, true and false. *ARTnews* (USA), 70 no. 8 (December 1971) 30–33, 65–66, 8 illus. (#1748).

1808

Unsigned article. Bolstering self-esteem. *New Yorker* (USA), 49 (17 March 1973) 32–33. (#1749).

1809

Butler, Joseph T. The American way with art. *Connoisseur* (USA), 184 no. 741 (November 1973), 205–209, illus. (#1751).

1810

Davis, Douglas. Masters of deceit. *Newsweek* (USA), 82 (23 July 1973) 49, illus. (#1751).

1811

Neugass, F. Truimph der Fälscher. *Weltkunst* (Germany), 43 no. 23 (1973), 2141, 2 illus; 43 no. 24 (1973), 2228–2229, 3 illus; 44 no. 2 (1974) 69, 1 illus. (#1751).

1812

Unsigned Article. Genuine fakes. *ARTnews* (USA), 72 (October 1973) 10–11, illus. (#1751).

1813

Unsigned Article. Fakes, forgeries and other deceptions. *Pantheon* (Germany), 31 no. 4, (1973), 454, 1 illus. (#1751).

1814

Gallego, Julian. Copias, replicas, pastiches. *Goya* (Spain), no. 120 (May–June 1974) 374–375. (#1752).

1815

Bosson, V. Kopier, repliker, pastischer, forfalskingar (Copies, replicas, pastiches and forgeries). *Paletten* (Sweden), no. 1 (1974) 10–11, 6 illus. (#1752).
English abstract in ABM vol. 8 (1977) #5068.

1816

Bloch, Peter. Fälshung und Forschung. *Jahrbuch der Berliner Museen* (Germany), no. 9 (1977) 2–3, 2 illus. (#1754).

1817

Hornig Sutter, M. Kritische Betrachtungen zur Austellung Fälschung und Forschung. *Keramos* (Germany), no. 75 (1977) 21–26, 6 illus. (#1754).

1818

Koschatzky, W. Echt oder Falsch. Zur Ausstellung des Folkwang-Museums in Essen. *Weltkunst* (Germany), 46 no. 21 (1976) 2100–2102, 6 illus. (#1754).

1819

Schälicke, B. Essen. Museum Folkwang. Ausstellung: Fälschung und Forschung. *Pantheon* (Germany), 35 no. 2 (April 1977) 158, 1 illus. (#1754).

1820

Wiegand, Wilfred. The art of forgery: authentic & false. *Encounter* (England), 48 (May 1977) 42–45, 4 illus. (#1754).

1821

Zoege Von Manteuffel, C. Fälschung und Forschung. *Kunstchronik* (Germany), 30 no. 6 (1977) 265–268. (#1754).

1822

Unsigned Article. Forgeries. *AB Bookman's Weekly*, (USA), 60 (21 November 1977) 2986. (#1755).

1823

Butler, Joseph T. The eye of the beholder: fakes, replicas and alterations in American art. *Connoisseur* (USA), 195 no. 785 (July 1977) 224–225, 1 illus. (#1756).

1824

Sherrill, S.B. Southport-Westport antiques-show loan exhibition. *Antiques* (USA) 111 no. 4 (April 1977) 686, 688, 1 illus. (#1758).

1825

Ashbery, J. Forging ahead. *New York* (USA), 11 (3 July 1978) 63–64, illus. (#1760).

1826

Stevens, Mark and McGuigan, Cathleen. The Spanish Forger. *Newsweek* (USA), 92 (10 July 1978) 67, illus. (#1760).

1827

Unsigned Article. My friend the Spanish Forger. *ARTnews* (USA), 77 (September 1978) 30, illus. (#1760).

1828

Unsigned Article. "Caveat lector." *AB Bookman's Weekly* (USA), 65 (17 March 1980) 2058. (#1761).

1829

Howarth, David. Now you see it . . . . *Country Life* (England), 170 no. 4378 (16 July 1981) 164–165, illus. (#1763).

1830

Conheim, Maryanne. The art you see, is it fake or real? *Philadelphia Pennsylvania Inquirer,* August 10, 1982 [Newspaper]. (#1766).

1831

Penny, Nicholas. London. Townley at the B.M. and Cavaceppi at the Clarendo Gallery. *Burlington Magazine* (England), 126 no. 970, (1984) 55–56, 2 illus. (#1767).

1832

Norrie, Jane. Real fakes: Michael Shepherd plays 'spot the difference'. *Arts Review* (England), 35 no. 2 (11 November 83) 629, 2 illus. (#1768).

1833

Sherrill, Sarah B. American decorative arts: fakes and forgeries. *Antiques* (USA), 125 no. 1, (January 1984) 68, 72, 1 illus. (#1769).

1834

Howard, Tom. Museum displays forgery collection. *Billings Montana Gazette,* November 4, 1985. [Newspaper]. (#1771).

1835

Walden, Sarah. The reproductive urge. *Times Literary Supplement* (England), 17 October 1986, p. 1165. (#1774).

AUTHOR INDEX

Reference is to entry number.

Aagard-Morgensen, Lars, 4, 18
Abbott, Craig S., 1402
Accorsi, C., 243, 244
Aitken, Martin, 619, 710
Akerman, John Yonge, 769
Akston, J.J., 1633
Albizzati, Carlo, 1022
Alden, John, 1554
Allegro, John Marco, 1471
Allodi, Mary, 455
Allport, Susan, 1110
Alscher, Ludger, 482
Alsop, J.D., 1482
Alsop, Joseph, 108
Althöfer, H., 245
Alvey, R.C., 807
Amandry, Pierre, 932, 933
Amar, S.S., 1247
Amyx, D.A., 495
Anderson, Lanie, 1634
Anderson, Richard Lloyd, 1403
Andren, Arvid, 689
Andrews, John F., 1477
Androsov, S.O., 496
Angeli, H.R., 15555
Angst, Walter, 1109
Anscombe, Isabelle, 620, 1198
Appuhn, H., 497
Arafat, W., 1404
Archibald, M.M., 808
Arias, C., 621
Aries, R.S., 179
Arnau, Frank, 78, 79, 80, 81, 82, 83, 1613
Arnold, Paul, 809
Ashbery, J., 1825
Ashmole, Bernard, 483
Atkin, E.J., 1536
Atkins, Guy, 225
Atkinson, R.J.C., 1038
Atlee, W. Dudley, 1221
Aubert, Fritz, 810
Austen, B., 1097
Austin, G., 1172
Austin, Pat, 1173
Auxion de Ruffé, R.d.'., 124
Avermaete, R., 180

Babelon, Jean, 811
Bachler, Karl, 19

Backhouse, Janet, 1483
Baer, Ilse, 943
Bahn, Paul G., 711
Bailey, D.M., 622, 623, 624, 625, 626
Bailey, Randy, 1039
Bailly, Robert, 627
Bainbridge, Henry Charles, 1019
Balan, Ernst-Henri, 812
Ballo, Guido, 84
Balog, Paul, 780
Banfield, Edward C., 20
Banister, Judith, 1004, 1005
Banti, Luisa, 498
Bapi, L., 1174
Barber, Edwin Attlee, 1776
Barends, F., 684
Barker, Harold, 1296
Barker, Nicolas, 1389, 1537
Barker-Benfield, Bruce C., 1405
Barnard, Noël, 974, 975, 1297
Baron, Hans, 1406
Bassani, Ezio, 1141
Batlle, Columba M., 1164
Battie, David, 600
Battin, M., 21
Baughman, Roland, 1556, 1557
Bauman, Lawrence Scott, 1635
Baumann, Peter, 630
Baynes-Cope, David, 1636
Bazarov, K., 22
Beale, Arthur, 489
Beardsley, Monroe C., 5
Becker, C.J., 813
Becker, Helen, 1407
Becker, Klaus, 598, 628, 629
Bedinger, Margery, 1133
Behrens, Gustav, 814
Belknap, George N., 1484
Bell, Lynne, 246
Bendall, Simon, 781
Bender, C., 247
Bendikson, L., 1594, 1595
Benjamin, Susan, 1098
Benjamin, Walter, 6
Bensch, F., 1040
Berger, Ursel, 199
Berkowitz, Rhoda, 1637
Berlo, Janet Catherine, 1142
Bernareggi, E., 782
Bernstein, Cheryl, 7
Berton, Paul, 500

Bertram, Fritz, 991
Bertrand, G., 248
Beurdeley, Michel, 601
Bevan, J. and Shapiro, I.A., 1485
Bharadwaj, H.C., 815
Bianchi, Bandinelli R., 1041
Bieber, Margarete, 484
Biesantz, Hagen, 1033
Biship, Bobbie, 1294
Bissell, E.E., 1558
Black, Lydia, 1486
Blacking, John, 712
Blair, Claude, 1023
Blankenhorn, V.S., 1263
Bleck, Rolf-Dieter, 1306
Blegen, Theodore C., 690
Bliss, A.S., 1596
Bloch, Peter, 8, 23, 24, 125, 490, 501, 502, 969, 1816
Block, Steven D., 1264
Blom, J., 1780
Blümel, Carl, 503, 504
Blunt, Anthony, 249, 1175
Blunt, C.E., 816
Bochicchio, Sergio, 1614
Boden, G., 631
Bogdan, Radu, 250
Bogucki, Peter I., 713
Bolken, Kandyce Smith, 1058
Bolz, Norbert, 1408
Bonci, Attilio, 817
Bonner, Gerald, 109
Boon, George C., 818, 820
Boone, Elizabeth H., 691
Boone, George C., 819
Booth-Jones, T., 1286
Borelli Vlad, Licia, 1307
Börker, C., 1246
Borsos, B., 714
Bosch, Lodewyk, 251
Bosson, V., 25, 1815
Boucard, Philippe, 680
Bovi, Giovanni, 821
Bower, Anthony, 126
Boylan, Leona Davis, 1000
Brachert, Thomas, 252, 253, 254
Bradshaw, Peter, 602
Brandhof, Marijke van den, 181
Brandi, Cesare, 110, 111
Brandone, A. 1308
Brandow, Wendy Waldron, 1615
Brandt, Walfried, 226
Brealey, John M., 255
Breek, R., 256
Bresc-Bautier, Geneviève, 1356
Breuil, Abbé, 715
Bromley, D. Allan, 257
Brommer, Frank, 505

Brook, G.L., 1390
Brooke, Christopher Nugent Lawrence, 1487
Brooks, John, 1059
Brooks, Valerie F., 258, 506, 1638, 1639
Brown, David, 1176
Brown, Jonathan, 452
Brown, Raymond Lamont, 1111
Brown, T.J., 1597
Brownlee, Marina Scordilis, 1409
Brox, Norbert, 1359
Brunet, Marcelle, 603
Brunetti, L., 822
Buchanan-Brown, John, 1163
Buchholz, Hans-Günter, 507
Buehler, M., 1298
Bunney, Sarah, 259
Burgess, Anthony, 1488
Burke, J., 704
Burroughs, Alan, 182
Busch, R., 1199
Bushell, Raymond, 1251
Butler, Joseph T., 1809, 1823
Buttrey, T.V., 823
Byvanck-Quarles van Ufford, 508

Cagiano de Azevedo, Michel-Angelo, 509
Cagiano de Azvedo, Michelangelo, 261, 260
Cahill, James, 262
Cahn, Joshua Binion, 1640
Cahn, Steven M., 26
Calico, F. Xavier, 824
Cannoo, Jean-Marie, 934
Cantera y Burgos, Francisco, 510
Caraci, Guiseppe, 1489
Carder, James Nelson, 1074
Carroll, Diana Lee, 1042
Carson, R.A.G., 825
Carter, John, 1538, 1539, 1540, 1541, 1542, 1543, 1544, 1559, 1560, 1561, 1562, 1563
Cashin, Edward J., Jr., 1490
Castelin, Karel, 826
Castiglione, L., 511
Cellini, Pico, 512
Cesano, S.L., 827
Cescinsky, Herbert, 1087
Ceysson, Bernard, 27
Challis, C.E., 783
Chamberlain, Betty, 513, 1641, 1642, 1643
Chambers, Sir Edmund Kerchever, 1391, 1360
Chamoux, Francois, 28
Chandra, Moti, 227
Chang, Shih-Hsien, 976

Chanin, A.L., 1782
Chapman, B., 935
Charles, J., 1785
Chase, W.T., 977
Chastel, André, 127, 263
Chatelain, Jean, 1608
Checkland, S.J., 264
Cheney, C.R., 1491
Christiansen, T.E., 1075
Cillario, A., 1644
Citroen, K.A., 681, 682, 1006
Clark, Kenneth, 128
Clines, Francis X., 265
Cole, Ann Kilborn, 1099
Cole, Sonia Mary, 85, 1792
Colin, Ralph F., 29, 266, 1645, 1646
Collingwood, F., 1564
Collis, J., 828
Colton, Harold S., 1134
Conheim, Maryanne, 1830
Constable, William George, 86, 267
Conway, James V.P., 1590
Cook, Brian, 514
Cook, P., 1200
Cooney, John D., 716, 717
Cope, L.H., 829, 830
Corbett, P., 762
Corbett, Patricia, 515
Coremans, Paul B., 183, 268
Cornet, Joseph, 1143
Corradini, Juan, 184
Cotter, Maurice J., 185, 186, 228, 269,
    270, 271
Courtney, Neil, 30
Coutot, Maurice, 187, 272
Cox, J.T., 1568
Craddock, Paul T., 962, 963
Crawford, Tad, 1616
Crawley, G., 718
Crawley, W., 1088
Cremaschi, L., 831
Croft-Murray, Edward, 1794
Cudworth, Charles L., 1265, 1266
Culican, William, 1024
Czerner, Olgierd, 31

d'Incerti, Vico, 833
Dabo, Leon, 448
Dahl, Edward H., 1210
Daniels, Vincent D., 1299, 1309
Dantzig, Maurits Michel van, 189, 188
David, Emmanuel, 112
Davidson, Harold G., 229
Davidson, R., 456
Davies, R.A., 1357
Davis, Douglas, 1810

Davis, Frank, 129, 130, 516, 517
Dawson, Giles E., 1410
Dearden, James S., 1569, 1570, 1571
Deblaere, A., 277
Decker, A., 278
Decoen, Jean, 190, 191, 192
Dedera, Don, 1135
DeGaigneron, 32
Degrada, F., 1267
Deighten, E., 1649
Del Renzio, T., 34
De Marly, Diana., 273
De Meredieu, 33
Demeure, Fernand, 87
Demortier, G., 1043
Denton, J.H., 1492
De Pradenne, A. Vayson, 692
Des Fontaines, Una, 605
De Towarnick, Frédéric, 274
Deutsch, Otto Erich, 1493
Devoe, Alan, 1392
De Wild, A. Martin, 275, 276
Di Peso, C.C., 632
Dickey, Herbert Spencer, 1144
Dickinson, A.D., 1411
Dieffenbacher, Alfred, 770
Dimitrijevic, S., 832
Dinkel, J., 1076
Dixon, K.A., 518
Döhmer, Klaus, 35
Dokíc, Dušan, 279
Dolley, R.H.M., 834, 835
Donno, Elizabeth Story, 1393
Donson, Theodore B., 1165
Dornberg, John 1310
Doty, Richard G., 784
Doudart de la Grée, Marie Louise, 194,
    193
Dow, Sterling, 633
Drachsler, Leo, 1609
Dreyer, P., 1177
Dreyer, Peter, 457
Duboff, Leonard D., 1617, 1618, 1619,
    1620, 1650
Ducret, S., 634
Duffy, Robert E. Jr., 1651
Duffy, Robert E., 1621
Dunn, Peter J., 1044, 1045, 1046
Duplessy, Jean, 836, 837
Dupont, Joan, 1178
Dupont-Sommer, A., 693
Duthy, Robin, 1145, 1200, 1287
Dutton, Denis, 1, 36

Easby, Dudley T., Jr., 519, 1652
Ebeling, H.J.M., 838

Ecke, Gustav, 520
Edge-Partington, James, 1146, 1147, 1148
Efremov, A., 280
Ehresmann, Donald L., 113
Ehret, G., 636
Ehrsam, Theodore George, 1361, 1362
Ekholm, Gordon, 724
Ekkart, R.E.O., 1179
Elbern, Victor H., 521, 1060, 1077
Elsen, Albert, 1653
Emerson, A.R., 1034
Emery, John, 1001
Ennimigazai, M., 1112
Epperson, Gordon, 37
Erkelens, J., 281
Esterow, Milton, 131, 282
Ettmayer, Peter, 945
Evans, Nancy Goyne, 992
Evers, J.H., 839, 840
Ewald, F., 283
Ewing, Robert, 284

Faider-Feytmans, Germaine, 970
Failing, Patricia, 522
Fales, Martha Gandy, 1007
Farrar, R.A.H., 725
Farrer, James Anson, 1363
Faxon, Alicia Craig, 114
Feest, Christian F., 604
Fehrenbacher, Don E., 1494
Feldhaus, F.M., 1654
Feldman, Franklin, 1622, 1655
Fell, H. Granville, 38, 132, 285, 458
Feller, Robert L., 286, 287
Fernier, Robert, 230, 288
Ferré, Jean, 195
Ferretti, Fred, 289
Ferrua, Antonio, 763
Field, R., 39
Fillitz, Hermann, 1008
Findlay, George, 133
Fischer-Graf, Ulrike, 1009
Fleming, Stuart J., 134, 290, 523, 637, 638,
    639, 978, 1295, 1300, 1311, 1312,
    1313, 1314
Fletcher, E.G., 1572
Fletcher, H.G., 1223
Folkenflik, Robert, 1412
Fong, Wen, 291, 292
Fontander, Björn, 694
Fonti, D., 524
Foucart, Jacques, 293
Fournier, Francois, 1224
Foxon, D.F., 1545, 1573
Fraenkel, Eduard, 1413
Frankel, Richard, 1315
Frankfurter, Alfred M., 294, 525, 1784

Frankis, P.J., 764
Franzoni, Lanfranco, 526
Fraser, Peter Marshall, 705
Freeman, Arthur, 1574
Freeman, Kenneth A., 640
Frel, Jiří, 527
Fridrich, J., 528
Friedman, Joan M., 1394
Friedrich, Otto, 1495
Frinta, Mojmír Svatopluk, 295, 296
Frisch, Bruce, 1316
Frisch, H., 1236
Fritz, R., 135
Froentjes, W., 297, 1656
Fruman, Norman, 1414
Fu, M., 231
Fuhrmann, Horst, 1472
Fulford, Michael, 726
Fuller, Peter, 40, 459
Fúster, Luis Fernández, 727

Gaborit-Chopin, Danielle, 1078
Gairola, T.R., 1317
Galbraith, V.H., 1496
Gallego, Julian, 1814
Gamberini di Scarfèa, Cesare, 772, 771
Gans, L.B., 685
Gans, M.H., 1002
Ganzel, Dewey, 1364, 1415
Garbini, G., 529
Gardner, Howard, 9, 10
Garrod, Dorothy, 728
Gathercole, Peter, 1136
Gearty, Thomas, J., Jr., 1575
Gedai, I., 842
Geiger, Hans-Ulrich, 843
Gerascenko, I., 298
Gerasimov, Todor, 729, 844
Germann, Sheridan, 1268
Getlein, Frank, 299
Gettens, Rutherford J., 641
Gettens, Rutherford John, 971
Gettins, Rutherford John, 972
Getz-Preziosi, Patricia, 530
Gibson, Michael, 1657
Gilbert, Anne, 1101, 1102
Gill, William J., 300
Gilles, K.J., 785
Gillespie, R., 1318
Gilmour, P., 136
Gimlin, Joan S., 137
Gingerich, Owen, 1282, 1283
Gjodesen, Mogens, 531
Glaster, Georg, 841
Glückselig, Josef, 88

Göbl, Robert, 845, 846
Godden, Geoffrey Arthur, 606
Goldman, Judith, 1180
Goldstein, Sidney M., 1061
Goll, Joachim, 89
Golvin, J.C., 730
Goodacre, S.H., 1416
Goodman, Nelson, 11, 41
Goodrich, David L., 90
Goodrich, Lloyd, 232, 1623
Goodspeed, Edgar Johnson, 1365
Gordon, Arthur Ernest, 759
Gordus, Adon A., 786
Goshen-Gottstein, Moshe H., 1497
Gould, Cecil, 138
Graak, K., 42
Grabar, Igor, 196
Gracia, J.J.E., 43
Grancsay, Stephen V., 936, 1775
Grant, Julius, 1658
Grasset, Jacques, 1225
Grebanier, Bernard, 1366
Grenberg, Y.I., 1319
Grice, J.W.H., 1113
Grierson, Philip, 787
Grigson, Geoffrey, 460
Grimwade, Arthur, 1010
Gros-Galliner, Gabriella, 1056
Gross, Karl-Heinz, 1114
Gross, M.J.H., 1576
Grotemeyer, Paul, 936
Grotz, George, 1103
Grummond, Nancy Thomson de, 979
Grundl, R., 301
Grundmann, Günther, 302, 303
Grunfeld, Frederic V., 532, 1081
Gualazzini, Ugo, 1473
Guarducci, Margherita, 760
Guerassimov, T., 937
Guglielmi, Stephen, 980
Gwinnett, A. John, 533

Hachmann, Rolf, 1025
Hackenbroch, Yvonne, 1026
Haedeke, H.U., 993
Hall, E.T., 731
Halliday, F.E., 1395
Hamilton, Charles, 1367, 1474, 1593
Hammond, Dorothy, 1089
Hamp, E.P., 765
Hanson, Victor F., 1320
Harasowski, Adam, 1498
Haraszti, Z., 1417
Harbottle, G., 1321
Harper, J. Russell, 233
Harper, Mr., 1322

Harris, Leon, 304
Harris, Richard, 139
Harrison, John, 305
Harrison, Wilson R., 1591, 1591
Harrisson, Caviness M., 140
Hartmann, A., 1027
Harvey, Brian, 1659
Haskell, Francis, 1795
Hauben, R., 44
Hayden, Arthur, 1166
Hayes, John, 234, 453
Hayward, John F., 642, 947, 994, 1028
Haywood, Ian, 1418, 1419
Hazen, Allen T., 1420, 1598
Headington, Ann, 141
Hector, Leonard Charles, 1475
Heichelheim, F.M., 1011
Heinz, Wolfgang, 1085, 1086
Hejna, Antonín, 847
Held, Julius S., 142
Helft, Jacques, 683
Heller, David, 1055
Helwig, Hellmuth, 1255
Hepper, F.N., 848
Herbert, Robert L., 306
Herchenroder, Christian, 115
Hersey, Irwin, 1150
Herst Jr., Herman, 1237
Herz, Norman, 1323
Herzer, H., 534
Hess, Thomas B., 1660
Higgins, Reynold, 1035
Higgins, Thomas, 1499
Hill, Philip, 773
Hilliard, Celia, 1577
Hillier, Bevis, 607
Himmelheber, G., 1115
Hirt, R., 1661
Hoaglund, John, 45
Hochfield, Sylvia, 307, 308, 309, 310, 535, 1662, 1663
Hodes, Scott, 1624, 1625, 1664, 1665, 1666
Hoffmann, Herbert, 1047
Hofrat, Becker, 849
Högberg, Th., 850
Högye, István, 851
Hollander, Barnett, 1626
Holm, Knud., 643
Holstein, Mark, 1421
Holzmair, E., 852
Homann-Wedeking, Ernst, 536
Homer, William Innes, 1201
Homma, Kunzan, 948
Honey, W.B., 608
Hoover, Eleanor, 311
Hope, Donald J., 788
Hopkins, F.M., 1422, 1578

Hopkinson, Cecil, 1500
Hormats, Bess, 312
Hornig Sutter, M., 1817
Horský, Zdeněk, 1284
Horton, Anne, 1202
Hosang, Joachim, 1226
Houlberg, Marilyn Hammersley, 1151
Hours, Madeleine, 197
Houseman, Lee Ann, 1667
Houtchens, Lawrence H., 1423
Hoving, Thomas, 143, 1012, 1073, 1668
Howard, Davis S., 644
Howard, Tom, 1834
Howarth, David, 1829
Howell, Standley, 1269
Hoyt, Edwin P., 789
Huart, Suzanne d', 1501
Huarte, José María de, 853
Hubbard, Clyde, 854
Hughes, Graham, 1800
Hughes, Merritt Y., 1424
Hume, Ivor Nöel, 706
Hunnisett, B., 1181
Huszár, Lajos, 855
Hutchinson, John, 313

Ilisch, P., 790
Ingalls, Daniel H.H., 1425
Ingleby, Clement Mansfield, 1368
Irving, Clifford, 314, 1369
Ishikawa, R., 949
Isnard, Guy, 91, 198, 199, 315, 1669, 1670, 1786
Ivins, William M., Jr., 46

Jack, R.I., 1502
Jackson, Betty, 686
Jacques Callot, 1182
Jaeckel, Peter, 856
Jaeger, Jerome Thomas, 92
Jahn, M.E., 695, 732
Jahr, Dan, 1270
Jänichen, Hans, 1478
Janson, H.W., 12
Jay, B., 1203
Jedzejewska, Hanna, 316
Jenkins, G.K., 857
Jensen, Carl Christian, 696
Jensen, Oliver, 1212
Jeppson, Lawrence, 93
Johansson, J.V., 1503
Johnsen, Thomas C., 1504
Johnson, Ben, 1324
Johnson, Franklin P., 537

Johnson, James R., 1048
Johnson, Lee, 1288
Jones, Brenda, 144
Jones, W.R., 1426
Joni, Icilio Federico, 200
Jordon, H., 1671
Jorgensen, Peter A., 1427, 1428
Joy, E., 1104, 1116
Jucker, Hans, 538
Jurukova, Jordanka, 858

Kaiser, Bruno, 1370
Kallfass, Monika, 859
Kalma, J.J., 145
Kaplan, J.H., 1429
Káplár, L., 860, 861
Karásek, Jan, 1227
Karsch, F., 1183
Keating, Tom, 201
Keck, Sheldon, 317
Keerdoja, Eileen, 318
Keisch, Bernard, 235, 319, 320, 1301, 1325
Kelly, Francis, 116
Kemp, J., 1430
Kendall, L.H., 1579
Kennick, William E., 13, 47
Kent, F.W., 1505
Kent, Norman, 146
Ketchum, Linda E., 1672
Kiejman, Mme Georges, 1673
Kiersnowski, Ryszard, 862, 863
Kilbracken, John Raymond Godley, Baron, 208, 207, 203, 204, 206, 205, 202
Kincaid, Robert M., Jr., 1674
Kind, J., 1184
King, Stuart Dale, 1137
Király, Ferenc, 864
Kisch, Guido, 938
Klein, John W., 1506
Klüssendorf, N., 791, 792
Knight, G.W., 1431, 1432
Knode, Harry C., 950
Knut, Nicolaus, 321
Koch, Bernhard, 865
Koestler, Arthur, 48
Kohler, Ellen L., 539
Kondratiev, Alexi, 1433
Koningsberger, Hans, 236
Korabiewicz, W., 1152
Kormarik, Dénes, 1326
Korski, Witold, 866
Koschatzky, W., 1818
Kosean-Mokrau, Alfred, 1479
Kotljar, N., 867

Kotschenreuther, H., 147, 540
Kowalski, H., 868, 1327
Kraay, Colin M., 869
Kraft, Konrad, 793
Krajick, Kevin, 148
Kraumann, František, 870
Krohner, Anita, 322
Kroll, R., 1117
Krueger, William C., 1599
Kruger, Gerhard, 981
Kubler, Arnold, 149
Kuhn, Katherine, 1185
Kulka, Tomas, 49, 50
Kurtz, Otto, 94, 95, 96, 209, 210, 461, 541

La Dassor, Gray, 733
La Moureyre-Gavoty, Francoise de, 491
Lacy, G.J., 1600
Lacy, Norris J., 1507
Lafaurie, J., 794
LaFontaine Dosogne, J., 1243
Lagerqvist, Lars O., 871
Lancaster, Paul, 1508
Lane, Alvin S., 1675, 1676
Lang, Berel, 51
Lange, Thomas V., 1434
Lanmon, Dwight P., 1062, 1063
Lapouge, Gilles, 150
Lapp, John C., 1509
Lappe, L., 323
Lappe, Ulrich, 1064
Lari, G., 324
Larsen, Erik, 1783
Lauant, A., 1244
Laufer, Berthold, 1049
Laurie, Arthur Pillans, 237
Lauter, Hans, 485
Lavanchy, Charles, 872
Lazović, Miroslav, 325
Lee, B. North, 1257, 1258
Lee, Ruth Webb, 1090
Leerinck, Hans, 151
Leeuwenberg, Jaap., 1079
Lefferts, Kate C., 542
Lehmann, Henry, 609
Lehmann, Paul Joachim Georg, 1371
Leichty, Erle, 734
Leisching, Eduard, 152
Lerner, Judith A., 543
Lerner, Ralph E., 1627
Lessing, Alfred, 52
Levantal, P., 326
Levenson, J.D., 766
Levinson, Jerrold, 53
Lewin, Robert, 1271, 1272, 1273, 1289
Lhotka, J.F., Jr., 873

Libman, Mikhail Iakovlevich, 97
Lifson, B., 1204
Lill, Georg, 1050
Lin, Ching-Chang, 1435
Lindemann, B.W., 544
Lindgren, Torgny, 874, 939
Linnenkamp, Rolf, 54
Lippens, Jan, 940
Lizardi, Ramos Cesar, 735, 1510
Lluis y Navas-Brusi, Jaime, 876, 877, 879, 878, 875
Lockner, H.P., 153, 964, 965, 982
Loew, Fernand, 154
Lomize, O., 327
Loomes, Brian, 1118
Lorini, M. Campbell, 1105
Loughrey, Brian, 328
Love, Iris, 545
Love, L.J., 880
Lowe, Robson, 1228
Lucheschi, Dino, 881
Lugt, Frits, 238
Lund, Marsha Mayer, 1132
Lutterotti, Otto, 117
Lutz, Cora Elizabeth, 1480, 1511
Lynch, Katherine L., 1436
Lynes, Russell, 546
Lyon, Marjorie, 1328

Macdonald, Hugh, 1513
Mackenna, F., 645
Mackenzie, D.N., 1514
Mackenzie, Norman H., 1601
MacLeod, Ian D., 882, 883
Mahon, Denis, 462
Mailfert, André, 211, 212
Mair, John, 1372
Makes, Frantisek, 155, 329
Makomaski, Waclaw, 884
Malaro, Marie E., 1628
Mallat, Jon M., 736
Mallon, P., 547
Maltese, C., 213
Marabottini, A., 55
Marceau, Henri, 330
Marconi, Bohdan L., 331
Marcuse, Michael J., 1439, 1440
Marder, Louis, 1441
Margolis, Joseph, 56
Marguerite, Antoine, 549
Marijnissen, Roger H., 332, 333, 1119
Marinho, João Augusto, 1229
Markbreiter, S., 646
Marsh, John, 885
Martin, Daniel L., 1677
Martindale, Percy H., 1167

Mathey, Francois, 1787
Matthys, A., 886
Mattingley, Harold B., 887
Maurer, Evan, 1153
Mayer, A.W., 737
Mayer, L.A., 795
Mayhew, N.J., 888
Mazzolai, Aldo, 548
McCrone, Walter C., 1213
McDonald, Dwight, 1580
McDonald, G.D., 1437, 1438
McFee, Graham, 57, 58
McIntyre, Arthur, 334
McKay, D.A., 1512
McKay, Shona, 1678
McKerrell, H.V., 738, 739
McKusick, Marshall, 740, 741
McLeod, M.D., 966, 1154
McWhirter, William A., 335
Meder, M.D., 1373
Mehlman, Felice, 1120
Melot, Michel, 59
Mendax, Fritz, 98, 99, 100, 101
Merryman, John Henry, 1629, 1679
Mesuret, Robert, 336
Metcalf, D.M., 889, 890
Metz, Peter, 14
Metzger, B.M., 1442
Meulenkamp, W.G.J.M., 464, 1777
Meyboom, P.G.P., 463
Meyer, Karl E., 102
Meyer, Leonard B., 60
Meyerstein, Edward Harry William, 1374
Michálek, Miroslav, 891
Mikolajczyk, A., 892
Miles, Charles, 742
Millán, Clarisa, 893
Mills, John FitzMaurice, 103, 1014, 1065,
    1091, 1092, 1281
Mishara, J., 983
Mitchells, K., 61
Miyoshi, Tadaki, 337
Moiseiwitsch, Maurice, 214
Moltesen, M., 550
Momigliano, A., 1443
Mommsen, H., 796
Montseny, Monné, Antonio, 1230
Moorey, P.R.S., 551
Moraes-Passos, Alfonso de, 647
Morahan, Richard E., 1375
Morgenstern, R., 894
Morrissette, Bruce Archer, 1377, 1376
Morse, Earl, 156
Mortlock, A., 610
Morton, A.H., 895
Mueller, H., 157
Muether, H.E., 338
Muir, P.H., 1581

Mumford, Lewis, 3
Murari, Ottorino, 898
Muscarella, Oscar White, 552, 648, 697,
    707, 708
Musper, Theodor, 158
Mustilli, Domenico, 118
Myers, P. Gay, 215, 1013

Nagel, Charles, 553
Natanson, Ann, 554
Naveh, Joseph, 743, 767
Neave-Hill, W.B.R., 611
Negri Arnoldi, Francesco, 555
Negus, James, 1231
Nercessian, Y.T., 797
Neuburger, Albert, 104
Neugass, Fritz, 339, 340, 465, 556, 1811
Neuwirth, Waltraud, 599, 612, 649, 650,
    651, 652, 653, 687, 997, 1066
Neve, Christopher, 341
Newman, William S., 1274, 1275
Nguyet, T., 557
Nicol, Andrew, 1681
Nicolay, Jean, 1093, 1094
Nicolson, Benedit, 466
Niggemeyer, Hanneliese, 1293
Nilsson, Martin, 1036
Nixon, H.M., 1256
Noble, Joseph Veach, 486, 558
Nogéus, Gunilla, 1238
Norman, Frank, 342
Norman, Geraldine, 216, 343
Norman, Philip, 1444
Norrie, Jane, 1832
North, Anthony R.E., 951
Nougayrol, J., 744
Novello, E., 899

O'Brien, Mary Louise, 1252
O'Connor, Rod, 344
Oddy, W.A., 798, 900, 1329
Ogden, Jack, 1037
Oldman, William, 1155
Olin, Charles, 1630
Oliver, A., 654
Olson, Roberta Jeanne Marie, 467
Oman, Charles, 1121
Osborne, Harold, 119
Osman, Colin, 1205
Ost, Hans, 449, 468
Otto, Helmut, 984

Paley, Morton D., 1445
Panciera, Silvio, 761

Pantazzi, Sybille, 345
Paras-Perez, Rodolfo, 469
Pariser, Maurice, 1583
Park, Julian, 1584
Parlasca, K., 346, 559
Parronchi, Alessandro, 560
Parsons, Harold W., 561
Partington, J.R., 1330
Partington, Wilfred George, 1547, 1546
Paul, Eberhard, 698, 699, 700
Pauwels, H., 1290
Payne, Joan Crowfoot, 655
Peacock, D.P.S., 745
Pedley, Katharine Greenleaf, 1548
Pei, W.C., 656
Pellan, Francoise, 1446
Pelzel, T., 347
Penelope, M., 1682
Penny, Nicholas, 1831
Perlman, Isadore, 1302
Peroni, Adriano, 562
Perrig, Alexander, 454, 470
Perzynski, F., 563
Pesce, G., 901
Peterson, Arthur G., 1067
Peterson, Frederick A., 1156
Peterson, H.L., 1095
Petráček, Karel, 564
Petschek, W., 159
Peukert, Karel, 902, 903
Peyrefitte, R., 217
Philip, Peter, 1122
Phillips, H., 1515
Piatkiewicz Dereniowa, M., 657
Pickering, Paul, 348
Pieper Lippe, M., 688
Pieper, Paul, 349
Piggott, S. William Stukeley, 1447
Piniński, J., 904
Piper, Towry, 1276
Plenderleith, H.J., 658, 1779
Poli, Kenneth, 1206
Pollard, Graham, 1259
Pollock, Phillip, 1683
Pomerantz, Louis, 1804
Pope-Hennessy, John, 492, 565
Porda, Edith, 746
Porkay, Martin, 218, 219
Potin, V., 799
Potratz, Johannes A.H., 985
Powell, John S., 905
Power, Robert H., 967
Prag, A.J.N.W., 566, 567
Pratt, Nancy, 1123
Pressouyre, Léon, 568
Price, Cheryl A., 1602
Prince, D., 1082
Probszt, Günther, 800, 907, 908

Puraye, Jean, 952

Quercu, Matthias, 1378
Quesnell, Quentin, 1516

Rabinowicz, O.K., 1517
Radcliff, Anthony, 569
Radford, C.A. Raleigh, 659
Radford, Colin, 62
Ragghianti, Carlo Ludovico, 351, 1684
Raines, Robert, 352
Ralls, Anthony, 63
Rambaud-Buhot, J., 1448
Rancoule, G., 909
Rapport, Leonard, 1518, 1603
Rasky, F., 1685
Ratchford, Fannie E., 1549, 1550
Ravier, André, 1476
Raynor, Vivian, 1806
Raynor, William, 353
Reberschak, S.F., 160
Reese, K.M., 1051
Reily, Duncan, 1519
Reith, Adolf, 701, 702
Renfrew, Colin, 747
Resolato, G., 64
Rewald, John, 355
Reyman, Janusz, 910
Rheims, Maurice, 15
Rhodes, Henry Taylor Fowkes, 1379
Rhyne, Charles B., 471
Rice, D.G., 613
Richter, Ernst Ludwig, 998, 1003
Ricke, Helmut, 1968
Riederer, Josef, 1303, 1331, 1332, 1333,
    1334, 1335, 1336, 1337, 1338, 1339,
    1340
Ringler, William, 1449
Ripin, Edwin M., 1262, 1277, 1631
Ripley, John W., 1285
Rizzi, A., 571
Robbins, Chris, 161, 356
Robinson, David M., 941
Robinson, E.S.G., 911
Rodee, Marian E., 1138
Rodger, William, 472, 1450, 1520
Rodgers, W., 1186
Roe, F. Gordon, 1131
Roettgen, S., 357
Rogers, Derek, 162
Rogers, Sherman E., 1239
Röntgen, Robert E., 614
Rooney, Dawn, 1139
Rosemberg, Jakob, 473

Rosen, David, 1341
Rosenbaum, Lee, 120
Rosenberg, Pierre, 358, 1253, 1254
Roskill, Mark, 239
Ross, M.C., 660
Rossi, Francesco, 986
Rossi, P.A., 572
Rossmann, Ernst, 359
Rostand, André, 570
Roth, Cecil, 1124
Roth, Toni, 360
Roushead, William, 1380
Rousseau, Theodore, 361
Rowe, John H., 748
Rowlett, Ralph M., 1342
Rudner, Richard, 16
Rudolph, Richard Casper, 987
Ruggles, Mervyn, 1686
Russell, John, 362
Russoli, Franco, 474

Sacharow, S., 1187
Sack, Harold, 1125
Sagoff, Mark, 65, 66, 67, 68
Saidenberg, N., 69
Sainsburg, W.J., 661
Sakař, V., 749
Salamon, Ferdinando, 1168
Salamon, Harry, 1188, 1189, 1190
Salomon, Richard G., 1451
Salzmann, D., 573
Sammler, Wilhelm R., 175
Sanders, Horace, 944
Sani, Bernardina, 574
Sapunov, B., 953
Satō, Masahiko, 615
Saunders, Laura, 1687
Savage, George, 105, 121, 163, 164, 363,
    364, 616, 1106, 1796
Saville, Marshall H., 662
Schaffer, Simon, 750
Schälicke, B., 1819
Schedelmann, Hans, 954, 955, 956
Scheper, Hinnerk, 365
Schimmel, S.B., 1452
Schlüller, Sepp, 220
Schneider, H., 912
Schnitzler, Hermann, 1080
Schoenbaum, S., 1453
Schofield, M., 1604
Schoske, S., 751
Schottenloher, K., 1454
Schrade, Hubert, 165
Schulder, Diane, 1688
Schüller, Sepp, 106, 107
Schultze-Frentzel, Ulrich, 664, 663

Schumacher, John N., 1455
Schur, Susan E., 1343
Schurr, Gérald, 366
Schuyler, Jane, 493
Scott Kenneth, 775
Seaby, W.A., 913
Secrest, Meryle, 367
Sedova, E.N., 240
Seeden, Helga, 575
Seiberling, Dorothy, 475
Seidel, Linda, 576
Seifert, Traudl, 1214
Seitz, Heribert, 957
Sejbal, Jiří, 914
Seling, H., 1015
Selinova, T., 1248
Severin, Hans-Georg, 942
Severova, M., 915
Sewell, Brian, 368, 369, 0447
Seyffarth, Richard, 370
Seymore, Charles Jr., 371
Shapiro, I.A., 1521
Shapiro, Maurice L., 577
Shaplin, P.D., 665
Shell, E.R., 1605
Shelton, K.J., 916
Shepard, Richard F., 372
Sheppard, Leslie, 1278
Sherrill, S.B., 1824, 1833
Shiel, N., 917
Shientag, Florence, 1689
Shirey, David L., 373
Short, Hugh de S., 776
Shortt, H. de, 918
Sieveking, Ann G., 752
Sikorski, Kathryn Ann, 1140
Simpson, Colin, 166, 578
Sipos, George, 70
Sirén, O., 579
Sjögren, P., 1522
Skelton, R.A., 1208
Sklenář, Karel, 703
Skolnik, Peter Barry, 1690
Skupinska-Lovset, I., 580
Skutil, Josef, 920
Slánský, B., 167, 374
Ślesiński, Marek, 168, 1344
Smeets, R., 666
Smith, Robert Metcalf, 1381
Smythies, Evelyn Arthur, 1232
Snow, Dean R., 753
Snowman, A. Kenneth, 1020
Solomon, Stephen, 169
Sonnenburg, Hubertus Falkner von, 378,
    377, 376, 375
Soper, Alexander C., 988
Southern, R.W., 1523
Spawforth, A.J.S., 1481

Spencer, Charles, 379, 1805
Spencer, Hazelton, 1456
Spencer, J.R., 921
Speyer, Wolfgang, 1382
Spielman, Heinz, 476, 477, 478
Spielmann, Heinz, 380, 381, 382, 383, 384
Squire, John P., 385
Staccioli, R.A., 581
Stalker, Douglas F., 71
Stamp, A.E., 1383
Stankiewicz, Daniela, 386
Stara, D., 995
Starr; Phyllis, 1457
Starretts, Vincent, 1396
Stechow, W., 241
Steele, Hunter, 72
Stein, Anne-Marie, 221
Stein, Claire, 1691
Stein, Harry J., 922
Steinke, Richard, 923
Sterba, Günter, 667
Sterling, Charles, 387
Stevens, Mark, 1029, 1826
Stolow, Nathan, 1692
Storm, C., 1397
Strauss, Irmgard, 1345
Strehlke, C.B., 582
Strieder, Peter, 1191
Strini, A., 1606
Strom, Deborah, 583, 584
Strommenger, E., 709, 754
Stross, Fred H., 1346
Sturt-Penrose, Barrie, 1279
Šujan, V., 668
Šujskij, K., 388
Swanson, V.G., 389
Swarzenski, H., 1260

Tannenbaum, Samuel Aaron, 1384, 1398
Tatlock, John, 1385
Taxay, Don, 777
Taylor, Gary, 1524
Taylor, John Russell, 1207
Tedeschi, G., 1693
Teodosiu, A., 390
Terry, K.W., 924
Teteriatnikov, Vladimir, 1084
Thiel, Albert Willem Rudolf, 617
Thomas, Alan G., 1399
Thomas, D., 1192
Thomas, John P., 1458
Thomas, Ralph, 1386
Thompson, C., 73
Thompson, J., 1525
Thompson, J.D.A., 925
Thompson, Lawrence S., 1400

Thompson, R.F., 1553
Thompson, S.O., 1459
Timpanaro, S., 1460
Tobler, Edwin, 926
Todd, William Burton, 1551, 1552, 1585, 1586
Tölle, R., 585
Tolstoy, Nikolai, 1461
Tout, T.F., 1462
Trautscholdt, Eduard, 1169
Trevanian, Michael, 1587
Trevor-Roper, Hugh, 1463
Trucco, Terry, 479
Truman, Charles, 1030
Trustman, Deborah, 1694
Turk, Frank, 1170
Turner, Evan H., 391
Turner, G.E.S., 1157
Türr, K., 487
Tyler, Varro E., 1233, 1240

Ucko, Peter J., 586
Unterkircher, Franz, 1261
Unverfehrt, Gerd, 17
Urdareanu, E., 428

Van Dalen, A., 928
Van De Waal, H., 1610
Van der Tweel, L.H., 1196
Van der Wiel, 801, 802
Van Dievoet, W., 1016
Van Dusen, Julie, 1159
Van Holst, Niels, 74
Van Luttervelt, R., 1127
Van Os., H.W., 429
Van Thiel, P.J.J., 430
Vana, Norbert, 1304
Vandersall, Amy L., 594
Varnedoe, J. Kirk T., 450, 1807
Vaulter, Roger, 929
Vegnet-Ruiz, Jean, 675
Velter, A.M., 930
Verlet, Pierre, 1107, 1128
VerMeulen, M., 1710
Verzele, M., 431
Vesela-Prenosilova, Zdenka, 1529
Vielhaber, CHR, 432
Vikan, Gary, 494, 1249
Vinter, Vlastimil, 174
Viscomi, Joseph, 1464
Voigtlaender, H., 778
Von Faber Castell, C., 676
Von Graevenitz, A., 1017
Von Habsburg-Lothringen, G., 1031, 1021

Von Steinwehr, H.E., 1052
Von Wilckens, Leonie, 1108
Vukanovic, T.P., 960

Waetzoldt, Stephan, 75
Wagner, Guenther A., 677
Walden, Sarah, 1835
Walker, Frank, 1280, 1530, 1531, 1532
Walker, Rainforth Armitage, 451
Walker, Richard W., 433, 1711
Wallach, Amei, 1712
Walters, Raymond Jr., 1465
Ward, William, 595
Warner, Glen, 1171
Warren, S.E., 755
Washburn, Wilcomb E., 1209
Waterman, Edward C., 434
Watt, Robin, 1160
Wear, Bruce, 488, 1632
Webster, Robert, 1053
Webster, William E., 76
Wehlte, K., 435
Weil-Cachin, Francoise, 436
Weiller, Raymond, 803
Weinberg, R., 437
Weisburd, S., 596
Wells, Anna Mary, 1466
Wells, T., 1589
Wenn, L., 1129
Werner, A.E., 223, 1072
Werner, O., 989, 1352, 1353
Werthmann, B., 1607
West, Janet, 1083
Wever, Gayle, 961
White, Newman I., 1387
Whitehead, John, 1388
Wicker, Brian, 438
Wieck, R.S., 1250
Wiegand, Wilfred, 1820
Wilda, Tadeusz, 439
Willett, Frank 1161

Williams, Leon Norman, 1234
Wills, G., 618
Wilson, J. Dover, 1467
Wilson, John A., 756
Wilson, Robert A., 1401
Windler, F.J., Jr., 779
Winkelmeyer, D., 1130
Winter, Paul, 1533, 1534, 1535
Wintersgill, Donald, 1292
Wiske, Eva, 1790
Witt, P., 176
Wolfe, Lester, 440
Wood, Susan, 597
Woods, William W., 1354
Wormser, R.S., 1468
Wraight, Robert, 122
Wreen, Michael, 77
Wright, Christopher, 224, 441, 442, 443
Würtenberger, Thomas, 1611, 1612, 1713
Wykes-Joyce, M., 177

Yap, C.T., 678, 679
Yates, Raymond Francis, 1096
Young, D.G., 1162
Young, Mahonri Sharp, 1032
Young, William J., 973, 1305
Yule, Paul, 757

Zakrzewska Kleczkowska, J., 931
Zall, P.M., 1469
Zedelius, V., 804, 805, 806
Zeri, Federico, 123, 242
Zevi, Franco, 178
Zimmerman, David W., 1355
Zink, H., 1018
Zoege Von Manteuffel, C., 1821
Zschelletzschky, H., 1197
Zug, Charles G., III, 1470
Zurcher, E., 444